A CONTEMPORARY IN DISSENT

A Contemporary in Dissent

JOHANN GEORG HAMANN

AS A

RADICAL ENLIGHTENER

Oswald Bayer

• •

Translated by

Roy A. Harrisville *&* Mark C. Mattes

WILLIAM B. EERDMANS PUBLISHING COMPANY

GRAND RAPIDS, MICHIGAN / CAMBRIDGE, U.K.

Originally published in German under the title
Zeitgenosse im Widerspruch. Johann Georg Hamann als Radikaler Aufklärer,
Piper Verlag, 1988.

This English translation
© 2012 Roy A. Harrisville and Mark C. Mattes

Published 2012 by
Wm. B. Eerdmans Publishing Co.
2140 Oak Industrial Drive N.E., Grand Rapids, Michigan 49505 /
P.O. Box 163, Cambridge CB3 9PU U.K.

Printed in the United States of America

18 17 16 15 14 13 12   7 6 5 4 3 2 1

Library of Congress Cataloging-in-Publication Data

Bayer, Oswald.
[Zeitgenosse im Widerspruch. English]
A contemporary in dissent: Johann Georg Hamann as a radical enlightener /
Oswald Bayer; translated by Roy A. Harrisville & Mark C. Mattes.
p.   cm.
Includes bibliographical references and index.
ISBN 978-0-8028-6670-7 (pbk.: alk. paper)
1. Hamann, Johann Georg, 1730-1788 — Criticism and interpretation.
I. Title.

PT2287.H9B3913   2012
193 — dc23

2011027509

www.eerdmans.com

Contents

Contents

Abbreviations

BW   *Johann Georg Hamann. Londoner Schriften.* Historisch-
      kritische Neuedition by Oswald Bayer and Bernd
      Weissenborn. Munich: Beck, 1993.

Dickson   *Johann Georg Hamann's Relational Metacriticism.* Berlin:
           Walter de Gruyter, 1995.

DWb   *Deutsches Wörterbuch* of Jacob and Wilhelm Grimm,
       Leipzig 1854ff.

H   Johann Georg Hamann, *Briefwechsel,* volumes IV-VII.
     Edited by Arthur Henkel. Wiesbaden: Insel-Verlag, 1959;
     Frankfurt: Insel-Verlag, 1965-1979.

Haynes   *Hamann: Writings on Philosophy and Language.* Edited by
          Kenneth Haynes. Cambridge: Cambridge University Press,
          2007.

HH   *Johann Georg Hamanns Hauptschriften erklärt,* volumes I-
      III, edited by F. Blanke and L. Schreiner; volumes IV-VII,
      edited by F. Blanke and K. Gründer. Gütersloh: Gütersloher
      Verlagshaus, 1956-1963; published volumes: I, II, IV, V, VII
      (cited by prefixing the interpreter's name).

Jerusalem   Moses Mendelssohn, *Jerusalem or On Religious Power and
             Judaism,* translated by Allan Arkush. Hanover, NH, and
             London: Brandeis University Press, 1983.

JubA8   Moses Mendelssohn, *Gesammelte Schriften*
         (Jubiläumsausgabe), vol. 8, *Schriften zum Judentum II*
         (revised by A. Altmann). Stuttgart–Bad Cannstatt, 1983.

LW   *Luther's Works* [American edition], 55 volumes. Philadelphia: Fortress and St. Louis: Concordia, 1955-86.

N   Johann Georg Hamann, *Sämtliche Werke*. Edited by J. Nadler. Six volumes. Vienna: Im Verlag Herder, 1949-1957.

Smith   Ronald Gregor Smith, *J. G. Hamann, 1730-1788: A Study in Christian Existence, with Selections from His Writings*. New York: Harper & Brothers, 1960.

WA   *D. Martin Luthers Werke: Kritische Gesamtausgabe* [Schriften], 65 vols. Weimar: H. Böhlau, 1883-1993.

WA DB   *D. Martin Luthers Werke: Kritische Gesamtausgabe* [Die Deutsche Bibel], 12 vols. Weimar: H. Böhlau, 1906-1961.

WA TR   *D. Martin Luthers Werke: Kritische Gesamtausgabe* [Tischreden], 6 vols. Weimar: H. Böhlau, 1912-1921.

WdF   *Johann Georg Hamann* (*Wege der Forschung*, volume 511). Edited by R. Wild. Darmstadt: Wissenschaftlich Buchgesellschaft, 1978.

ZH   Johann Georg Hamann: *Briefwechsel*, volumes I-III, VI. Edited by Walther Ziesemer and Arthur Henkel. Wiesbaden: Insel-Verlag, 1955-1957, 1975.

Introduction

The journalist and writer Johann Georg Hamann (1730-1788), equal in stature to Kant and Hegel, is a radical enlightener. He was the brightest intellect of his time, wrote Goethe, who owed him decisive impetus, as did Herder, the *Sturm und Drang* movement, the Romantics, and above all, Kierkegaard. Goethe's judgment runs counter to another more widespread one, namely, that Hamann is opaque, even irrational. True, Hamann erects barriers for his readers. He wants to hinder them from mere consumption or a quick read that would only keep them the same, and not alter them. Hamann waits for active readers who not only want to welcome him but work through what he offers so that they can arrive at their own judgment, or at the very least, to a critical self-awareness.

The uniqueness of Hamann's writings consists in the fact that, as no other did, he discovered viewpoints of an aesthetics of receptivity and let himself be guided by them. "The idea of the reader is the muse and helpmeet of the author" (*Leser und Kunstrichter*, 1762). "Writer and reader are two halves whose needs are related to each other and have their uniting as their common goal."

"To speak is to translate," just as hearing is also translating. In terms of this apt word of Hamann, the aim of the present book is to serve as broker and negotiator between old texts and new readers. It seeks to bring to light possibilities of understanding that have been submerged, as well as alternatives to current intellectual perspectives.

More than any other author, Hamann does not want to be parroted but creatively heard and represented. His intellectual physiognomy cannot be made to suit mere repetition. Thus, the portrait offered in this book is the result of a longstanding association with Hamann's provocative thoughts, which sct free as well as constrain one to give one's own judgment.

Unlike Kant in Philosophy, Goethe in German Studies, and Schleiermacher or Luther in Theology, Hamann is not a recognized authority. Whoever is concerned with them is deemed at the outset to be a serious academic who needs no justification for such concern. This is not true for Hamann. Only of late has research turned to him. Students of German, philosophers, and theologians meet regularly at the International Hamann Colloquium. Likewise, the growth of interest in and enthusiasm for Hamann outside the university, already developed in Hamann's lifetime, is not to be underestimated. Still, an author such as Hamann who gives himself to such concentration in his written word could not be a mass attraction. Of course, he wanted to be and will be heard and understood. But not at any cost. Certainly not at the cost of truth. In what way Hamann is bound to it can be summarized in three comprehensive themes.

Independence and Freedom

Compared with his contemporaries, even with such relatively free and lively, critical and self-reflective intellectuals as Lessing and Kant, Hamann's independence and freedom are striking. He exercises judgment with a self-reliance whose critical power in a certain sense exceeds and also deepens Kant's. Since Hamann does not oppose the rational to the irrational but holds together understanding and sensuousness, time and eternity, contingent truths of history and necessary truths of reason, attitudes and activities in a living whole — in a "marriage" — he shows what it means to be a radical, consistent enlightener. He is such because he holds reason and sensuousness together by means of the appropriate word *(im treffenden Wort)*. In the appropriate word the clarity of ideas and the rigor of feelings participate in each other, are involved in an exchange.

Hamann is not opaque, as his writings might suggest at first glance. However, he does not evince that Apollonian lucidity of thought that allows the otherness of sensuality, passion, pain, and complaint to be silenced and turn pale. If Goethe calls Hamann the brightest intellect of his time,[1] he means in the sense of that phrase with which he cites Hamann, "Clarity is a suitable distribution between light and shade," and then adds, "Take note!"[2]

As a Dissenter

Hamann's clarity, which appropriately separates light from shade, and with which he spoke, wrote, and thought, with which he knew how to share the word in a way that often pained him and stood his readers on their heads, is not achieved in a linguistic and cultural ghetto. Rather, it penetrates every ghetto and leads to an unprecedented breadth and freedom of thought, or better, to a comprehensive aesthetic, to a perception involving heart, mouth, and hands, of what the metaphysicians conceived as their triple-starred "God, self, and world" in an alleged purity, abstracted from everything sensuous, empirical, and historical, from tradition, experience, and language. The dissent that Hamann voices when he deems it necessary works no diastasis but leads precisely to an understanding, not, of course, to a confirmation of what was always known, which would merely be submerged and needed only to be recalled. Rather, the dissent serves a new hearing and learning, which is neither mere construction nor mere anamnesis. If Hamann, in his innermost self a contemporary, scandalizes his philosophical and moralistic century, as he says, he seeks understanding in a purposive dissent. He wants to convince his recipients, to alter them, to change their one-sided analytical orientation — which merely cultivates the spirit of observation — into a total perception of life. He wants to convert their art of separation *(Scheidekunst)*, hostile to life, into an art of marriage *(Ehekunst)*, hospitable to life.

Hamann's dissent applies solely to disassociation, indeed, to every separation, whether it consists in the sexual, familial, social, political, world-historical arena and in relation to nonhuman fellow creatures. What Hamann promotes as a contemporary in dissent is a comprehen-

---

1. Kanzler Friedrich von Müller, *Unterhaltungen mit Goethe*, 2nd edition, furnished with notes and edited by R. Grumach (Weimar: H. Bölhaus, 1982), 109 (December 18, 1823).

2. Johann Wolfgang Goethe, *Maxims and Reflections*, trans. Elisabeth Stopp (London: Penguin, 1998), 28. Compare ZH VI, 235, 1f. (to Jacobi; 1786).

sive integration. What is dismembered and torn in pieces through extreme analysis is to be linked again in thought, in a total context of life that cannot be gathered through construction or reconstruction, not in intuition or in an irrational way, but rhetorically arranged, in the medium of history, philosophy, and poetry, and in the logic of the image and of thought.

The dissent of this contemporary is not, say, an end-in-itself, but a necessary means to serve life in its wholeness and to fend off disunion, atomizing, and dismemberment. The perspectives and dimensions to which Hamann's works lead, as brief as they are, intend to be seen in their fullness and diversity.

The present book seeks to do justice to this diversity, though in a selection that indeed claims to be representative of the entire corpus and its encyclopedic scope, and to have met the thematic chief points. Whoever sees how Hamann perceives the most varied themes, which in current scientific inquiry fall under the jurisdiction of a series of disciplines such as Theology, Philosophy, German Studies, Psychology, Sociology, Law, History, Mathematics, and Physics, and thus often unravel, will not hesitate to see in him, the customs official, the man in a subordinate position, a "stifled existence,"[3] as the world-renowned Berlin professor Hegel disdainfully judged it, a *uomo universale* ("Renaissance man"). In any case, Goethe admits to having learned from Hamann that everything isolated is reprehensible and what is at issue is the combination of all powers and their interplay.[4] Hence, one may for a moment be tempted to speak of a "universal genius." But the language game and life within which one would find oneself would be immediately met with the irony of the third act of *Wolken,* the *Nachspiel Sokratischer Denkwürdigen:* "Don't seek a blond . . . among the playmates of Apollo. . . . Don't stare at me just because I'm dark, for the genie has burnt me so."[5]

This encodes Hamann's encounter with God in the word from the cross. The following sentence is moved by the confession that "the foolishness of the genius" is "rich enough to replace the wisdom which comes to mind through the combining of universal truths."[6] In what

---

3. *Hegel on Hamann,* trans. Lisa Marie Anderson (Evanston, IL: Northwestern University Press, 2008), 41.

4. *Goethe's Autobiography: Poetry and Truth from My Own Life,* trans. R. O. Moon (Washington, DC: Public Affairs Press, 1949), 452.

5. "Wolken," in N II, 107, 3-6.

6. "Wolken," in N II, 107, 7-9; compare 1 Corinthians 1:25.

does the true universality and with it the true wisdom consist? Hamann contradicts the "common minds," "our current surveyors and metaphysicians,"[7] with the word from the cross. He refuses to obey their "rules of art" and "critical laws,"[8] because they practice the art of separation and not the art of marriage.

The Root of Freedom for Criticism

Hamann was given license for his disobedience and dissent as one who was once himself a "fratricide," had gone astray in disassociation, had practiced and suffered the art of separation, but had been brought to the art of marriage through the gospel, had been brought to communion with God, the neighbor, and all creatures. Here, in the irrevocable life-change at London and its literary documentation fortunately handed down to us, is to be sought the root of Hamann's independence and freedom over against his contemporaries, the root of his capacity for criticism in the service of a universal "aesthetic," of an impartial and richly structured perception.

This root also yields a clear answer to the obvious contemporary question, whether Hamann's work is to be identified as postmodern in the eighteenth century. In addition, one could refer to Hamann's delight in the mask and pseudonymity, to his "cento" (interwoven carpet) style, to his art of citation and notation, and to his "collage" technique, coupled with the intent to provoke disaffection. Hamann is concerned that tradition and the present, author and reader, are not melded into each other but that a distance remains between them. But above all, reference should be made to Hamann's criticism of the Cartesian method of explanation and demonstration, his criticism of the construction of a unity of self-consciousness, his dismissal of the principle and talk of the whole or the unity of reality, even talk of God as the "unity of reality," his validation of the otherness of reason, sensuousness, his work in mythology, his emphasis on human corporeality, on sensuousness, on human fundamental connectedness to all fellow creatures, from which it may not be separated through instrumental reason.

As much as this contemporary of the eighteenth century is a contem-

7. "Wolken," in N II, 106, 9ff.
8. Cf. "Socratic Memorabilia," in Dickson, 393 (N II, 75, 3-5).

porary of postmoderns, and possibly even their "forefather,"[9] their ancestor — and indeed he is such in a specific way — so little does Hamann's work adhere to what is popular and nonobligatory, to that intellectual and bodily vagabonding connected with the quest that calls itself "postmodern."

Certainly, whoever joins with Hamann in his dissent against his age will by all means speak of the "crisis" of the Enlightenment and its "dialectic," indeed, even of an "end" to modernity, which has so shaped the culture that our fellow humans have reciprocally become objects of human construction and our nonhuman fellow creatures have become sacrificial offerings as well as gods, as is indicated in the *Aesthetica in nuce*.

Nevertheless, Hamann's metacriticism of modernity, its testing, is not only postmodern, but simultaneously premodern, in the sense that it results from the conclusion of the *Aesthetica in nuce*: "Let us now hear the conclusion of his newest aesthetic, which is the oldest: Fear GOD, and give glory to him; for the hour of his judgment is come: and worship him that made heaven, and earth, and the sea, and the fountains of waters!"[10]

The oldest aesthetic lies in fearing, loving, and trusting solely in God above all things. But what is oldest is at the same time the eschaton, the last, the newest of all, the absolutely new, which never ages.

Since Hamann allows the Bible to be his concrete historical a priori, he is led into an inexhaustibly spacious area of experience. Luther spoke of it as the "divine Aeneid," whose comprehensiveness cannot be mastered.[11] Nevertheless, in its breadth and depth this inexhaustible comprehensiveness is not vague and indefinite. Rather, it has its precision throughout, which however does not conform to the Cartesian ideal of method. It is precision of a sort in which logic is by no means excluded, but is safeguarded in a constitutive association with poetry. Not least in this way, Hamann takes care that the question about method is not isolated from the question about truth.

9. *Goethe's Travels in Italy*, trans. Charles Nesbit (London: George Bell & Sons, 1885), 182.

10. Haynes, 95 (N II, 217, 15-19).

11. "Table Talk," in LW 54:476 (WA TR 5, 317f. [Number 5677]).

Contemporary

The question about truth is the question about the true intellectual present. To take a position toward it involves awareness of the dual meaning in the title of this book. First, *a contemporary in dissent* denotes a contemporary of the eighteenth century — of the moralistic, illumined, enlightened century Hamann wanted to scandalize, a contemporary of the *siècle philosophique* (philosophical century). Second, it denotes our present contemporary. Indeed, the distance from the eighteenth century cannot be overcome. In what follows we will consistently seek to take that into account. Still, we have by and large the same problems that like the ecological crisis have only become more pronounced. And even today people like Hamann want to hear the prophetic word of the Bible and be interpreted by it. But even others who maintain a distance toward the Bible will not deny its wide-ranging cultural significance and recognize that it contains experience and makes new experience possible.

What benefit may we expect from an engagement with this contemporary of the eighteenth and twenty-first centuries? The author of this book cannot deny that he is a theologian, specifically, a systematic theologian. In one of the many possible answers to the question as to its benefit he points to Hamann's concept of science yoked to Hamann's association with the Bible. "The man to whom history (by virtue of its name) yields science, and philosophy knowledge, and poetry taste not only becomes eloquent himself but almost the equal of the ancient orators. They used occasions and events as the basis and made a chain of keys which became decisions and passions in their audience."[12]

In this trajectory it is clear how problematic it would be to isolate the central field, that is, to isolate philosophy as the arena of observation, hypotheses, theories, and systems[13] (what one usually deems to be "science") from the past and future, from poetry and history. All three dimensions belong together, may not be isolated and thus positioned as absolute. Otherwise all three are ruined, the poets together with the orators, historians, and philosophers. "From orators were made talkers; from historical experts, polyhistors; from philosophers, sophists; from poets, wits."[14]

---

12. "Cloverleaf of Hellenistic Letters, Second Letter," in Haynes, 46-47 (N II, 176, 20-24) (translation altered). Cf. below chapter 12, "Created Time," notes 45-57.

13. "Cloverleaf of Hellenistic Letters, Second Letter," in Haynes, 44 (N II, 175, 6f.). Cf. below chapter 8, "History and Reason," note 83.

14. "Cloverleaf of Hellenistic Letters, Second Letter," in Haynes, 47 (N II, 176, 25ff.).

Hence, beginning with my own profession, with systematic theology, I maintain that the question regarding the benefit of an intense encounter with the work of Hamann is as follows: If what is to be learned from Hamann is true, then all three dimensions named together belong to science; they will not be sterile but fruitful, and not dead but living. This holds even when scholarship, institutionalized in the university, for various reasons must especially cultivate and emphasize the rational element, that central field, philosophical knowledge.

In the present book Hamann is chiefly described and interpreted. His historical and systematic significance, his relevance, are developed. But he is not performed only in those instances in which he is quoted. It was noted, however, that this could most often happen. But even to perform him in a small group in which one tries to decipher Hamann texts would on no account mean to copy him and overcome the distance between him and us. "His style should be no model for others, but as his style it is quite becoming."[15]

Everything depends on perceiving both nearness and distance, and not the one without the other. Due to the unique provocations and stimuli by which Hamann moves us to reflect today over what we could scarcely hear and learn elsewhere, *his* style is becoming.

However, he is digestible only if we avoid "Hamannizing"[16] and becoming a "Königsberg sect" of "little Hamanns," whose invasion of the republic of letters frightened a reviewer in the *Teutschen Merkur* as early as 220 years ago.[17] Unjustifiably. Through his style, Hamann prevented his becoming a model for others. Whoever copies him makes him or herself ridiculous. Even in his life, above all in his "marriage of conscience," he was not concerned with furnishing a model for others.[18]

Just as Hamann himself respects the unique strangeness of another's style and histories, so today we do right by Hamann if we observe not

---

15. "Philological Ideas and Doubts," in Dickson, 476 (N III, 36) (from the *Göttingischen Anzeigen von gelehrten Sachen* coined for Herder, used by us in view of our relation to Hamann).

16. "Zweifel und Einfälle über eine vermischte Nachricht der allgemeinen deutschen Bibliothek," in N III, 173, 31.

17. "Königsbergsche Zeitungen," in N IV, 315, 4f. Cf. "Zweifel und Einfälle über eine vermischte Nachricht der allgemeinen deutschen Bibliothek," in N III, 173, 20ff. Cited by R. Unger, *Hamann und die Aufklärung. Studien zur Vorgeschichte des romantischen Geistes im 18. Jahrhundert,* 2nd edition (Halle, 1925), 430.

18. H IV, 327, 36–328, 1 (to Reichardt; 1781).

only the distance from his time, the eighteenth century, but also the distance from his person and individual style, allowing him his "most exact locality, individuality, and personality."[19] If we observe the distance that the intractable Pan[20] deliberately created toward his contemporaries of that time, then we make use of the freedom for distinguishing *(krinein)* and for criticizing that Hamann advocated to such degree and practiced himself.

A Contemporary in Dissent. This title reflects the character of the book, which is to avoid expropriating the historical individuality and personality of Hamann for one's own already preconceived interests, but rather to allow him his style and locality, and on the other hand to listen to him today and, moved by common questions, to take him seriously as our contemporary in the twenty-first century.

In the crisis of a common cultural perspective, Hamann opens us to possibilities for a new perception of self and world. Though engaged with Herder, Lessing, Mendelssohn, Frederick the Great, Kant, Jacobi, and many others, it is not only in contact and in disagreement with them, but also with us that he publishes what he has to say about a responsible perception of fellow creatures, of nature, reason and language, time and history, sexuality and marriage, of human rights and politics. If we encounter in the figure of Hamann both a comprehensive representation of and a critical breach with the intellectual and political world of the eighteenth century, he is also our contemporary, in any case to the degree that the problems of the Enlightenment are our own, whether they deal with the constitution of subjectivity in the unity of self-consciousness, with "freedom" as the fundamental concept of anthropology, ethics, politics, and the philosophy of history, or with the modern concept of nature and its crisis.

The third, most comprehensive section of this book (Chapters 4–12) is dedicated to the corresponding great controversies. It indicates in a special way that Hamann, taking up wide-ranging themes, establishes connections and thus is not merely an aphorist as most have supposed. In this section where possible, a systematic ordering of the material is attached to a chronological sequence, as can easily be seen in the timetable offered in the appendix.

19. "Ein fliegender Brief," in N III, 352, 25f. Cf. H V, 316, 10ff. (to Jacobi; 1785).
20. "Kreuzzüge des Philologen," in N II, 113. Cf. below chapter 1, "Life and Work," note 42.

The second section (Chapter 3), whose theme is "original motif," points to the root of what is developed in the following nine chapters. Hence this comprehensive chapter is given special place. Here, the distance from a contemporary of the eighteenth century is more reduced than in the other chapters. It shows that Hamann's *Thoughts about My Life* offer an answer to the contemporary question about identity.

The first section, which includes the first and second chapters, provides an overview of Hamann's life and work, and seeks to present the style and shape of his authorship as journalist and writer in a comprehensive way.

The book originated in lectures held during the summer semester of 1987 at the University of Tübingen in the *studium generale* (general studies curriculum), open to members of all faculties. Thanks are due the initiative of the publisher that the publication appeared in its present form.

I wish to thank Dr. Wolfgang-Dieter Baur as well as Dr. Elfriede Büchsel, Dr. Paul Ernst, Dr. Johannes von Lüpke, and Dr. Reinhard Merkel, the first critical readers of this book. Thanks are due also to Mrs. Gisela Hauber and Mrs. Isolde Thill for their careful copyediting of the manuscript, and to Mrs. Thill for setting up the index of persons.

Not last but first of all I thank my wife, who with clear head and true heart energetically promoted the formation and completion of this book in a timely manner.

Tübingen, Germany
Autumn 1987

I am greatly pleased that this book is now accessible to English-speaking readers. I am indebted to Eerdmans Publishing Company for adopting it into its program. Most of all I need to extend hearty thanks to colleagues Prof. Dr. Roy A. Harrisville and Prof. Dr. Mark C. Mattes for translating this text with considerable sympathetic understanding and meticulousness, and for sparing no pains in doing so. May the book find many readers whom the Magus can provoke to critical thought.

Oswald Bayer
Tübingen/Hennef, Germany,
October 31, 2010

Chapter 1

Life and Work

The prejudice that Hamann is opaque stubbornly persists to our day. In terms of an opaqueness laden with mystery many hear the sobriquet "Magus of the North," known to everyone who has heard anything at all about Hamann.

This sobriquet given by the Schwabian Carl von Moser to the man from Königsberg and which he gladly received has nothing to do with magic. It will do nothing more than recall the story of the Magi, the "wise men," told in the Gospel of Matthew. A magus is one who has seen the star of Bethlehem and "overwhelmed with joy" worships the child in the manger, as indicated in the story (Matt. 2:10). "Magus" is thus simply the designation for a Christian whose name is always involved in specific stories and cannot even be thought of apart from them. This uniqueness characterizes Hamann's life, work, and achievement in a special, most provocative way. Hamann learns that he is interpreted by specific histories, events, and guises, which one may call "typological," whether they are the "Magi from the East, to Bethlehem," Socrates, or Amos and John the Baptist who pronounce judgment, or Matthew, a tax collector like Hamann, of whom it is said that Jesus "saw a man called Matthew sitting at the tax booth, and he said to him, 'Follow me.' And he got up and followed him" (Matt. 9:9). Hence, instead of signing his letters with his name, Hamann signed them with the self-appellation, "*Magus in telonio,*" at the tax booth.[1]

---

1. H V, 291, 17 (to Kraus; 1784).

Now the star of Bethlehem has not simply enlightened the whole world. Rather, it shines "in a dark place, until the day dawns . . ." (2 Peter 1:19).[2] So, Hamann knows that he belongs to a race[3] that lives in the twilight, *"entre chien et loup"* (between dog and wolf), as he signs an important letter in which he critically scrutinized Kant's famous "Answer to the Question: What Is Enlightenment?" *(Beantwortung der Frage: Was ist Aufklärung?).* *"Entre chien et loup,"* between day and night, between the times, no one can say whether the gloaming turns into an eternal night or an eternal day, unless one attends to the light of the prophetic word, "shining in a dark place. . . ."[4]

It is thus no miracle that a specific darkness, the darkness of the world situation, is not to be denied. Writers who are honest, subject to no illusion or guile, must account for it in the way in which they write. Reviewers of Hamann's *opuscula* (little works) such as Moses Mendelssohn faulted "the darkness and mysteriousness" of his style.[5] Hamann responds, speaking of himself in the third person with irony, as he often does, "in order to arrive at the wonderful economy of his style: thus after deducting $666\frac{2}{3}$ typographical errors it appears to suit precisely the darkness of his whole situation."[6]

In any case, the brightest intellect of his time knew of its opacities, above all, of his own. He confesses that self-knowledge is a descent into hell.[7] And in Goethe we find not only the judgment that Hamann is the brightest intellect of his time but likewise the reference that Hamann saw also the shadows: "Clarity is a suitable distribution between light and shade."[8]

The journalist and writer Johann Georg Hamann spoke, wrote, and thought clearly. In a clarity that pained him and turned his readers on their heads, he knew how to rightly divide the word. But even he often failed and let his literary essays lie as torsos.

---

2. Cf. for example "Essay of a Sibyl on Marriage," in Dickson, 508 (N III, 200, 25.39 [important to Hamann from the *Biblische Betrachtungen* and on]).

3. Cf. "Philological Ideas and Doubts about an Academic Prize-Winning Essay," in Dickson, 491 (N III, 51, 21f.): Herder writes for "an evil and adulterous generation." Cf. also H VII, 424, 23 (to Jacobi; 1788).

4. "Philological Ideas and Doubts," in Dickson, 488 (N III, 48, 16f.). (Cf. note 2 above.)

5. "Verurtheilung der Kreuzzüge des Philologen," in N II, 264, 32.38.

6. "Zweifel und Einfälle über eine vermischte Nachricht," in N III, 187, 18-21.

7. Cf. "Kreuzzüge des Philologen," in N II, 164, 18.

8. Goethe, *Maxims and Reflections* (compare above Introduction, note 2).

"We live here from crumbs. Our thoughts are nothing but fragments. Indeed our knowledge is a patchwork."[9] "I am not up to universal 'truths, fundamental principles, systems,' instead I am up to crumbs, fragments, whims, thoughts."[10] To this corresponds the character of his public writings, which often, but by no means always, had a difficult birth. They are intentionally brief occasional pieces, "arising from special occasions in my life,"[11] "full of personality and locality, full of relationship to similar appearances and experiences, but at the same time full of allusions to the world of literature in which he lived."[12]

In an unprecedented way Hamann was always a listener and reader first of all, and then spoke and wrote. Not coincidentally many of his works are formal reviews or can be best understood as such. Since he was always a reader first of all, and then an author, in writing he related himself at the outset to his reader, just as a letter writer relates to the one with whom he or she speaks. Not coincidentally, many of his works and ahead of them all the first writing, *Socratic Memorabilia* (1759), grew from his correspondence and from it allow their origin to be known.

It is true that Hamann criticizes the author's dependence on the reader and compares it to the relationship of a god to the one who offers sacrifice; the gods and their devotees are mutually dependent on each other. But Hamann does not criticize the author's dependence on the reader on the assumption it could be annulled and the corresponding attention avoided. The reader is not to be thought away. The reader belongs to the author essentially, not casually. "The idea of the reader is the Muse and help meet of the author."[13] The reader belongs to the author as the wife to the husband (Gen. 2:18). In Hamann's speaking and thinking the metaphors that stem from the sphere of sexuality and hark back to it play a key role.

Though Hamann maintains he was not equal to systematic thought, he is nonetheless systematic precisely in the fact that thoroughly oriented to the aesthetics of receptivity he has the relationship between author and reader in mind from the very first. This relationship is not guaranteed through an a priori universality of thought or through rigid,

9. "Fragments," in Smith, 161 (N I, 299, 27-29) (translation altered).

10. ZH I, 431, 29f. (to Lindner; 1759).

11. H V, 314, 10f. in context 9-14 (to Jacobi; 1785).

12. Johann Georg Hamann the Younger, *Hamann's Schriften*, ed. F. Roth (Berlin: G. A. Weiner, 1821-43), VII Sections, 1821-23; Vol. I, Section VIII; Preface.

13. "Leser und Kunstrichter," in N II, 348, 10.

established definitions of words. Rather, it is first established. In order for the intended communication to succeed, the author must not yet definitively establish connection with the text. Author and reader can only form it together as husband and wife form a marriage. "Writer and reader are two halves whose needs are related to each other and have their unification as a common goal."[14] No one is a self-sufficient individual able to exist all by oneself. Together they form an indissoluble, fruitful unity in their medium, the book.

Locality, Individuality, Personality

In contrast to his contemporary Kant, and to Hegel, Hamann establishes relationships in such a way that they cannot be presumed to be a system originating with the author. The relationships he establishes are not generalizations in the sense that they can be cut away from the "profound particularity" that Hegel so severely criticized in his lengthy review of Hamann's writings, edited by Friedrich Roth in 1821-25.[15]

It was not least against philosophers and systematic theologians that Hamann writes in his bequest, the *Fliegender Brief:* "I know nothing better than to oppose the universal chatter and the index finger aiming beautifully from the distance into the wide world . . . than the most precise locality, individuality, and personality."[16] In the same context Hamann points to the place of his birth, "the most dilapidated building of the old city bath situated by the Pregel and the Katzbach,"[17] to that world captured by Johannes Bobrowski's poem.[18]

Hamann
That
one world,
roads, ways today

14. "Leser und Kunstrichter," in N II, 347, 22-24.

15. Cf. below chapter 2, "Style and Form," note 56.

16. "Ein fliegender Brief," in N III, 352, 23-26.

17. "Ein fliegender Brief," N III, 350, 36f.

18. This poem has been deciphered by B. Gajek in "Autor — Gedicht — Leser. Zu Johannes Bobrowskis Hamann-Gedicht," in *Literatur und Geistesgeschichte. Festgabe für H. Burger,* ed. R. Grimm and C. Wiedemann (Berlin: E. Schmidt, 1968), 308-24. Cf. Ruth and Matthew Mead in the volume *Shadow Lands* by Johannes Bobrowski (New York: New Directions, 1994), 99.

Wasianski is coming — who
wrote the Lives
and who the poems à la Grécourt,
between Lizentgraben and
Katzbach the whole, what do I know, world.

But a bird sings
through the night, in the
too heavily pruned trees,
summerlong this bird,
it does not wake my son,
but I — so I shall
go, I fish for a dish of
will-o'-the-wisp in the meadows
behind the ditch.

World. I see in the rain
a white cloud. It is I.
Down the Pregel
the boat. From the mists. World.
A hell, in which God dwells.
World. I say with Sancho:
God, I say: he understands me.

The world conversation in which Hamann lived is defined by the most exact personality, individuality, and locality in which he lived. Born on August 27, 1730, in Königsberg, East Prussia, he was the son of a public bath administrator and surgeon, whose father was a pastor in Lausitz and whose brother, likewise named Johann Georg Hamann (1697-1733), was a literary figure. His mother hailed from Lübeck. The father's occupation earned Hamann the title he proposed for a selection of his writings planned by his pupil and friend Johann Gottfried Herder. The title was "Quackery" or "Little Metacritical Tub."[19] As the father bathed everyone in a tub, so the son will test and metacritically treat all, including Kant, the critic of pure reason.

Hamann's youth in the port, government, and university city is played out in an atmosphere in which Pietism and Enlightenment are

19. H V, 350, 19-27; cf. 403, 1-9 (to Herder; 1785).

woven together without significant conflict. At the age of sixteen, in 1746, Hamann begins the study of theology and philosophy, then changes to law and political economy. Chiefly, however, he studies literature, philology, and rhetoric, but also mathematics and the natural sciences. He drops out of the university without a diploma, as an *"Invalide des Apoll,"*[20] as he calls himself in a letter to the king. Afterward, he resides for a longer time as a home tutor on Baltic estates.

In these years (1752-56) Hamann's baroque encyclopedic erudition is broadened. He obtains the most varied bibliographic tools, scholarly lexicons, review periodicals, and dictionaries. Characteristic of Hamann's authorship is the combination of philological detail with philosophical insight and breadth, of work in detail with a profound systematic interest.

Hamann's studies in this period are devoted chiefly to texts in political economy. His first larger publication is the translation of a manuscript in political economics, to which he adds his own appendix.[21] Correspondingly, in 1756 he is employed by the Berens Trading Firm in Riga. While a student in Königsberg, he is befriended by Johann Christoph Berens, and together with Berens, Johann Gotthelf Lindner (1729-1776), and others he publishes the weekly *Daphne*. The learned tutor becomes a businessman.

In 1757 the Berens firm sends Hamann to London with a commission apparently having to do with political economy. There he completely loses his bearings. He fails both professionally and personally. Yet his life is changed. Among the many books, those "miserable comforters,"[22] he finds his way to the one book, finds his way from distraction to concentration on the one thing needful, from unbearable unrest to certainty. He finds that in the Author of the Bible he has met the Author of his life-story through the "descent into the hell of self-knowledge";[23] has met a friend who interprets and understands him. Having become the reader of the one book, this reader of many books learns that in reading he is read and in understanding is understood.

That the knots were untied "on the evening of March 31," 1758, while he meditated on the story of the fratricide in Genesis 4 does not mean that Hamann had this experience in an isolated moment or as pure intu-

20. ZH II, 226, 11f. (to the *Königlich-Preussische Kriegs- und Domänenkammer*; 1763).
21. "Beylage zu Dangeuil's Anmerkungen . . ." (1756), in N IV, 225-42.
22. Cf. "Thoughts about My Life," in Smith, 152 (N II, 39, 27) (translation altered); cf. Job 16:2.
23. "Kreuzzüge des Philologen," in N II, 164, 17f.

ition.[24] He did not experience it unmediated, but in the context of a profoundly penetrating and extensive reading and writing, just as Martin Luther witnessed to the "reformational change" in himself and his theology.[25] While reading, Hamann writes the *Biblische Betrachtungen (Biblical Meditations of a Christian)*,[26] in the form of a diary[27] and not intended for publication, along with a pietistic general confession titled *Gedanken über meinen Lebenslauf (Thoughts about My Life)*,[28] and other texts,[29] among them the *Brocken (Fragments)*, all of which not only prepare for Hamann's later work but in essence already contain it. The life-change from the many books to the one book witnessed to in these texts does not nullify the old books but transforms their study and allows entry into a newly established context.

Socrates in Königsberg

The coincidental beginning of Hamann's actual authorship indicates its enduring peculiarity. After his return from London to Riga, the Bible reader, the one understood by God, senses the old spirit opposing his new experience. His old friends Johann Christoph Berens and Immanuel Kant now see in Hamann only a "Schwärmer," and a man of no civil use. In the context of this dispute, Hamann's courting of Catharina Berens, in whom he saw the bride "according to God's will," fails in 1758.[30] The two friends seek to return Hamann to the Enlightenment. The ensuing conflicts involving the fundamental one between Enlightenment and Christianity are witnessed to in a series of comprehensive letters, chiefly to Johann Gotthelf Lindner, who mediates between Hamann and the two friends. The *Socratic Memorabilia*[31] are born in 1759 out of the work on this basic conflict.

---

24. "Thoughts about My Life," in Smith, 153 (N II, 40, 38ff.). He structures the meditation on Deuteronomy 5:17 on the basis of Genesis 4.

25. LW 34, 338 (WA 54, 186, 25-29).

26. "Schlusswort," in N I, 327.

27. "Biblische Betrachtungen," in N I, 7-249.

28. "Thoughts about My Life," in Smith, 139-57 (N II, 9-54).

29. "Betrachtungen zu Kirchenliedern," in N I, 250-309.

30. ZH I, 288, 14 (to his father; 1759). Cf. N II, 52, 34-53, 27.

31. "Socratic Memorabilia," in Dickson, 375-400 (N II, 57-82). The following citations in this section can be found at 59, 26; 59, 24; 59, 19; 59, 30.

In this writing Hamann deals with the language of the eighteenth century inspired by the figure of Socrates. By means of the spirit of the time and through the general public he seeks to reach his friends, Berens and Kant. The twofold inscription, "with a double dedication to the public, or to no one" and "to two" corresponds with this attempt. The two friends cannot be directly reached, but only indirectly. At heart they share in the publicity. In essence they belong to the general public. But the general public has power. It fascinates and creates dependence.

With the publication of the *Socratic Memorabilia* Hamann intends to liberate his friends from enslavement to the general public, "to purify" two "of your devotees . . . from service to your vanity." The public, the omniscient No One, is to be conquered from within by the unknowing Socrates, to be struck with its own weapon. In remembrance of the beloved figure of Socrates, Hamann offers the insatiably inquisitive general public a "gift," a "sacrifice," which it is to desirously accept and allow to be tasted. But the sacrificial gift is a "pious fraud," has a barbed hook, is a "Greek gift" (Trojan horse). Hamann's Socrates, a contemporary in dissent, lurks behind the customary readership. Moloch, the "public," gulps what brings its downfall. The societal general public, perceived by Hamann in its artificiality and power with a visual force comparable to Hobbes's *Leviathan,* is seen as an idol, is exposed with biting irony, is to burst and at least set the two friends free. With his authorship of the *Socratic Memorabilia,* Hamann intends to entangle the "omniscient No One" and the "unknowing Socrates" to the effect that Kant and Berens will step out of the no man's land, out of the fascination of the anonymity that knows much but understands nothing, and become individuals who have grown skeptical of their own knowledge and confessed their own ignorance, in order to make room for faith.

Hamann adopts the following proposition from David Hume, whose skepticism had special significance for him: "the final fruit of all worldly wisdom is the observation of human ignorance and weakness." So, according to Hamann, the philosopher "falls on the sword of his own truths."[32] "Reason is holy, right, and good; but through it comes nothing other than the recognition of thoroughly sinful ignorance. . . . Therefore, let no one be deceived. Whoever among you thinks to be wise, let that one become a fool. . . . The office of philosophy is the embodied

---

32. ZH I, 355f. (to Lindner; 1759).

Moses, a stubborn and severe teacher of the faith."[33] Hamann has no illusion about the success of his indirect sermon and on the title page sets as a motto the opening lines of the *Satires* of Persius: "Who then will read something like this? — Are you asking me? — Nobody, by Hercules! — Nobody? — Perhaps two or perhaps no one!"

The witness to which Hamann was called by his conversion in London did not lead him, a stutterer all his life, to a public office in the church. It is as a writer that he was a *"minister verbi divini,"* a servant of the divine word, in this, as in many other ways comparable to Kierkegaard. Authorship is a preaching office of its own. So Hamann's language does not take the usual shape of the Reformation tradition of preaching. The graphic language of the Luther Bible is rather woven into the life-story of the author, in concrete situations of conversation, encounters, journalistic constellations, reviews, replies, in anti- and metacriticism. Hamann engages his opponent with irony and ridicule, parodying and satirizing, scolding and flattering. In this way, still living in the *respublica litteraria* (republic of letters) before the time of the collapse of the rhetorical tradition, he makes use of the means of rhetoric — situated within the strategy of his witness.

Since his collaboration on the *Daphne* while a student journalist, then in later years an editor and subsequently for fifteen years author of numerous reviews for the *Königsbergsche Gelehrte und Politische Zeitungen*,[34] Hamann at the core of his being had communication in mind. The newly emergent sensitivity in which the educated of his time engaged in the processes of communication, in friendly conversation and correspondence, in the relation between author and reader, not least in the art of reviewing, reaches its zenith in Hamann.

The apex of the critical-political existence of this Christian, his reading and writing, is a *metacriticsm* of Kant's *Critique* and also the political system of Frederick the Great.[35] Hamann was a contemporary of both, not merely in a chronological sense. He participated to the inmost degree in what they represent. Kant's "Answer to the Question: What Is Enlightenment?" (1784), especially his *Laudatio* (encomium) of the Age of Frederick, strikes him "in the very soul." Kant speaks of self-inflicted immaturity instead of self-inflicted tutelage. By such an

---

33. "Wolken," in N II, 108, 19-28.
34. "Königsbergsche Gelehrte und Politische Zeitungen," in N IV, 257-435.
35. Cf. below chapter 6, "Criticism and Politics," and chapter 9, "Reason Is Language."

unexpected metacritical development Hamann proves to be a radical enlightener.

The unheard-of claim of Hamann's metacriticism is not at odds with his outwardly unglamorous life. For many years he remained a "lover of leisure," of spare time for reading; he cared for his sick father, and worried about his brother who was becoming feeble-minded, but had assumed no useful vocation acceptable to the middle class. In 1767, through Kant's mediation, he receives the post of translator in customs administration controlled by Frederick's counselors, and in 1777 is promoted to "warehouse steward." He remains "sitting in the custom house" *(in telonio sedens),* in a subordinate position, with scanty income, for which he must struggle against the *"Arithmétique politique,"* the economic-political arithmetic of the state. In 1787 his request for a leave of absence for a long-planned visit to the circle of friends around the Princess Gallitzin in Münster is given with his dismissal and a modest pension. He never legalized his "marriage of conscience" with Anna Regina Schumacher, his father's maid and the mother of his four children, not only but also as a protest against the double standard of his well-mannered age.[36]

Hamann was not a theologian of the academic guild nor an officially called man of the church, but an *"homme de lettres"* (man of letters). So he was addressed, and so he occasionally called himself. "For me, every book is a Bible."[37] Totally fascinated by books and the one Book, he was first of all always a reader, and then only an author. His love was directed to the word. He was a philologist, a "lover of the word." To want to be more would mean to want to be more than Creator of the world, who is the "author" who addresses and understands me, the "Poet," who does what he says and says what he does. To want to be less would contradict the dignity of the human, in essence a creature of language. With Luther, Hamann stresses that "the human has no more powerful or nobler work than speaking."[38] The human as an *animal rationale* is a creature of language, one who is addressed and thus able to answer, but also obliged to be re-sponsible.

As a philologist Hamann sought the proper word, *"le mot propre."*[39]

36. Cf. below chapter 11, "Essay of a Sibyl on Marriage."

37. ZH I, 309, 11 (to Lindner; 1759).

38. LW 35, 254 (WA DB 10/I, 100, 12-14). Cf. "Königsbergsche Gelehrte und Politische Zeitungen," in N IV, 425, 39f.

39. "Über das Spinozabüchlein Jacobis," in N IV, 457, 30; 458, 15.21f. Cf. 459, 28-31.

He often found it, though often with pain. For him the proper word was the living word, the salient point, from which a conversation, a letter, a book is organized, becomes intelligible in its shape and can be evaluated. Thus to the proper word belongs its development, its emergence. It gains its reality in process. "The delivery makes the point just like the clothes make the man. Every point is an invisible embryo, whose concept and content must first come, into the world, as it were, and be evident through the delivery. Hence, that witty thought of the wise man: speak that I may see you,"[40] an apothegm attributed to Socrates.

The way in which Hamann sought the proper word in others and himself gave offense, just as Socrates once gave offense with his type of questioning. Socrates' appearance, which did not conform to contemporary ideas of a handsome man, was as offensive as his penetrating style of questioning. Yet, as Alcibiades said in Plato's *Symposium,* on the inside, through his words, through his questions Socrates was beautiful, just as the luminous idol inside Silenus's chest. In this perplexing discrepancy between inner and outer lies the essence of the comparison drawn by Hamann between his vocation as a writer and the vocation of Socrates. "In short, all my *Opuscula* (little works) make up an Alcibiadic chest. Everyone has found fault with the Façon of the Satyr or Pan and no one has thought of the old reliquary of Luther's *Small Catechism.*"[41]

In this letter, Hamann alludes to the above-named Friedrich Carl von Moser on the title vignette of the *Crusades of the Philologist* (1762). It provides a hideous ram-faced satyr signed "PAN," and thus illustrates the offensive form and content of Hamann's writings in conflict with the taste of his century. This title page can be understood from the background of baroque emblematic. The title to which the offense aroused by the philologist points is reflected in the repulsively ugly Pan of the vignette as the *picture,* while the motto from Virgil underscores the title's war motif *(Kreuzzüge):* "Still other wars will come and again a greater Achilles will be sent to Troy."[42]

The tenacity and offensiveness of his writings, depicted in the title vignette of *Crusades of the Philologist,* has Hamann himself in view with

---

40. "Über das Spinozabüchlein Jacobis," in N IV, 456, 16-19. Along with it cf. chapter 4, "The Modern Concept of Nature in Crisis," note 31.

41. ZH III, 67, 9-13 (to Moser; 1773).

42. Title page, "Kreuzzüge des Philologen," in N II, 113.

its formulation. Harking back to it he asks, "is not the word of the cross in the inscription of his book a scandal to the Jews and foolishness to the Greeks?"[43]

The hidden beauty and solid core of the *Crusades of the Philologist* is thus the word of the cross taken up in Lutheran tradition. For Hamann that word is the source of his authorship and so aptly describes him in the eyes of others that it (1 Cor. 1:23 and 27) was etched on his gravestone in Münster in 1788. It was thought to write "the Philosopher and Theologian," but remarkably a *viro Christiano* (Christian man) was decided on, thus: Johann Georg Hamann, Christian. Hamann wanted expressly to be a *Philologus crucis* (philologist of the cross). From the cross comes the power of criticism in a critical philology.

In his commentary, referring to himself in the third person, Hamann uses the passage from the Epistle to the Hebrews (4:12), which speaks of a "critical" word of God and joins it to the sign of the cross: "But what should we say now about the taste of the philologist? Firstly his name suggests a lover of the living, emphatic, double-edged, penetrating, crucial, and critical word, before which no creature can hide but everything lies open and in cross-section before his eyes. Before long in the standard of his flying collection glitters that sign of scandal and foolishness, in which the smallest art critic is victorious with Constantine and the oracle of judgment leads to victory."[44]

If, without detriment to his philology of the cross, Hamann was not an official academic theologian or a man of the church called to the official preaching office, but rather an *homme de lettres,* then we can see that he is not only of interest to theologians but also above all to scholars of German Studies. Moreover, if we keep in mind Hamann's struggle against the forgetfulness of language in Kant's transcendental critique of reason as concentrated in his proposition that "reason is language,"[45] then even the interest of philosophers can be understood. Obviously, whoever like Hamann subordinates thought to language and being to the word does not achieve philosophical approval from all quarters. At the height of his authorship Hamann was Kant's friend and opponent, his "meta-critiquer." Shortly before his death he signed his *Letztes Blatt,*

43. "Göttingische Anzeige, und vorläufige Beantwortung der Frage: Wo?" in N II, 255, 24f.

44. "Verurtheilung der Kreuzzüge," in N II, 263, 49–264, 1. Hebrews 4:12 is cited here as well as the *"in hoc signo vinces"* of the Roman emperor Constantine.

45. Cf. below chapter 9, "Reason Is Language."

an entry in the poetry album of the seventeen-year-old Marianne von Gallitzin in Münster as a *"metacriticus."*

Justice to the interdisciplinary significance of the Königsberger Socrates will only be done by those who trespass the boundaries of the academic disciplines, who venture beyond enforced borders. I hope to do justice to this requirement — even if I can and will not deny that I am a theologian.

Physiognomy of the Writings

The issue and linguistic shape of the writings in which Hamann's intellectual shape is transmitted to us show that they are indissolubly united in their literary form. The various forms of Hamann's authorship appear in the titles. To Hamann's mind, all his writings can be viewed from them and their mottos. Their title is their face, their "physiognomy."

This has already been seen in the *Socratic Memorabilia.* After searching for a motto and "explanation of its title" Hamann took the title of *Fragments* from John 6:12. The title of Kierkegaard's *Philosophical Fragments* emulates it. "We live here from crumbs. Our thoughts are nothing but fragments. Indeed our knowledge is a patchwork." "I am not up to universal 'truths, fundamental principles, systems,' instead I am up to crumbs, fragments, whims, thoughts."[46] Accordingly his writings bear titles such as *Imaginary Thoughts (Chimärische Einfälle), Philological Thoughts and Doubts (Philologische Einfälle und Zweifel), Doubts and Thoughts (Zweifel und Einfälle).* Nearly all the titles of Hamann's writings reveal that they are answers, imitations, free associations. The *Aesthetica in nuce* (1762) borrows its title from the book of a contemporary. The writing "To the Solomon of Prussia" *(Au Salomon de Prusse)* alludes to the conclusion of Voltaire's ode to Frederick's assumption of the throne in 1740: "The Solomon of the North brings the light." The planned *Courageous Letters Concerning Natural Religion (Freimütigen Briefe, die natürliche Religion betreffend)* reverse the anonymously published (1780) *Courageous Letters Concerning Christianity (Freimütigen Betrachtungen über das Christentum)* of the Freemason and professor, court preacher, and Hamann's father confessor, Johann August Starck (1741-1816), and at the same time are related to Hamann's translation of

---

46. Cf. above notes 9 and 10.

Hume's *Dialogues Concerning Natural Religion*, in which he sees crucial help in his struggle against the representatives of "natural religion."

The writing *Golgatha and Scheblimini* (*Golgatha und Scheblimini! Von einem Prediger in der Wüsten . . .*) has an especially eloquent title, appearing in 1784 in the "desert," that is, in rationalistic Berlin, and as an answer to Moses Mendelssohn's *Jerusalem or on Religious Power and Judaism* (1783). It is written, like all Hamann's writings, in "cento" style. It is "inlaid," a mosaic (in 1762 Hamann had published a collection of his French writings under the title *Essais à la Mosaique*). "This little mosaic writing is assembled from known passages of Mendelssohn's *Jerusalem,* and opposed to Wolff's subtleties, by which he sought to cloak his ignorance of Judaism and his enmity against Christianity, which he calls religious power."[47] With the Old Testament (Ps. 110:1: *Scheblimini* = "Sit at my right hand!") Hamann opposes enlightened Judaism on behalf of Christianity. Its center lies in intertwining the event of the crucifixion (Golgatha) and resurrection of Jesus Christ *(Scheblimini),* in the "earthly crown of thorns and heavenly crown of stars and in the transverse relation of the deepest humiliation and most noble exaltation of the two opposite natures."[48] This center, given shape in the title of the writing, defined Hamann's life, reading, and writings to their subtlest ramifications. The reciprocal participation of the properties of the divine and human natures, "this *communicatio* of divine and human *idiomatum* is a fundamental law and the master-key of all our knowledge and of the whole visible economy."[49] (*The Last Will and Testament of the Knight of the Rose-Cross* [*Des Ritters von Rosenkreuz letzte Willensmeinung über den göttlichen und menschlichen Ursprung der Sprache,* 1772].)

Golgatha and Scheblimini is "the true content of my entire authorship, which has nothing other than an evangelical Lutheranism in its center."[50] The uncompleted *Disrobing and Transfiguration: A Flying Letter to Nobody, the Well Known* (*Entkleidung und Verklärung. Ein Fliegender Brief an Niemand, den Kundbaren,* 1785-87) serves the "disclosure of my little authorship and clarification of its purpose, to renew

---

47. "Golgatha and Scheblimini," in N III, 319, 1-5. Cf. below chapter 10, "Natural Right and Social Life."

48. "Ein fliegender Brief," in N III, 405, 29-407, 3.

49. Cf. "The Last Will and Testament of the Knight of the Rose-Cross," in Haynes, 99 (N III, 27, 11-14).

50. H VI, 466, 22-24 (to Schenk; 1786).

misjudged Christianity and Lutheranism, and to remove the misunderstandings opposed to it."[51] It concludes with the confession that it is "Christianity" in terms of "Lutheranism," which "for over a quarter of a century made of my secret authorship its coat of arms."[52] Above all, in its "taste and power alone Luther's *Small Catechism* is a match for the murder by Pope and Turk in every aeon," and which, according to Hamann's own testimony, is hidden within the "alcibiadic chest" of his rude writings, like the idol in Silenus's chest, and in this chrysalis shape smuggled out of a religious ghetto into the public light becomes "a proper scandal of our prophets of lies, appearances, and mouths."[53] Beyond the vigorous language of the Luther Bible, in the midst of "our philosophical and enlightened century," Hamann repeats Luther's rough gesturing by way of language. But he is not concerned with literary shadow boxing but with the seriousness of convicting false prophecy and with the struggle against idolatry. "For what is the highly touted reason with its omnipotence, infallibility, effusiveness, certainty, and evidence? An *Ens rationis*, an oil god, to which a shrill superstition of irrationality imputes divine attributes."[54]

"The fear of the Lord is the beginning of wisdom, and this wisdom makes us cowardly about lying and lazy about versifying"[55] — lazy about the versifying of the literati and philosophers, who in an uncritical use of their reason are without the necessary skepticism and have become "orthodox" in their dogmatism. By contrast, Hamann wants to recognize "no other orthodoxy than our Lutheran Small Catechism."[56] If the orthodoxy of "healthy reason" sought to govern every area of life and even to intervene in vernacular language with a puristic zeal for reform, Hamann made himself the advocate of the inconspicuous, of what is offensive to pure reason, of the contingent. He authored a New Apology for the Letter h, the elimination of which at the middle and end of a syllable was forced on orthography by one of the many proposals for re-

---

51. H VII, 43, 36–44, 2 (to Jacobi; 1786).

52. "Ein fliegender Brief," in N III, 407, 16-18.

53. ZH III, 67, 2-14 (to Moser; 1773).

54. *Konxompax. Fragmente einer apokryphischen Sibylle über apokalyptische Mysterien*, 1779, in N III, 225, 3-6. Translator's note: *Ölgötze* is a sixteenth-century German word denoting an oil icon depicting a god that is not living, but stiff and dead.

55. H V, 291, 24-26 (to Kraus; 1784).

56. "Zweifel und Einfälle über eine vermischte Nachricht der allgemeinen deutschen Bibliothek," in N III, 173, 7f.

form that came into vogue. In "New Apology of the Letter h by himself" the little "h" defends itself against the violent and enthusiastic improvers of language: "My existence and preservation is a matter for him who bears all things with his strong word and who has sworn, saying 'Till heaven and earth pass, one jot or one tittle shall in no wise pass.'"[57]

Hamann diagnoses as virulent a reason that compels to universality and necessity, to purity from everything contingent and unique. He draws a parallel between the Enlightenment and Roman Catholicism from the viewpoint of their striving for universality, their method of abstraction connected with it, and the despotism of their system effected by it. He struggles against the domination of instrumental reason that shapes the modern dealing of humans with their fellow creatures — in the "coherent and systematic conclusiveness of Roman and metaphysical catholic despotism whose transcendental intellect itself prescribes its laws of nature."[58]

Hamann's struggle against "Roman and metaphysical catholic despotism" comes to a head in his metacriticism of Kant's *Critique of Pure Reason*. The salient point lies in the "purity," as the title already indicates: *Metacriticism of the Purism of Reason* (*Metakritik über den Purismum der Vernunft* [1784]). The purity assumed by Kant is due to an abstraction, just as his assumption of the goodness of the will. Hamann evaluates Kant's *Groundwork of the Metaphysics of Morals* (*Grundlegung zur Metaphysik der Sitten* [1785]) in comparison with the *Critique of Pure Reason:* "Instead of *pure reason* the talk here is about another fancy and idol, the *good will*."[59] He writes to Scheffner, "*Pure reason* and *good will* are always just words for me, whose concept I am not in a position to arrive at with my senses, and I have no *fidem implicitam* (implicit faith) for philosophy."[60] "Without experience and tradition," Hamann has "no concept" of reason.[61] The revolution in philosophical perspective concentrated in Hamann's *metacriticism* struggles against the forgetfulness of language in the transcendental critique of reason. It is chiefly concerned with the philosophical doctrine of God, logic, ontology, and hermeneutics. In its thematic connection with the philosophy of

---

57. "New Apology of the Letter h," in Haynes, 160 (N III, 105, 10-13).
58. "Golgatha and Scheblimini," in Haynes, 171 (N III, 297, 15-18) (translation altered).
59. H V, 418, 21f. (to Herder; 1785).
60. H V, 434, 24-26 (to Scheffner; 1785).
61. H V, 448, 25f. (to Jacobi; 1785).

right[62] as developed in *Golgatha and Scheblimini,* the programmatic proposition of the *Zwei Scherflien* ("Two Mites") sounds out what merely makes its appearance in the *Metacriticism:* "Without language we would have no reason, without reason no religion, and without these three essential components of our nature we would have neither spirit nor social bond."[63]

Hamann's life, reading, and writing occur in the unique freedom that makes up the humanity of the human. In debate with Herder's anthropology and interpreting the commission to rule in the biblical primeval history, Hamann refers to Aristotle and maintains "that the true character of our nature" consists "in the *judicial* and *administrative* dignity of a *political animal.*"[64] This dignity is not self-acquired[65] but is given to the human. With this power the human is moved beyond mere receptivity and mere spontaneity. We are neither merely readers nor authors but both at the same time. Our freedom is a communal interplay between what is given beforehand and what is acquired, what is received and what is passed on. We do not have power over the beginning and end of this interplay. We remain learners, but learning "in the true understanding is neither *invention* nor sheer *recollection.*"[66]

The communal interplay does not take place in a space free of rule and does not live from anticipating this freedom. It is defined in such a way that others have power over me and I over them, as lord and servant, simultaneously a free lord over all things and subject to none and a dutiful servant to all and subject to everyone. "Everyone is his own legislator but also the first-born and the neighbor of his subjects."[67]

Hamann uses this freedom in his French writing "To the Solomon of Prussia" *(Au Salomon de Prusse),* which he combined with the "Philological Thoughts and Doubts" *(Philologische Einfälle und Zweifel)* into twin publications. Hamann appeals to the king, who stops "his ears from all cries of his subjects and tax servants,"[68] addresses the first servant of the state as such, as the lowest servant, and urges him to become

---

62. Cf. below chapter 10, "Natural Right and Social Life."

63. "Zwei Scherflein zur neusten Deutschen Literatur," in N III, 231, 10-12.

64. "Philological Ideas and Doubts," in Haynes, 114 (N III, 37, 24-26); cf. below chapter 6, "Criticism and Politics," note 29.

65. "Philological Ideas and Doubts," in Haynes, 114-15 (N III, 37, 28–38, 3).

66. "Philological Ideas and Doubts," in Haynes, 119 (N III, 41, 10-12).

67. "Philological Ideas and Doubts," in Haynes, 115 (N III, 38, 16f.).

68. H V, 208, 34f. (to Bucholtz; 1784).

what he already is by virtue of the humiliation and exaltation of Jesus Christ. "Sire . . . You have humbled Yourself and being found in fashion as an unhappy Prussian, You will at last succeed in becoming our FATHER, who will know well how to give good things, like our Father who is in Heaven. . . ."[69] In such freedom the "magus" speaks, the one who has seen the star (Matt. 2:10), a *vir christianus*. Hamann found no publisher for his daring twin publications.

---

69. "To the Solomon of Prussia," in Haynes, 141 (N III, 57, 1.58, 22-26); cf. below chapter 6, "Criticism and Politics," note 49.

Chapter 2

Style and Form

The style and forms of Hamann's literary works, his "authorship," as he happily put it, are not easy to analyze. Moreover, every analysis kills the liveliness of whatever is made an object. Only in a somewhat artificial distinction can there be inquiry first into the style and then into the forms.

Rhetoric and Romanticism

The study of literary style or "stylistics," cultivated today among the philological disciplines in the university, is the successor of rhetoric, whose literary theory long ago developed in antiquity was, given certain changes, in effect up to the eighteenth century. Rhetoric united all the sciences. Hence, the significance of the dissolution of the tradition of rhetoric that occurred with Romanticism can hardly be overestimated. With the rise of the doctrine of the "genius," for which the *Sturm and Drang* period conscripted Hamann, as well as of the individualization of literary work, the system of rhetoric with its fixed principles of genre and its normative principles of style collapse. The newly emerging stylistics finds its central concept in the "expression" *(Ausdruck)*. This is characteristic of the hermeneutics of Romanticism and with it of Schleiermacher's hermeneutics, which is still effective up to the present, even in theology. Later, the concept of "experience" *(Erlebnis)* pioneered by Romanticism is connected with it. The work of art to be interpreted is understood as an expression of experience. In a "hermeneutic of retrogression" one moves back from the expression to the motive, to the original liveliness that led to this expression. At the same time the organological achieved categorical significance. One saw the work of art or the text sprung from a "germinal resolve," like an organism growing, blooming, and arriving at maturation.[1]

In order to understand Hamann's style, it is important to see that above all, Romantic hermeneutics together with its effects saw itself verified by Hamann's work. But it completely failed to recognize that Hamann was still fundamentally defined by the tradition of rhetoric, and accordingly still lived in the ancient *respublica litteraria* (republic of letters). Hamann is altogether defined by the rhetorical tradition, and does not at all express himself in a free-floating subjectivity. So, in order to understand him, we must not go back to a primal experience of a biographical or other sort in terms of a "hermeneutics of retrogression."[2]

Indeed, to a degree the Romantics were justified in appealing to Hamann, perhaps to his commentary on Buffon's oft-cited proposition *"Le style est l'homme même,"* as found in the Academy Speech of 1753. Hamann, who guided the Königsberg student and later professor Kraus in a translation of the entire *Discours sur le style,* and along with a few notes allowed it to be published as an appendix to the sixth to tenth fascicles of *Königsbergsche Gelehrte und Politische Zeitungen* of 1776, gives his opinion:[3] If the overall subject of a literary work, as Buffon states, is outside the person, but the person itself is altogether style, and cannot be stolen, kidnapped, or expropriated, then the life of style depends "on the individuality of our concepts and passions, and on the same apt application for the knowledge and revelation of objects through comparable means. Internal self-knowledge seems to be the unity which determines the measure and content of all external knowledge, just as self-love is the basic drive of all of our reality. 'There are

---

1. Friedrich Schleiermacher, *Hermeneutics and Criticism and Other Writings,* trans. Andrew Bowie (Cambridge: Cambridge University Press, 1998), 116. See also the Introduction by the editor Manfred Frank in F. D. E. Schleiermacher, *Hermeneutik und Kritik* (Frankfurt am Main: Suhrkamp, 1977), 19.

2. Cf. S. A. Jørgensen, "Zu Hamanns Stil," in *Germanisch-romanische Monatsschrift,* N.F. XVI, vol. 4, 1966, 374-87. Cf. further the epilogue by Jørgensen in Johann Georg Hamann, *Sokratische Denkwürdigkeiten/Aesthetica in nuce* (Reclam Universal-Bibliothek 926) (1968), 163-91.

3. "Königsbergsche Gelehrte und Politische Zeitungen," in N IV, 424, 34f.; cf. Buffon, *Discours sur le style* — a fascimile of the 1753 12th edition (Hull, UK: Department of French, University of Hull, 1978), xvii.

sixty of the queens and eighty of the concubines, and countless virgins. But one is my Muse! — who breaks forth like daybreak, beautiful like the moon, elect like the sun, frightful like the army's vanguard.' "[4]

Naturally, *Sturm und Drang* and Romanticism understood such expressions as a manifest of its own view, such as Hamann's first remark on the publication of the translation of Buffon's speech *Über den Stil*. Here, in the name of good "taste,"[5] understood as a faculty of judgment, issuing from both head and heart, he turns against the acceptance of a regulation established purely a priori. Regarding the following proposition of Buffon, "the order in which one seeks to situate his thoughts must be preceded by a still more general arrangement of fundamental ideas and categories," Hamann remarks, "the thought here is not of a web of dispositions [when Hamann speaks of 'dispositions' he is thinking of Spinoza's *Ethics*, later of Kant],[6] all of which ends in gross mechanism[7] and tiresome materialism of the school and trendy joke. What is really here is reference to what after the analogy of the whole of nature and its organization for life is the *punctum saliens* ['the salient point': the point in which the chicken begins to live in the yoke] and the *prima stamina*[8] of the embryo in the soul of an author."[9]

As much as Hamann is concerned to encounter the living word — the salient point, from out of which a speech, a letter, a book is organized, becomes intelligible, and can be evaluated[10] — just as much does there belong to this *punctum saliens*, this embryo, its particular type of development, its linguistic emergence by sounds and letters even up to the tittle (Matt. 5:18). But for Hamann such reading and writing is subordinate to the "great law of parsimony."[11]

---

4. "Königsbergsche Gelehrte und Politische Zeitungen," in N IV, 424, 43-50. Cf. Song of Solomon 6:8-10.

5. "Fünf Hirtenbriefe," in N II, 372, 22. Cf. ZH II, 85, 23 (to Lindner; 1761).

6. Cf. "Das Triumvirat," in N IV, 460, 31f.: "dangles a spider on a blessed thistle by a thread of its caprice." Cf. "Ein fliegender Brief," in N III, 401, 16f.: "to build systems like spiders and theories like nesting birds."

7. Cf. "Wolken," in N II, 97, 31 ("mechanism of its concepts").

8. *Stamen* (noun): a warp on a loom; threads on a spindle, a weave. According to N VI *Lebensfaden* are *"prima stamina"* the beginnings of the threads of life. Cf. "Philological Ideas and Doubts," in Haynes, 116 (N III, 39, 13). In addition, E. Büchsel, HH IV, 222, note 3.

9. "Königsbergsche Gelehrte . . . ," in N IV, 419, 42-46.

10. Cf. above chapter 1, "Life and Work," note 39.

11. Cf. above chapter 1, "Life and Work," at note 40 and below chapter 4, "The Modern Concept of Nature in Crisis," note 31.

In his economy of style Hamann is linked to Persius,[12] his "first beloved poet," to whose "motto" he often states he wants to be faithful: "*Minimum est quod scire laboro*" (a minimum is what I labor to know). What Hamann shares with Persius in matters of style is surprising. It is present in the brevity, laconic style, and the *stylus atrox* (atrocious style),[13] "in the frequent, not always clear interweaving of erudite allusions and proofs, in the boldness and strangeness of metaphors, tropes and epithets, in the dramatic attitude of conceiving and describing psychic and physical conditions in their external manner of appearance,"[14] thus not at all to be subjectivized, but perceived in a conscious shaping from their surface.

In what is this relationship of choice between the Christian, Hamann, and the heathen, Persius, grounded? Hamann, like Kierkegaard, took to heart the word of Jesus: "I tell you, on the day of judgment you will have to give an account for every careless word you utter; for by your words you will be justified, and by your words you will be condemned" (Matt. 12:36-37).

On October 24, 1783, Hamann writes to his son Johann Michael, who had learning difficulties: "My dear child, I advise you to use both the *evangelical law of parsimony* in reading and writing, accounting for every useless, idle word, — and *Economy of Style*. In these two mystical words can be found the whole art of thinking and living. Everything that Demosthenes thought of in the threefold repetition of a single artistic word, these two words *economy* and *style* are for me."[15]

Speech Is Action

To understand the emphasis Hamann places on the "economy of style" we need to decipher the above-cited reference to Demosthenes, who in answer "to the question, what is most essential for the speaker, gives first place to the delivery [*hypokrisis (= actio)*], and second to the delivery, and third, again, to the delivery."[16]

---

12. Cf. L. Schreiner, HH VII, 172ff. On Petronius: "Königsbergsche Gelehrte," in N IV, 423, 42f. Cf. with H V, 358, 5-11 (to Scheffner; 1785).

13. "Königsbergsche Gelehrte," in N IV, 421, 53ff.

14. L. Schreiner, HH VII, 173.

15. H V, 88, 15-22 (to Johann Michael Hamann; 1783); cf. "Zweifel und Einfälle," in N III, 187, 26.

16. A. Schaefer, *Demosthenes und seine Zeit* (Leipzig: B. G. Teubner, 1856), vol. 1,

Beyond the obvious point of comparison, Hamann is fundamentally interested in the *hypokrisis* given such stress by Demosthenes. This concept allows him to perceive rhetoric and dialectic, logic and aesthetics, poetry and politics in their interrelationship, and it decisively shapes his style.

By attending to detail, above all to etymology, Hamann develops the boldest systematic concepts. So, by exhausting the meanings of a single Greek word, the term *"hypokrisis,"* he arrives at a fundamental anthropological description of reality as an ambivalent process of communication. By taking up the facets of meaning in *"hypokrisis,"*[17] this process can be described thusly: Every person answers to a question challenging him or her, by evaluating and thus interpreting what is heard. Such a responsive *actio* of the person as speaker is also a mimetic depiction, the action of an *akteur,* an actor, who plays a role, with which the person need not be identical but can be distanced from it and thus "feign" it.

Hamann understands all human life-expressions, including learning and teaching, reading and writing, as "actions."[18] By doing so he incorporates the earlier mentioned experience of the orator Demosthenes, who when unsuccessful represented an actor whose actual importance in speaking has to do with "delivery," with the *"hypokrisis,"* the *"actio,"* the "action." It is the motive power of Hamann the author "who loves action"[19] and thus speaks happily of his "actions as author *(Autorhandlungen)."*

Hamann's actions as author never appear in thick books, but always only in little writings: "Even I was once in the Arcadia of literature and mixed with the legions of anonymous and pseudonymous scribblers, sought in small volumes to labor with doubts and imaginings against the dictators of pure teaching and reason, against the demagogues of the Ephesian tabernacle and miracle smiths. I too offered hecatombs (100 sacred oxen) to No one, to the knowable, as one of my brothers called the attic public of our enlightened century. Not in stout bulls and fat oxen, but rather in small wafers, small pates, and thin flat cakes, not in large sacks of marketable coins, but in old copper pennies, and in *urceis*

297f. (with numerous examples). ZH II, 69, 10f. (to Lindner; 1761): "Decorum is also perhaps the soul of action so praised by Demosthenes."

17. G. W. Benseler, *Griechisch-Deutsches Schul-Wörterbuch* (Leipzig: B. G. Teubner, 1882), 854, 1.

18. Cf. below chapter 9, "Reason Is Language," notes 30-47.

19. "Kreuzzüge des Philologen," in N II, 116, 18f.

(little pitchers) of broken shards, but not in thick-bellied amphora of a widely traveled and well-read fabricator of legends."[20]

Not thick-bellied books, but "flying leaves" comprise Hamann's actions as author, answers kindled by a specific occasion, which then, however, represents the spirit of the entire age. These actions do not unfold a system, but are rather rhapsodic, even fragmentary. They are imaginings, whimsies, crumbs,[21] but are combined in an unheard-of fashion, concentrated on a single word, on the proper word, *"le mot propre."* Kierkegaard, by his own testimony greatly indebted to Hamann in the indirect disclosure of existence, the pseudonymity of his writings, the concept of "anxiety," and so forth, penetratingly observed: "I do not wish to deny that I admire Hamann. . . . But the primitivity of genius is in his brief sentences, and the pregnant form is in entire correspondence with the desultory flinging out of a thought. With all his life and soul, to the last drop of blood, he is concentrated in a single word, the passionate protest of a highly gifted genius against an existential system. But the System is hospitable; poor Hamann, you have been reduced to a paragraph by Michelet. Whether any monument has ever marked your grave, . . . but this I know, that you have been with satanic might and main forced into the paragraph uniform, and stuck into the ranks"[22] by the historians, who care for order through their classifications.

Kierkegaard makes use of Hamann in order to fight Hegel, the system. He enlists Hamann as an ally in his criticism of Hegel but with reservation, and remarks that Hamann's protest against the system is not sufficiently systematic, that "the elasticity of his thoughts lacks evenness and his supernatural buoyancy lacks self-control, in case he should have had to work in a coherent manner."[23]

In this judgment, Kierkegaard falls in with Hegel, whose review of Hamann's writings contains the criticism that he is mired in a concentration of "his deep particularity," admittedly "original," but does not, as would correspond to Hegel's own philosophizing, move in "the form of universality" and "the expansion of thinking reason."[24]

If Hamann were an "original," then he could not *live* so much *from*

---

20. "Das Triumvirat," in N IV, 460, 39–461, 4.

21. "Fragments," in Smith, 161 (N I, 299, 27-29); ZH I, 431, 29ff. (to Lindner; 1759).

22. *Concluding Unscientific Postscript to the Philosophical Fragments*, trans. David Swenson (Princeton: Princeton University Press, 1941), 223-24.

23. Kierkegaard, *Concluding Unscientific Postscript*, 242.

24. *Hegel on Hamann* (cf. above, "Introduction," note 3), 6.

citation as he does. All his writings are collages, montages of quotation, unless one assumes that the manner of dealing with quotation makes up what is original. Hamann's style is through and through defined by the insight that the "wealth of all human knowledge . . . rests on the *exchange of words*."[25] Therefore the quotation is neither an ornament nor a superficial display of erudition, but a sign of an elementary and unavoidable dependence. The author is primarily a hearer and reader. His writings are thus "a faithful impression of the capacities and inclinations with which one has read and can read."[26] I can only think because something is given me beforehand. I can only hear because I am addressed. If, according to an appropriate remark of Hegel taken from Buffon that Hamann's writings do not have a genuine style but are style through and through,[27] and if this style is not only occasional and marginally cento,[28] then to designate him as an "original" would run counter not only to Hamann's self-understanding but to his analyzable style, to what is "objectively" clear from the texts. Hamann's actions as author, not only factually but deliberately and consciously, move within a context and thus make known that every author and every human in his or her finitude is referred to another. To stylize the praxis in use since Descartes and flourishing since Romanticism as an original and independent free-thinking phenomenon corresponds neither to the insight into the fundamental human condition nor to virtue as conceived by philosophical ethics.

Since the wealth of all human knowledge lies in the exchange of words, the quotation is neither ornament nor embellishment but the sign of an elementary and indissoluble dependence. It is Hamann's peculiarity to enrich "his writings not only with quotations and allusions, but actually to construct them in great measure."[29] According to Hamann an author is as good as he or she can read and hear: "The true genius knows . . . his dependence."[30]

---

25. "Word Order in the French Language," in Haynes, 20 (N II, 129, 6f.).

26. "Leser und Kunstrichter," in N II, 341, 16-18.

27. *Hegel on Hamann*, 6.

28. The Latin term *cento* denotes first of all a fabric woven together from different pieces, for example, a rag rug; but it is then used to describe poems combined from individual verses of various poetical works.

29. Cf. Reiner Wild, *Die neueren Hamann-Kommentare* in *Johann Georg Hamann* (*Wege der Forschung* 511), ed. R. Wild (Darmstadt: Wissenschaftliche Buchgesellschaft, 1978), 403.

30. "Verurtheilung der Kreuzzüge," in N II, 260, 22-24; Cf. "Wolken," in N II, 98, 1off.

This phrase of Hamann indicates the magnitude of the perversion that immediately began with Herder, his pupil and friend, when Hamann's discourse about "genius" was taken up and he became the ancestor of the *Sturm und Drang*. Hamann's concept of genius is bound to the ability to read and the desire to hear stated above, and is not to be separated from either. He has no originality in mind that belongs to beginning or being able to begin with oneself. This would be empty subjectivity. By contrast, Hamann's writings adhere to concrete dependencies and references.

Accordingly for their part they are designed to be taken in. They intend to give food for thought, to encourage, or shock. They establish relationships, are open for the interference of the reader; they do not cut off any further threading by means of a systematic development in terms of a "construct," perfectly anticipated by the author. They thus have their communicative power precisely through their particularity, through what Hegel criticized in Hamann. The particular is the author as well as his authority, the occasion for speaking, the *"Sitz im Leben"* of the text, its cause, its place, its first addressee and the later reader reached as later addressee.

A communication that adheres to such particularities can only be regarded as "unsystematic" when measured by the philosophical thought of Hegel and his successors. In the communication promoted by Hamann there occurs what Hegel's systematic development precisely hinders. It cannot be separated from concrete experience, opportunity, and locality. In this way, it resists abstraction, taking flight to the universal; it resists even the thinking of Hegel, who wants to take the finite seriously but in fact overplays it in thought.

Alienation

Hegel's judgment on Hamann's work, in which he misses development or universality, corresponds exactly to his assessment that Hamann's authorship was unsuccessful. "Such essays could produce no effect of any kind, either with influential individuals or with the general public. The particularity of the interest . . . is here far too preponderant, and there is, moreover, no evidence of any other content."[31] Hegel complained about

---

31. *Hegel on Hamann*, 32.

Hamann's "surliness" as his "hostile sentiment toward the public for which he writes. Having expressed a deep interest in and thus associated himself with the reader, he immediately thrusts the reader away with a grimace, farce, or a scolding which is not made better by his use of biblical expressions, or he does so with a certain derision and mystification, and destroys in spiteful manner the sympathy he awakens."[32]

But whoever is not moved within the universality of thought without resistance, weightlessly as it were, but wants to change, to shatter, to comfort and at the same time does not want to bind the reader to his own person, needs an alienating style. Chief elements in Hamann's authorship and his style can be compared with Berthold Brecht's thoughts on epic theater and alienation, though Hamann as Lutheran distinguishes himself from Brecht's moralistic intent in a remarkable way. The alienating style does not enable the reader to identify with the author, but to come to his or her own judgment, because distance is given to the reader by the author himself through his style of parsimony, ellipses, and laconic utterances; indeed distance is actually forced on the reader. Hegel's remark is on target to the effect that Hamann thrusts his readers aside after he has awakened their interests. But this happens, though Hegel overlooks it, with the goal of making the reader independent, bringing the reader to his or her own judgment and not to repeat in thought or speech what another thought before. Often Hamann intentionally uses dashes and in another way takes care that readers are set free to develop their own fantasy and intervene with their own judgment. So it is precisely "what is surly" that serves the process of communication and is not an indication of unsystematic thought.

Hamann does not assume he is in agreement with his reader from the outset. And he does not anticipate a final successful understanding, an ideal point of convergence in communication, an imaginary but as it were necessary point of unity and agreement. He does not advocate a communicative a priori. Rather he hopes that precisely by virtue of the dissent and the crisis, understanding and being understood will come about. At the same time, he is borne by hope in the merciful judgment of God, the ultimate judge and interpreter.

Hamann's uniqueness in writing and his stated intent is only to make a clenched fist and leave it to the reader to unclench it with an open

32. *Hegel on Hamann*, 40.

hand, to use the ancient figure. For Hamann the clenched fist, the core of truth, lies in the detail, in the contingency of the word, of time, of person, and of action — unbearable for a generalizing way of thinking. The contingencies and particularities are taken seriously and staged linguistically. Accordingly Hamann wants to be read and deciphered micrologically. In the process of such reading the truth is, however, unfolded in another way than Hegel sees it unfolded and thinks of as system.

Form: Flying Leaves

Hamann called his little writings "Flying Leaves,"[33] not only the published *opuscula* collected in the *Crusades of the Philologist*. Under the title "Flying Leaves," he proposed a publication of his works.[34] As pamphlets and leaflets they serve the day, that which is or should be timely. They are up to date, offering "modes, opinions, novelties."[35] They are *"neue Zeitungen."*[36] Already as a student Hamann collaborated on the weekly journal *Daphne* (1749-50), and, not incidentally, was editor of the new *Königsbergsche Gelehrte und Politische Zeitungen,* for only a brief time (1764) however. But for fifteen years, until 1779, he was a reviewer for this newspaper.

"Flying Leaf" was the contemporary term for "leaflet." Lessing uses the word, as does Goethe who asks: "Are there not so many newspapers, monthlies, and flying leaves now?" The entries in the *Deutsches Wörterbuch*[37] clearly indicate the transfer from "flying" or "winged words," "flying talk," and "report." Hamann calls his writings "flying leaves" because he sees the word in motion — the word, which like the wind, "blows where it wills" (John 3:8). "Regardless of whether one hears it blowing; so one looks to the fickle weather-cock to find out where it comes from, or rather, whither it is going."[38]

In its actuality such a flying word and leaf is transitory, a bird in flight, a tangent that only touches the circle, ephemeral, for just this day,

---

33. "Göttingische Anzeige," in N II, 255, 17-25; "Beylage zur Denkwürdigkeiten," in N III, 113, 4; "Zweifel und Einfälle," in N III, 188, 29; cf. H V, 4, 7 (to Reichardt; 1783).

34. H IV, 400, 3f. (to Herder; 1782); cf. H V, 313, 14-18, 10ff. (to Jacobi; 1785).

35. "Königsbergsche Gelehrte," in N IV, 265, 3f.

36. DWb 31, 591-93.

37. DWb 3, 1785f.; here also reference to the question of Goethe is cited.

38. "Aesthetica in nuce," in Haynes 73 (N II, 203, 11-13).

in this moment only emerging as real from the many possibilities. It is a sound, a tone, which in the next second is no longer given the senses, but can only but be remembered, and this only with toil. When the Princess von Gallitzin requests from Hamann "all my *Opuscula profligata* together with a small *historia arcana* of my circumstances and ways of thinking,"[39] fulfilling this request, he admits to Herder, becomes really "sour," because "the remembrance of all situations, misunderstandings, contingencies to which so much and most relates die out and I am no longer able to find out or fill up the whole."[40] He writes to Scheffner, "It really was a Herculean task for me to go through what I have written from 1759 to 1783, because it is all related to the actual situations of my life, to moments false, to crooked, faded impressions, which I am no longer able to refresh. I no longer understand myself, understand myself quite differently than I did then, some things better, some worse. What one doesn't understand one had best leave unread, and it should have remained unwritten, still less have been published."[41]

Such reliance on the given moment with its contingencies, harshly rebuked by Hegel in his review, actually raises the question whether Hamann mastered contingency or rather was mastered by it.[42] Accordingly, do Hamann's writings lack a dignified content, a universal thought, lasting longer than the flash of its origin?

Hamann was aware of the character of his writings. In 1773 he wrote a short piece titled *Monologue of an Author (Selbstgespräch eines Autors)*[43] by which he wanted to induce the Berlin bookdealer, publisher, and writer Friedrich Nicolai to publish his *Philological Thoughts and Doubts*. Along with the *Monologue* he undertook a last attempt to find a publisher for it. Filled with self-irony he begins: "Do you still hold fast to your weakness, dear heart? Of becoming a known author in a great quarto?"[44] Then again, addressing Nicolai: "So mine Herr, do not laugh too much at a foreigner who in the author's shape of the small gray nightingale [not, say, of the proud peacock][45] seeks to commend himself

39. H V, 348, 13-15 (to Herder; 1785).
40. H V, 348, 29-33; compare the apparatus in N II, 394.
41. H V, 358, 12-18. On the subject cf. *ibid.*, 358, 30–359, 2 (to Scheffner; 1785).
42. Cf. below chapter 8, "Reason and History."
43. "Selbstgespräch eines Autors," in N III, 76-79.
44. "Selbstgespräch eines Autors," in N III, 69, 3ff.
45. "Selbstgespräch eines Autors," in N III, 75, 32-34. An allusion to a contemporary poem.

to its eighteenth century in Europe more by a flighty leaf than by a thick volume. . . ."[46]

A brief comparison of Hamann's flying leaves with the bulky volumes of Hegel, who has much in common with Hamann but at the same time sharply distinguishes himself from him, can clarify the matter further.

Hegel admires Hamann for not being concerned with empty subjectivity or pure existence but with connections, with the interweaving of thought and existence, understanding and intuition, concept and sensuousness, thinking and feeling, faith and knowledge, intention and action, with "these historical truths, temporal and eternal,"[47] with God and humanity, humiliation and exaltation, as implied in the title of *Golgatha und Scheblimini*.[48] So, in his review of Hamann, Hegel finds that it "is extraordinary to see here how in Hamann the concrete idea ferments and turns against the divisions of reflection, how he opposes them with the true purpose,"[49] namely of creating "coincidences."[50]

But in spite of the fermentation of the concrete idea, what Hegel fails to see in Hamann is a "developed system."[51] Hamann has "only made a 'clenched fist' and anything further . . . left to the reader 'to unfold in the open palm.'"[52] This judgment of Hegel, in forming which he takes up the old image used by Hamann for the relation between dialectic and rhetoric, thoroughly corresponds to Hamann's self-understanding and the intent of his authorship. Nevertheless, in Hegel's judgment approval and criticism interpenetrate.

Approvingly, Hegel distinguishes the content of Hamann's writings as the "deepest of religious truth."[53] This depth in Hamann is not what irritates Hegel about his contemporary Romantics, that is, as something

---

46. "Selbstgespräch eines Autors," in N III, 75, 1-4. Cf. "Königsbergsche Gelehrte," in N IV, 460f.

47. "Golgatha and Scheblimini," in Haynes, 193 (N III, 311, 37).

48. Death and Resurrection, Exaltation and Humiliation; cf. below chapter 8, "History and Reason," notes 48ff.

49. *Hegel on Hamann*, 35.

50. *Hegel on Hamann*, 39.

51. *Hegel on Hamann*, 39.

52. *Hegel on Hamann*, 39. Here Hegel cites the end of the *Metakritik* to use Hamann against Hamann. Cf. "Metakritik über den Purismus der Vernunft," in N III, 289, 23f. Cf. O. Bayer, *Vernunft ist Sprache: Hamanns Metakritik Kants* (Stuttgart: Frommann-Holzboog, 2002), 418f.

53. *Hegel on Hamann*, 33.

empty; it is of "concentrated intensity."[54] However, and this criticism of Hegel's is stronger than his approval, Hamann's depth is without breadth. It "arrives at no sort of expansion,"[55] and remains "particular."[56] "For his part, Hamann did not take the trouble that, if one may put it so, God took, albeit in a higher sense, that is, with open palm to unfold the clenched core of truth which he is (ancient philosophers said of God that he is a round sphere)[57] in reality toward a system of nature, of the state, of justice and morality, of world history. . . ."[58]

System as a Hindrance to Truth[59]

What Hegel misses in the journalist Hamann, who does not conceive his age in ideas that require thick volumes but with flying leaves that provoke one to one's own judgments, is the labor to "reflect on" God's "revelation" "as the divine unfolding,"[60] in order to overcome in thought the separations that according to Hegel the deadening understanding of the Enlightenment brought about. Admittedly, Hegel himself had overcome the separations solely in the medium of thought. As criticized by Marx and other left-wing Hegelians, these separations remained stuck fast in the sensuous-political reality. By contrast, Hamann is concerned with the interrelation and interweaving of thought and sensuous-political existence, but not in the medium of thought alone.

Hence, many elements of the left-wing Hegelian criticism are already operative in Hamann, but not based on atheism. Hamann held the illusion of overcoming the separations by way of thought to be a flight into the system of pure conceptuality. He fights and resists this illusion and flight, and consequently what results are only *crumbs*, fragments, which in their linguistic form make clear that their author does not seek to overplay his finitude or need and refuses to be subsumed under universal categories.

Hamann, however, does not grant autonomy to his finitude or need.

54. *Hegel on Hamann*, 31.
55. *Hegel on Hamann*, 31.
56. *Hegel on Hamann*, 6, 31, 43.
57. Cf. M. Tullius Cicero, *De natura deorum*, I, 24.
58. *Hegel on Hamann*, 39.
59. H VI, 276, 15 (to Jacobi; 1786).
60. *Hegel on Hamann*, 39.

Nor does he generalize them, like Schleiermacher, into a structure of "absolute dependence" that could be universally demonstrated and recognized. His aversion to the system of pure conceptuality is not based on the desire to get back to a fundamental anthropological "structure." For this reason we cannot harmonize Schleiermacher and Hamann.

In his express criticism of the notion of "structure" as well as of "system" lies Hamann's theological and philosophical relevance. Against the ascent from a painfully particular existence to the universal of a rounded-out development of truth in a system[61] and thus against the thesis that the total is the truth, as well as against resorting to the primordial, Hamann, the Magus who sees the star in the darkness,[62] insists on the fleeting place of existence between what is allowed and what is appropriated, what is received and what is handed on.[63] In this way he affirms life as a process whose beginning and end and thus whose unity I do not have in hand, whose coherence is not guaranteed by any pure a priori and cannot be simulated through a historical reconstruction. "If his future will be like a thief in the night: then neither political arithmetics nor prophetic chronologies can make a day of it. . . ."[64]

It is from this eschatology of existence *entre chien et loup* (between the times[65]), together with a doctrine of creation in exact correspondence to it and an anthropology given with it, that the uniqueness of Hamann's *opuscula*, his "flying leaves," is to be understood.

If we now develop this thesis, which combines theological, philosophical, linguistic, and literary insights, then along with it the form-historical and form-critical approach takes on validity. Over a century ago, Franz Overbeck promoted it in the history of early Christian literature and New Testament studies. Overbeck's polemic against the "false theological idealism which regards religion as indifferent to its authentic forms,"[66] a po-

---

61. Cf. "Aesthetica in nuce," in Haynes, 73 (N II, 203 [against Kant]), but also, in anticipation, against Hegel's idea of a Christological-dialectical system.

62. Cf. chapter 1, "Life and Work," notes 1-3.

63. Cf. below chapter 5, "Freedom as a Fundamental Concept of Anthropology," note 68 and following.

64. H IV, 315, 3-5 (to Herder; 1781). Cf. Bayer, "Zukunft und Schöpfung," in *Schöpfung als Anrede. Zu einer Hermeneutik der Schöpfung* (Tübingen: J. C. B. Mohr [Paul Siebeck], 1986), 153.

65. Cf. below chapter 12, "Created Time," especially notes 21-29.

66. Oswald Bayer, *Theology the Lutheran Way*, 146-48 and 272f.; the reference of this and the following quotations appear there.

lemic directed against Hegel and his disciples, is of undiminished importance, because it is still not everywhere recognized that dogmatic as well as ethical propositions can be formed and answered only in exact relation to forms. For this reason it is necessary to emphasize Overbeck's viewpoint in Systematic Theology and Philosophy and not to surrender it to the study of literature alone. At the same time we can affirm Ludwig Feuerbach's polemic against Hegel's philosophy, which "maintains that philosophy has the same content as religion; it only strips away the form of sensuousness into which religion sinks this content."[67] Feuerbach is correct when he responds to Hegel: "This sensuous form cannot be separated from the content of religion, without canceling itself out," that is, without obliterating it. "It is absolutely essential for religion."[68]

The form absolutely essential to religion is individualized in Hamann's authorship. It is individual style and "anti-style" in the sense of his remarks on Buffon's *Discours sur le style.*[69] In, with, and under all individuality, in the particular situation of the one who lived in Prussian Königsberg *in telonio sedens* as an *"homme de lettres"* in his love for the word, admittedly appear the traits that without detriment to individuality are characteristic of every Christian, insofar as he or she is really a Christian, and that means truly human.

Documents of Finite Reason

We will now look first of all at Hamann's "flying leaves" from an anthropological point of view.

"Flying leaf" is a contemporary word for "leaflet." But in Hamann's usage it is also a Bible quotation. The transient and voided human being who is nonetheless immortal because God has addressed him and thus will have to do with him in eternity, whether in anger or in grace,[70] complains to God: "Will you frighten a windblown leaf and pursue dry chaff?" (Job 13:25).

Since Hamann relates this word of Job to his authorship and superficially exchanges the divine for the human judge, for the reviewer, the art

---

67. Oswald Bayer, *Theology the Lutheran Way,* 146-48.
68. Oswald Bayer, *Theology the Lutheran Way,* 146-48.
69. "Königsbergsche Gelehrte," in N IV, 425, 51.
70. Cf. Martin Luther, LW 5, 76 (WA 43, 481, 32-35 [on Gen. 26:24], 1541).

critic — "the seriousness of the art critic persecuted the bruised reed and every windblown leaf of my Muse"[71] — he seems to play with the serious text of the Bible. He does so throughout. But the joke is not without seriousness and thus with humor in which, as in the Book of Jonah, serious judgment is combined with "a ghost of a smile."[72] In humor the human becomes aware of its finitude. Humor stands in the tension between the nothingness of the human and the eternity of God, more precisely, at the point where I not only recognize but also acknowledge that I am nothing and transient, finite and mortal, and that my Creator is eternal.

This is what emerges from the context in the Book of Job, and Hamann always renders contexts in the present tense: The human who is as transient as a withered leaf that flies from a tree, "lives few of days and full of trouble, comes up like a flower and withers, flees like a shadow and does not last" (Job 14:1ff.). This human, this flying, lightweight leaf, comes to trace the eternal weight of God's address: "Do you," Job asks, as much astonished as shocked and weighed down, "fix your eyes on such a one that you bring me into judgment with you?" (Job 14:3).

This does not contradict the equally bewildered but uncomplaining and somewhat laudatory question of the human awarded dignity, dominance, and criticism: "What are human beings that you are mindful of them?" (Ps. 8:4). What am I that you remember me in this way, bestowing reason upon me?

What this astonished praise and no less bewildered complaint offers as paradigm of Hamann's authorship is the situation of response arising from hearing, and to which for Hamann the writing that arises from reading exactly corresponds. The situation of the author is that of a precisely qualified creatureliness. On its behalf Hamann appeals "to that stoic wisdom," "which alternately united the *imbecillitatem Hominis* and the *securitatem Dei*,"[73] and writes from his sickbed to Jacobi: "Ev-

---

71. "Ein fliegender Brief," in N III, 399, 21ff.

72. Gerhard von Rad, *God at Work in Israel*, trans. John H. Marks (Nashville: Abingdon, 1980), 65. Compare K. P. Hertzsch, *Der ganze Fisch war voll Gesang. Biblische Balladen zum Vorlesen*, 10th edition (Stuttgart: Radius Verlag, 1984), 53: "But God, who already knew the way, smiled at how Jonah ran."

73. "Zweifel und Einfälle," in N III, 189, 1-3. The quotation is from Seneca ad Lucilium, *Epistulae Morales* LIII, 12: "*Ecce res magna, habere imbecillitatem hominis, securitatem dei* ["Behold, what a wonderful thing to have the weakness of a man, but the

erything is good [Genesis 1:31] — everything is vanity [Ecclesiastes]! It is good for me that I am able to feel with equal intention the *imbecillitatem hominis* [the weakness of a man] and *securitatem DEI* [the strength of God that gives certainty]."[74]

As journalist and author Hamann consciously reckons with this precisely qualified creatureliness. His "flying leaves" are offensively impressive documents of finite reason, distanced as much from transient esoterics of pure reason as from the short-lived hustle and bustle and premature decision that give no time to play and joke and are therefore so humorless and bitter.

As such, the theological and anthropological viewpoint of creation is already an eschatological viewpoint: The Creator is the judge. Only through judgment does he permit the world to be perceived as creation. *Aesthetica in nuce* testifies to this truth with special emphasis. It concludes with a cento, in which the skeptical wisdom of Solomon the preacher and the Apocalypse of John allow the first commandment to be heard in a theological and eschatological accent on creation: "Let us now hear the conclusion of his newest aesthetic, which is the oldest: Fear GOD, and give him glory; for the hour of his judgment is come; and worship him that made heaven, and earth, and the sea, and the foundations of waters!"[75]

The first commandment is the alpha and omega of the authorship of Hamann, who memorized Luther's Small Catechism in confirmation instruction, took it to heart for life, and with his writings intended nothing other than to share it indirectly with the public.[76] The truth of this "Bible for children and laity"[77] means the truth of the Bible and the truth of the God to which it testifies. For Hamann it is summarized in Luther's explanation of the first commandment: "The fear of the Lord is the beginning of wisdom . . . : to fear and love him."[78] Correspondingly, he writes in a letter to Jacobi: "The fear of the Lord is the beginning of wisdom and his evangelical love of wisdom is the end and *punctum*. I recognize and am aware of no other *Dos moi pou sto* [i.e., another Archime-

---

serenity of a god]." Cf. ZH I, 329, 11: "I enjoy in equal measure the emptiness and abundance of humanity" (to Lindner; 1759).

74. H VII, 339, 7-9 (to Jacobi); cf. H V, 317, 14f. (to Jacobi; 1785).

75. N II, 217, 17-19; cited is Ecclesiastes 12:13 and Revelation 14:17.

76. Cf. above chapter 1, "Life and Work," note 41.

77. "Zweifel und Einfälle," in N III, 195, 4.

78. "Biblische Betrachtungen," in N I, 152, 22.31; cf. "Zwo Recensionen," in N III, 24, 3f.

dean point] than his Word, his oath, and his *I am* — and *will be. . . .*"
God is "the most perfect love, because it is everything in its Neighbor,
therefore alone deserves to be loved above all, and can rightly demand
to love the neighbor as one's self — but God himself before our own and
our neighbor's self."[79]

The intent of Hamann's authorship can be made concrete once more
in the *Aesthetica in nuce*. What the flying leaf bearing this title serves is
made expressly clear at the end just quoted, in the "conclusion" of the
aesthetic that corresponds to its beginning: "not a lyre! — nor a
painter's brush! — a winnowing-fan for my Muse, to purge the
threshing-floor of holy literature."[80] Parallel to this we read: "O for a
muse like a refiner's fire, and like a fuller's soap!"[81] What is cited is
Malachi's word of judgment (3:2ff.): "But who can endure the day of his
coming, and who can stand when he appears? For he is like a refiner's
fire and like fullers' soap; he will sit as a refiner and purifier of silver,
and he will purify the descendants of Levi and refine them like gold and
silver. . . ." Hamann is speaking in the guise of a prophet of judgment, in
that of John the Baptist who is co-defined by the word of Malachi. Elsewhere he sees himself as a type of Amos.[82]

Negotiation Discourses

The rhetorical means used to realize the idea of publication match the
intention served by such a flying leaf as the Königsberg journalist's
Aesthetica in nuce. The beginning of the *Aesthetica in nuce* can be
"compared with the beginning of an ancient legal discourse."[83] In view
of Hamann's solid rooting in the tradition of rhetoric I would like to
propose that all of his *opuscula* be understood as "negotiation discourses." In order to reflect on this form of Hamann's writings in a
scientific-theoretical way, we should recall the connection between rhetoric and dialectic that can easily be intimated from the structure of an
articulus, for example, of the *Summa Theologica* of Thomas Aquinas.
"The art of negotiation has been cultivated scholastically as 'dialec-

79. H V, 333, 16-27 (to Jacobi; 1785). Cf. ZH II, 331, 2-4 (to Herder; 1765).
80. "Aesthetica in nuce," in Haynes, 62 (N II, 197, 10f.).
81. "Aesthetica in nuce," in Haynes, 79 (N II, 207, 10f.).
82. "Kreuzzüge des Philologen," in N II, 115, 10f.
83. S. A. Jørgensen, "Zu Hamanns Stil" (cf. above note 2), 378.

tic.'"[84] This art takes on fixed form in scientific disputation, endemic to the university in the High and Late Middle Ages past the time of the Reformation and old Protestant orthodoxy and still residually at work. "Rhetoric as an art related to the individual discourse . . . is really a part of dialectic, insofar as the individual discourse is always oriented to the situation and the negotiation concerned with the situation."[85]

An important, clearer definition of "negotiation discourse" results from the distinction between "consumption discourse" and "conservation discourse." "The consumption discourse is a discourse which . . . the speaker holds once within a relevant historical situation (in the private or public sphere) with the intention of altering it, and exhausts its function corresponding to his or her intention . . . within this situation."[86] The consumption discourse is, however, consumed in its occurring, but has not been destroyed with the occurrence, insofar as it was necessary to alter the situation. The discourse is thus permanently preserved in the altered situation.

A wholly new aspect must be kept in mind if "negotiation discourses" are fixed in writing and handed on, or from the outset — such as Hamann's negotiation discourses available to us as works — are designed to be written. By this means these discourses cannot only be heard, but also seen. Time and space appear in a peculiar connection. Stated and published in writing, they are there for us for further use. However, in our actualizing them they appear again as "consumption discourse" such as is spoken and heard, say, in a lecture.

Hamann as author of the "negotiation discourse" is an accuser, defender, and judge in the office of reviewer, art critic, and *criticus*. He more closely describes himself as *meta-criticus*, that is, as a further-tester and further-judge, in this sense: a "relecturer." The compound draws our attention to the fact that the critic is not autarchous but relates to what is given, thus reads further,[87] but in doing so judges in freedom. This occurs in a judgment that in terms to be made precise in a chiefly eschatological way is preliminary and in this sense a pre-judice. If we seek a single comprehensive description of the multiform and multifac-

84. H. Lausberg, *Elemente der literarischen Rhetorik* (Stuttgart: Franz Steiner, 1982); here §7. Cf. also §8 on the three kinds of negotiating discourse.

85. Lausberg, *Elemente der literarischen Rhetorik*, §7.

86. Lausberg, *Elemente der literarischen Rhetorik*, §11 in relation to §§11-13 and 14ff.

87. Cf. "Ein fliegender Brief," in N III, 352, 16 ("further-reading," "relecture": "Nachlese").

eted brief writings of Hamann, we can define them according to their type of text as "reviews."

The Form of the Review

The characterization of the form and intent of Hamann's authorship just given can be summarized thus: Hamann's *opuscula*, "flying leaves," are the written negotiation discourses of a metacritic who knows the Creator of the world and its Judge, its *criticus*. His writings are reviews. To a great extent this also applies to his letters.[88]

To develop this thesis we need to ask about Hamann's understanding of *"criticism."* It is radical, insofar as in his enlightenment Hamann harks back to the root of the history of the concept of "criticism," that is, to Aristotle whose *Politics* had defined the full citizen by participation in judicial functions, in *krisis*, and in office, in *arche*. This participation defines the full citizen in contrast to the *metoeken* (small farmers), to the backbenchers, or even to the slaves. In his debate with Herder's anthropology,[89] Hamann expressly lays hold of this politico-legal definition of Aristotle but corrects and deepens it by assigning it together with the biblical primeval history to *everyone*. He asserts as basic to anthropology, "that the true character of our nature consists in the juridical and administrative dignity of a political animal," of the *zoon politikon*,[90] thus with judicial and authoritative rank.

This critical activity, essential to humankind, lies in making distinctions, linking differences, and thereby mastering them. The coherence between the critical and archontic shows itself in this way. Both together form the chief element of the Logos, the *ratio*.[91] In his "critical and archontic dignity" the human being is an *animal rationale*, a rational being, and simultaneously an *animal sociale*. The human is defined by the

---

88. His correspondence exists on wide stretches of the exchange over what has been or is still to be read.

89. "Philological Ideas and Doubts," in Haynes, 114-16 (N III, 37, 25f., 39f.); cf. Aristotle, *Politics*, The Loeb Classical Library, trans. H. Rackham (Cambridge, MA: Harvard University Press, 1967), 175.

90. "Philological Ideas and Doubts," in Haynes, 114 (37, 24f.) and 116 (39, 17f.). "The entire canon of human perfection consists in criticism and politics" (22ff.).

91. Cf. above chapter 1, "Life and Work," notes 64-67, and below chapter 5, "Freedom as a Fundamental Concept of Anthropology," as well as chapter 6, "Criticism and Politics."

fact that others have power over him and he over others, as lord and also servant, free lord over all things and subject to none and dutiful servant of all things and subject to everyone.

In their true relationship dependence and autonomy, authority and criticism do not exclude but include each other. But who brings them into their true relationship? The way in which Hamann, not only in the *Crusades of the Philologist,* "Philologus crucis" ("a philologist of the cross"),[92] answers this question Christologically, in a theologically Trinitarian and eschatological way, can be briefly characterized as follows: From the viewpoint of eschatology and the theology of creation, the human being, defined by the "critical and archontic dignity of a political animal," undergoes in the interlacing of creation and Last Judgment an orientation toward the cross of the One who as servant is Lord. The exinanition and humiliation of the triune God grants freedom to participate in the world as it is and thereby to suffer. Such freedom and love lives from faith in the hope of overcoming the world by engagement through suffering. The comprehensive perception of the world and myself in the experience of God undergoing articulation and reflection in an "aesthetics" of discipleship occurs as learning through suffering. Hamann speaks of the "obedience of the cross in aesthetic discipleship."[93]

Reviewer with Reservation

Now in order finally to state in what sense Hamann's writings are reviews and their author a reviewer we must anticipate what will next be made a specific theme under the title "Original Motif," that is, Hamann's life-change that occurred in 1758 in London and became constitutive for all his speaking and writing. In London Hamann's experience with the Bible was that in reading he is read, and in understanding, through the "descent into the hell of self-knowledge,"[94] he is understood better, more critically and mercifully, than he could understand himself. In dealing with the Bible Hamann encounters the *krités,* the Art Critic and Reviewer absolutely who as Author of his life history and history of the world is also the best Interpreter of his works and has the majestic

92. "Hamburgische Nachricht," in N II, 249, 31f.
93. Apparatus in N III, 459.
94. "Chimärische Einfälle," in N II, 164, 18.

39

right finally to interpret and judge them. Every human judgment accordingly becomes a provisional and revisable criticism: a pre-judice.

This characterization alludes to a letter to the Swiss Johann Caspar Häfeli in which Hamann impressively voices his understanding of the critic and reviewer, and for which purpose he uses the answer to the request for an interpretation of dreams in the biblical story of Joseph: "Do not interpretations belong to God?" (Gen. 40:8). The passage in the letter draws attention once more to the momentary character of the flying leaves: ". . . unfortunately our judgment depends upon a moment, on an often arbitrary point of view, that I almost despair of all human judgments or treat them like majestic rights, and with the patriarch Joseph would want to say that *interpreting* and *judging* belongs to God — ."[95]

If, as Hamann confesses, interpreting and judging belong to God and are his majestic right, then every human with his or her judgment about the greatness of a historical figure and the significance of its life work is under a decisive reservation, that is, in the expectation of "the thief in the night, who is still to come," of the last reviewer and judge.[96] Hamann's greatness and foolishness, his pride and humility, consist in interpreting, judging, reading, and writing, and "critically and politically" living in the recognition of this reservation.

Recognition of this reservation explains why Hamann does not assume he is in agreement with his reader from the outset. And he does not anticipate a final successful understanding.

Systematically, in Hamann the discourse on mercy, in which I do not initially understand but am understood, occupies the same place as the discourse concerning the transcendental ego in Kant's philosophy. On Easter of 1787 Hamann writes from his sickbed to Friedrich Heinrich Jacobi, with whom he carried on an intensive correspondence in the last years of his life but who did not understand him at decisive points: "With all my head-splitting I am in the same boat with Sancho Panza, that I finally must content myself with his *Epiphonem* [exclamation]: God understands me!"[97] "The transcendental philosophy of Sancho Panza is for me as holy as the Samaritan's oil and wine."[98]

"God understands me!" The author Hamann also claims this confes-

---

95. H IV, 314, 22-26 (to Häfeli; 1781). Cf. ZH III, 89, 30-32 (to Kant; 1774).

96. "Fünf Hirtenbriefe," in N II, 368, 9f. Cf. 1 Thessalonians 5:2f.; Revelation 3:3; 16:5; 2 Peter 3:10.

97. H VII, 135, 17 19 (to Jacobi; 1787).

98. H IV, 340, 5f. (to Herder; 1781).

sion for his readers. They are "readers in hiddenness, whom God knows and understands better than I."[99] In this lies their freedom. The truth that communicates itself does not force. For this reason its witness will not compel it. It occurs freely and is the majestic right of the Author, who finally interprets and judges.

99. "Das Triumvirat," in N IV, 460, 10-13.

Chapter 3

Original Motif

"God understands me!" This word of Sancho Panza, the simple squire of Don Quixote, is the brief formula for the "motif" of the journalist and author Johann Georg Hamann.

The German word "Motiv" has both a literary critical ("motif") as well as a psychological connotation ("motive"). It denotes the motivation for an activity and the type of a concrete situation, in contrast to a "theme" which, when compared to "motif,"[1] is abstract and points toward an ideal sphere. For example, the motif of the hostile brother and fratricide suits the "hate" theme. The story of Cain and Abel in Genesis 4 up to John Steinbeck's *East of Eden* is prompted by this motif. This example also allows us to see that the psychological and literary-critical connotations of one and the same German word "motif" are connected, insofar as the (literary) motif is determined by a motive, and the situation it indicates lives from a tension that requires a solution. A literary motif is not conceivable apart from a situation-altering power. It describes the moving power of action.[2]

The twofold connotation of the word accordingly applies to our question about Hamann's "motif" as well as the motivation for his written discourses as their literary forms. What creates Hamann's textual world is not, as for example, a primary experience detachable from the actions

1. For the concept "motif" cf. W. Kayser, *Das sprachliche Kunstwerk. Eine Einführung in die Literaturwissenschaft* (Bern: Francke, 1983), 60-62.

2. Cf. above chapter 2, "Style and Form": Negotiation Discourse, notes 83-87.

of the author that unfold in a quite different way. All these in turn betray a common motive, a single source, from which and — as Hamann says against the logic of imaging — toward which is poured out "the little brook of my authorship."[3] The word "motif" represents the indissoluble union of the origin of the author's action and the medium of its presentation, the indissoluble union of intention and means.[4] The origin cannot be separated as a pure "experience," for example, from the mode and medium of its communication as a mere "expression."

Against Monarchic Reason and Deadly Separation

In the sense in which we must now consider it, the motif cannot be considered in a more fundamental way. At issue is the motif of all motifs, that motif in relation to which nothing higher or deeper can be imagined. Viewed systematically, in the argot of Kant, it would put the question of transcendentality at the very same spot, that is, the question as to the condition under which the constitution of self- and world-relation and the relation to God is possible. What makes consciousness a unity? What makes systematic thinking and thus science possible?

Those who with Kant ask this question place themselves within a tradition two and a half thousand years old, in the tradition of reason's imperial desire for unity, the tradition of monarchic reason. It is not by accident that the Greek word *archē* denotes rule and principle. Monarchic reason is afraid of the polyphony of the manifold. It fears it as anarchy, as chaos. Reason is monarchic both as the ancient ontology of substance as well as the modern philosophy of subjectivity. It is the monarchic strain that unites so many disparate thinkers such as Aristotle, Descartes, Kant, and Hegel. Its concern is given classic expression at the end of Book XII of Aristotle's *Metaphysics*. This book, a "closed treatise in itself," which in its own way "traverses the entire range of subjects in metaphysical books" and hands on "the only complete statement of the doctrine of God"[5] in

3. "Ein fliegender Brief," in N III, 399, 19f. in conjunction with N III 399, 10–401, 7. Cf. ZH I, 345, 1-4 (including context, to Lindner; 1759).

4. "Cloverleaf of Hellenistic Letters, Letter 2," in Haynes, 45-46 (N II, 175, 35-37) and E. Büchsel, "Hamanns Autorschaft bestimmt nach der Absicht," in R. Wild, *Johann Georg Hamann*, (218-32), 178.

5. Aristotle, *Metaphysics* XII, trans. and with a commentary by Hans-Georg Gadamer (Frankfurt am Main: Klostermann, 1976), 7 (Introduction).

Aristotle, represents the apex of his philosophy and with it also his systematic approach to knowledge. The pinnacle of this apex, its striking conclusion, reads: "the things that are *(ta onta)* do not want to be ruled badly. 'The rule of many is not good; let one be the ruler!'"[6]

Hamann passionately resists this acclamation of monarchic reason in which Descartes, Kant, and Hegel are agreed. If we have understood this resistance and the position from which it emerges, we have understood the enormous philosophical achievement Hamann accomplished. Coherent with this philosophical dissent is that the form of its presentation is not the lordly gesture of the systematic thinker who creates order by way of a "cobweb of dispositions"[7] and "definitions," and which according to Hamann's apt remark "are laws and belong to the monopoly of monarch."[8] Though Hamann also masters this art and trots it out in order to parody it[9] and turn it into a farce,[10] in his flying leaves he prefers "to labor . . . with doubt and thoughts against the dictators of pure doctrine and reason."[11]

But what does Hamann offer in place of the dictates of pure doctrine and monarchic reason? The "exchange of words." Not, however, dialogue as principle. In that case dialogue would only serve the one truth and its monarchic claim again and fail to recognize the fundamental disturbance, distortion, even killing of communication denoted by the word "sin."[12] It is sin that forbids speaking of a "unity of consciousness" on which contemporary thought is so bent.[13]

In what shape Hamann encountered this will to unity can be seen from the sources richly welling up from his works and correspondence. To Jacobi he writes: What "I . . . have not been able to bear from my youth in the academy on" is the talk of "sufficient reason," of *ratio*

---

6. Aristotle, *Metaphysics* XII. Within the quotation a quotation from Homer (*Iliad* 2, 204).

7. "Königsbergsche Zeitungen," in N IV, 419, 42.

8. "Selbstgespräch eines Autors," in N III, 72, 7f.

9. Cf. "Selbstgespräch eines Autors," in N III, 72; "Beylage zum 37sten Stück der Königsbergschen gelehrten und politischen Zeitung, 1772," in N III, 20-24.

10. "Beylage zum 37sten Stück der Königsbergschen gelehrten und politischen Zeitung, 1772," in N III, 20, 8.

11. "Das Triumvirat," in N IV, 460, 40-42; cf. H VII, 419, 12ff.; 425, 2f. (to Jacobi; 1788).

12. Cf. "Biblische Betrachtungen," in N I, 220f. (on Acts 2): "a confusion of language" through the "misuse" of "freedom" given to Adam.

13. Cf. the note regarding Benson in the "Aesthetic in nuce," in Haynes, 73 (N II, 203). Cf. below chapter 9, "Reason Is Language," note 4.

sufficiens,[14] linked with the name Leibniz. Hamann's aversion to talk of sufficient reason lies in the fact that "without Manicheism," hence without being or becoming a Manichean, he "has everywhere found contradictions in the elements of the material and intellectual world."[15] For that reason, Hamann loves the *principium coincidentiae oppositorum,* which he has "always opposed to the *principiis contradictionis* and *rationis sufficientis.*"[16] Back of this philosophical position is the Christology of the communion and communication of the two opposite natures affirmed by Hamann, that is, the divine and human natures of Jesus Christ in one and the same person. In such a Christology is reflected the condition of communion in which the sinful human and the justifying God are intimate, are able to come together again, through deadly dissociation.

If we inquire after the "motif" of Hamann the journalist and writer in the radical way stated, thus after the "primary motif," then we come to the motif of sin and its overcoming. It defines Hamann's understanding of self, world, and God throughout.

For describing this primary motif firsthand, comprehensive texts have happily come down to us: the *Biblical Meditations (Biblische Betrachtungen),* the *Fragments (Brocken), Meditations on Church Songs (Betrachtungen zu Kirchenliedern),* a lengthy written prayer, and above all, the *Thoughts about My Life-Story (Gedanken über meinen Lebenslauf),* all of them texts that Hamann did not design for the public. They are fundamental for an understanding of Hamann's dissent regarding monarchic reason, a persuasion still operative in the assumption of a communicative a priori, whose representatives fancy themselves hermeneutically enlightened, but with their transcendental-hermeneutical notion of language bow to reason's imperious desire for unity and allow themselves to be forced to give an ultimate foundation.

The only "ultimate foundation" Hamann gave was given in the *Thoughts about My Life-Story,* that is, in the unusual form of a confession, a *confessio.* It is as worthy of thought as Blaise Pascal's *Mémorial.*

Based on this confession the viewpoint of Hamann's primary motif, which we just explained systematically, will in what follows be made clear in a fundamental anthropological actualization.

14. H V, 327, 14f.; 325, 30 (to Jacobi; 1785).
15. H V, 327, 16f.
16. H V, 327, 14. Cf. H IV, 287, 5-17 (to Herder; 1781).

Individuality and Sociality

Dietrich Bonhoeffer's impressive formulation cuts the shortest path toward understanding Hamann's *Thoughts about My Life-Story:*

> Who am I really, what others say about me?
> Or am I only what I myself know of myself?
> Who am I? They mock me, these lonely questions of mine.
> Whoever I am, Thou knowest, O God, I am Thine![17]

Who am I? Is this question appropriate in public? Doesn't it belong in the solitude of a soliloquy? Or in a conversation that has its unique time and place? Yet each of us has his or her name that identifies a specific life-story. And this story, in any event some stories from it, are more or less known to a more or less large public. Others participate in my story. But they do not do so without making a judgment about me in one way or another.

I am tossed about between others' judgments about me and my own judgments about myself. We will now look at these two sides that we may designate the side of individuality and that of sociality.

No one lives alone. I am not able to do without the network of relationships in which I find myself, to see through them and conform my behavior to them as much as I can. Based on my previous experience I can do no other than consider the probable answers of persons with whom I have to do, both with regard to the word I speak and the decision I make. If I live with other humans, if I answer to a request or some other summons, then I alter myself by so doing. I risk becoming another. I risk even becoming many others so that something such as my "I self," my identity, is wholly dissolved in constellations of relationships that are constantly changing, loses itself in them. Hence Hamann writes to his friend Jacobi: "Such individual personalities which wholly disappear from memory, were the ingredients of my composition, which more often relate to a very specific viewpoint or to an equally contingent frame of mind. I have made so many funny attempts at reading myself that I can almost as easily and spiritedly sympathize with the prejudices of my friends and enemies."[18]

---

17. Dietrich Bonhoeffer, *Letters and Papers from Prison*, ed. Eberhard Bethge (New York: Collier Books, 1971), 347-48.

18. H V, 316, 10-15; cf. II V, 317, 16ff. (to Jacobi; 1785); on the subject: ZH III, 246, 34-36 (to Nicolai; 1776).

Just as dangerous as this loss of self is the desire to maintain and save oneself as an "I self," to be bent on one's individuality and originality, steadfastly to crouch in on oneself, as it were, to be curved in on oneself. Fidelity to one's self can, however, mean something completely different. Most significantly, it furthers the relation to another human being when I remain true to my word, when I hold to my promise and preserve community. But in this I am no longer by myself, insofar as I am referred to the trust of the other, without which I can scarcely keep my promise.

All this requires a continual balancing act between the I and my fellow humans, between identity and sociality. Must we then be tightrope walkers? Daredevils, who in every moment must take care not to fall on the side of individualism or collectivism? No political engagement, no care for the well-being of the whole in which I am intertwined in suffering and forming can suppress the question, "Who am I?" In it the puzzle of our existence is expressed. No one can solve it through flight into the universal or particular of his or her empty subjectivity, crouched in oneself and stuck fast in it. Can I become certain of myself?

Understandably, to escape this deeply distressing question one seeks a socially established "counsel of conscience." But, "Am I really what others say of me?" Or must not Bonhoeffer's line, "Who am I? They mock me, these lonely questions of mine," be immediately followed with, "Who am I? They mock me, these shared questions"?

Those who hope to orient themselves to world society, to the nation, to an association, but above all to a group and in it promise themselves an answer to the question "Who am I?" expose themselves to a danger that is not merely evident today. It was already seen, for example, by the theological critics of specific forms of Pietism in the seventeenth and eighteenth centuries. In the Pietist's *Reskript*, of significance for the history of the Evangelical church in Württemberg, the section "On Testing the Condition of the Soul of Other Persons" reads:

> It is forbidden to induce others to tell of their so-called inner state of soul and secret conditions in the assembly and there to subject themselves to a counsel of conscience, classification, and prescription established by the group. Such matters belong in the presence of the preaching office or in a secret Christian confidentiality among a very few, for example, among two, three, or four persons,

not in an assembly of various persons who could see or interpret it in a number of ways.[19]

So it evidently occurred that one induced others to tell of their so-called inner state of soul and secret conditions in the assembly, that is, in the group to tell everything that was thought and felt and "to subject themselves to a counsel of conscience, classification, and prescription established by the group."

One can scarcely describe more precisely the matter in question. The counsel of conscience established by the group, the classification and regulation it establishes and to which one should subject oneself and on suggestion undertake is also found today, in the most varied shape, in the social interaction of a small group or even in advertising — for example, giving the housewife a bad conscience when she does not buy Mister Clean. So we need not think only of the large-sized conscience established by a group, and how it functions in specific political relationships, awaiting self-discipline and absolution received from the collective.

It is a main feature of theological anthropology to encounter every collectivism just as skeptically as every individualism. "Am I really what others say of me? Or am I only what I myself know of myself?" Neither is first or last. And there is no balancing act between the two. Psychology, sociology, and pedagogy have no more than this in view. Theological anthropology can do nothing but render this balancing act problematic, or more precisely, relativize it, relate it to the word of the One who can be addressed in complaint and praise, petition and thanks, in trust and certainty of being heard: "Whoever I am, Thou knowest, O God, I am Thine!"

If the balancing act between the I and fellow humanity, between identity and sociality is taken into such a prayer, it does not disappear. It remains a daily reality and task till death. But it is not the first and the last that would be said of us. This first and last is the God who promises himself to us, who has taken us into the history of his love and by it given us the primary motif and impulse of our life history.

Knowledge of God and knowledge of self are not to be separated. Their relation to each other is played out in a specific linguistic medium. It consists in the exchange of words between God and the human. This

19. *Das Württembergische Pietisten-Reskript vom Jahre 1743*, ed. Evangelische Oberkirchenrat (Stuttgart, n.d. [1978]), unpaginated facsimile [page 9].

is not a dialogue apart from world and history of an I and Thou pure of the It of nature and culture. It embraces the "world," discloses and shapes it. This exchange is literally "world shaping." One's own life-story is not only reflected in it but has its very existence in it, is formed in it and experiences its unity in it. This unity is not that of an "individual substance of reason"[20] that would accidentally have a history. No "I" that I myself would be is at the basis of my life-story. The fact, however, that the human is not an amoeba that dissolves and dwindles away in ever-changing shapes and relations, that in the midst of these changes a continuity nevertheless persists without there being any inherent power to change the self or integrate its changes, as with Proteus — all this results from the fact that God is the primary motif and motive of my life-story. He is Poet in the radical sense; he is Author.

God — an author! God — a writer! This is Hamann's answer to the question, "Who am I?" This is his answer to the problem to be developed below, and to which transcendental thought responds in a monarchical and monological way.

"Thoughts about My Life-Story"

In London, on April 21 and 24, 1758, Hamann dated an extensive piece of writing[21] which like Pascal's *Mémorial* was not intended for the public and first appeared in 1821.[22] The piece was "Thoughts about My Life-Story."[23]

That Hamann intends to have thoughts about himself not only to and before himself is indicated by the Psalm word that he sets under the title as motto: "When the cares of my heart (and of me, myself) are many, your consolations cheer my soul" (Ps. 94:19).

> I have drafted these thoughts about my course of life for myself or
> for my beloved father and brother; and I wish consequently that

20. Cf. the definition of "person" as *"rationalis naturae individua substantia"* [individual substance of a rational nature] in Boethius, *De persona et duabus naturis Jesu Christi*, Migne, Patrologia Latina 64, 1343 C.

21. "Thoughts about My Life," in Smith, 140 (N II, 9); cf. Smith, 154 (N II, 41, 22); "Gedanken über meinen Lebenslauf," in N II, 45, 7.

22. "Schlusswort," in N II, 381, last line.

23. "Thoughts about My Life," in Smith, 140-57 (partial translation) (N II, 9-44); continued in N II, 44-54.

they may serve the latter or my closest friends by being perused. I have in them spoken with God and with myself. With respect to my life I have justified God and accused myself, indicated and discovered myself — all for the praise of the solely good God, who has forgiven me, in the blood of his only begotten Son, and in the testimony which the Spirit of God confirms in his word and in my heart. God has poured me from one vessel into another, so that I do not accumulate too much scum and become stale without retrieval and should stink. Everything must happen for the best for us. Since our life turns out to be the death of sin, so must all sicknesses redound for the experience, the example, and the glorification of the same.[24]

In the thoughts about his life-story Hamann acknowledges the exchange of words between himself and God: "In them I have spoken with God and with myself." It is a rigorous conversation, a struggle, as Jacob had to undergo with God at the Jabbok (Genesis 32), a struggle in an exchange of words in which the old being is given over to death for the sake of the life of the new being. As in the experience of the Psalms (Ps. 51:5f.), of Paul (Rom. 3:4), and of Luther, this discourse consists in the confession of one's own sin and in praise of the God who forgives it.

"I have justified God and accused myself. . . ." The confession uttered here is developed in a long narrative of a distinctively particular individual history, that is, Hamann's individual history, which he nevertheless finds in the history of others and narrates in the motifs of these stories:

> I recognized my own crimes in the history of the Jewish people, I read my own course of life, and thanked God for his longsuffering with this his people, because nothing other than such an example could authorize my confidence for a similar hope. . . . With these reflections, which seemed to me so mysterious, on the evening of March 31 I read the fifth chapter of Deuteronomy [Hamann meant more precisely 5:17: "You shall not kill!"], and fell into deep thought.

24. "Thoughts about My Life," in Smith, 155 (N II, 42, 14-27) (translation altered). In fact, Hamann entrusted his thoughts to his "closest friend to peruse" but in so doing was disappointed in Johann Christoph Berens: ZH I, 308, 27-33; cf. ZH I, 304, 31-305, 12 (to Lindner; 1759).

I thought of Abel of whom God said [Gen. 4:11]: the earth has opened her mouth to receive your brother's blood — I felt my heart pound, I heard a voice sigh in its depths and wail as the voice of blood, as the voice of a slain brother, who wanted to avenge his blood, if I did not hear it betimes and went on stopping my ears to it, — saying that it was just this that made Cain restless and a fugitive [Gen. 4:12]. All at once, I felt my heart swell, and engulfed in tears, I could no longer — I could no longer hide from my God that I was the fratricide, the murderer of his only begotten Son. The Spirit of God proceeded, notwithstanding my great weakness, notwithstanding the long resistance, which I had earlier made against his witness and his moving, to reveal to me more and more the mystery of divine love and the benefit of faith in our gracious and only Savior.

With sighs that were brought before God by an Interpreter who is beloved and dear to him, I went on with the reading of the divine Word, and enjoyed that very help with which it was written as the only way to understand it, and with the divine aid I brought my work to an unbroken conclusion, on April 21, with extraordinarily rich consolation and quickening.

Now, thank God, I feel my heart more at rest than ever before in my life. At the times when melancholy has begun to arise I have been overwhelmed with a consolation the source of which I cannot ascribe to myself, and which no man can instill so inexhaustibly into his neighbor. I have been frightened by its abundance. It swallowed up all fear, all sadness, all mistrust, so that I could no longer find a trace of them in my spirit.[25]

Hamann confesses God as the One who comes to him in the prevenient word, in the histories narrated, anticipating him and being anticipated. God is met in histories and through them interprets the one who hears them in such a way that the hearer is changed, becomes a new being.

Entangled in Histories

To the extent Hamann tells of his own life, his individual history, to that extent this witness, if one looks to its structure, assumes universal significance.

25. "Thoughts about My Life," in Smith, 54 (N II, 40, 25–41, 30) (translation altered).

If we take Hamann's *Thoughts about My Life-Story* as a model of every life, as a universal answer to the question "Who am I?," then they verify the thesis that the I does not accidentally have a history but is history through and through, and in such a way that the I as my own history is interwoven with the histories of many others and cannot be loosed from them. This applies not only to my history as having happened or as happening, but to my history that is told. For my life history as having happened or as happening does not happen unless I tell it to others and to myself, unless it is told to me by others, unless it is more or less coherently preserved in my remembrance, sinks or is pressed into my subconscious, in order to emerge now and again, most of all condensed in special scenes and constellations that then are clear to us in all their details.

In some measure or other these recalled scenes and images always contain elements of objectifiable facticity. In their own way they are bound to a specific space and time. But the content of meaning of the whole scene can be altered; the perspective in which it emerges can be shifted. Hence, the narration of history belongs to history itself. A tells his life history to B expecting that B gives some response to it. Depending on how B hears, what he asks or does not ask, he impinges on the history of A and is entangled in it. The conversation that has been conducted is now a part of the history of both. In this situation it is not merely the case that "a history continues in the telling and hearing of it."[26] From the very outset it holds, as a fundamental anthropological rule, "that being human is exhausted by being entangled in histories, that the human being is one who is entangled in history."[27]

Yet as appropriate as it is to speak first of all of "histories," of an indeterminate and indeterminable plurality of histories, just as unavoidably the question arises, "How do the individual histories fuse into a comprehensive history of the one entangled in them?"[28] This can occur by means of an individual history, in which we then speak of a "fateful event." There are histories

> which stand as a single history at the center of an entire life, histories from which an entire life becomes intelligible, from which all

26. Wilhelm Schapp, *In Geschichten verstrickt. Zum Sein von Mensch und Ding* (Hamburg: Meiner, 1953), 2nd edition with a Foreword from H. Lübbe (1976), 107.

27. Schapp, *In Geschichten verstrickt*, 123. With this Schapp formulates the thesis of his entire book, a thesis he is able to make thoroughly illuminative.

28. Schapp, *In Geschichten verstrickt*, 128.

previous and subsequent histories alone receive their ultimate meaning. So it is with the great conversions, for example, the conversion of the Apostle Paul and St. Augustine. From the viewpoint of this conversion the whole life is divided into two parts, the first part stamped null and void and the second disclosing the authentic life of the saint. But with this disclosure the first part does not sink into an abyss, but remains within the horizon of the second. In a certain sense we can even say that it carries the second part along with it and that it belongs inseparably to the horizon of the whole life even after conversion, even by giving direction, though only in negation, perhaps one could also say in a support from which the saint tries to gain ever greater distance, but whose existence he never denies or tries to deny.[29]

We have before us such a history of conversion, of decisive change, in Hamann's *Thoughts about My Life-Story*. As to form, the uniqueness of a single and all-decisive change is not unique. No history of a life can be told without a viewpoint integrating everything. In his book *Analytic Philosophy of History* Danto shows that this also applies to the writing of history and can be identified in the reflection of scientific theory.[30]

Danto has examined the role of histories and narratives and made clear their relationship to historical explanation. He shows that statements that narrate history and histories comprise a temporal whole within which single parts, chiefly the beginning point and end point of a change, have their explanation. This occurs by locating a transition between the beginning and end point, and which combines both with the whole of the narrative context.

With Hamann in view let us take up the concept of "conversion." If used to narrate a life history, then it connects beginning and end by denoting a key event that discloses the meaning of events before and after, and allows anticipation of their completion.[31]

---

29. Schapp, *In Geschichten verstrickt,* 129ff.

30. Arthur Coleman Danto, *Analytic Philosophy of History* (Cambridge: Cambridge University Press, 1965).

31. Cf. below chapter 12, "Created Time," note 42.

The Poet of the World

The medium within which Hamann not only narrates his life together with the decisive change, but in which this history occurred and was able to occur at all, is the language of the Bible. In it are narrated histories into which God himself has entered. He has not only brought them about himself but at the same time has told of himself. As "Poet," God is creator and narrator alike.[32]

By titling God as "Poet"[33] Hamann in a luminous etymological depth of mind combines elements usually perceived as dissonant or as suppressing each other, that is, the word of command and the word of love, freedom and passion, creation as work and creation as word. Hamann intends to do the same thing with his strong emphasis on God's fatherliness and authorship which, joined with the thought of condescension, he understands constitutively and consistently as linguistic: God is a poet who speaks in the *genus humile* (in a humble way).[34]

What gives the pitch is the linguistic element, more precisely the element of address. In this way Hamann radically distinguishes himself from Whitehead, for whom God is likewise "the poet of the world."[35] In Whitehead, Christian faith, "a tender care that nothing finally perishes," "a wisdom, which uses everything which is merely rubble in the temporal world," and an "infinite patience" in which God "tenderly saves" the "confusion" of the world, is overlaid and encompassed by Platonism. That is, God is "the Poet of the World by his vision of truth, beauty, and goodness . . . in the patient operation of the overpowering

---

32. This lays claim to the dual meaning of the Greek *poietes* (the word for "Creator" according to the Nicene Creed).

33. "Aesthetic in nuce," in Haynes, 78 (N II, 206, 30f.) with explicit reference to 2 Corinthians 4:6; Haynes, 67 (N II, 200, 7f.) ("mighty speaker"), with reference to Psalm 33:9; "Über die Auslegung der heiligen Schrift" (N I, 5): "God an author! —" Cf. the reference to Ephesians 2:10 *(poiema)* in "Wise Men from the East," in Smith, 192 (N II, 140, 28-32).

34. Cf. especially "Cloverleaf of Hellenistic Letters, First Letter," in Haynes, 35-42 (N II, 169-73) and below, notes 37-38. In his imitation of ordinary colloquial language the "*genus humile*" [the humble species], the "lower style of speech," is used to tell of events taking place in the low social order.

35. Alfred North Whitehead, *Process and Reality: An Essay in Cosmology*, ed. David Ray Griffin and Donald W. Sherburne (New York: The Free Press, 1978), 346. Cf. *Timaeus* 28c.

rationality of his conceptual [!] harmonization," but not as in Hamann, in sensuous speech to the creature through the creature.[36]

History that has occurred and been narrated, history that is occurring and discloses itself in address are interwoven. Only the violence of artificially dissecting observation tears apart what belongs together in the Trinitarian event.

"God a writer! The inspiration of this book," as well as its understanding, "is just as great a humiliation and descent of God as the creation of the Father and the incarnation of the Son."[37]

> How has God the Father abased himself, when he not only formed a lump of clay but even ensouled it with his breath. How has God the Son abased himself! He became a human, the most humble among beings, he took the form of a servant, became the most unfortunate of beings. He was made sin for us. In God's eyes he was the sinner of the whole people. How has God the Holy Spirit humbled himself, when he became a historian of the smallest, most despised, most insignificant events on earth, to reveal to humans in their own language, their own history, their own paths, the counsels, the mysteries and the ways of divinity?[38]

The implication respecting his own self-knowledge is that "I know my own crimes in the history of the Jewish people, I read in it my own course of life and thank God for his patience with this his people, because nothing but such an example would be able to confirm me in hope."[39]

It is extremely important for Hamann that the Bible as a book of stories does not exclude the world of nature and history in all their breadth, but at the very first discloses them.[40] From the Bible one recognizes oneself and other histories, "our own life and other objects, peoples and

---

36. Cf. below chapter 4, "The Modern Concept of Nature in Crisis," notes 35-44.

37. "Über die Auslegung der heiligen Schrift," in N I, 5.

38. "Biblische Betrachtungen," in N I, 91, 7-17; cf. "Thoughts about My Life," in Smith, 156 (N II, 43, 28-40), especially (36-40), and "Biblische Betrachtungen," in N I, 99, 24-100, 19.

39. "Thoughts about My Life," in Smith, 153 (N II, 40, 25-29) (translation altered); in the context from Smith, 153-54 (N II, 40, 25-29–41, 30) (translation altered). Cf. Smith, 155 (42, 27-29).

40. Cf. below chapter 4, "The Modern Concept of Nature in Crisis," notes 12-15.

events": "We have a great prejudice in the view which limits God's effect and influence merely to the Jewish people. He has wanted to explain to us openly in the example of the same the hiddenness, the method, and the laws of his wisdom and love, make them meaningful, and allow us to appropriate them for our own life and for other objects, peoples, and events."[41]

Hamann does not perceive his own life story in isolation because he perceives it as the history of Israel in miniature. This does not narrow the history of Israel to, say, the history of the soul of one individual. Rather, through it and the God speaking in it an individual person with its concrete life-story experiences being led out from pure subjectivity or self-preoccupation and desolate depth into the breadth of creation and history. In this way Hamann has surpassed the opposition of particularity and universality on the basis of which Hegel judges him. Hegel sees Hamann in an "abstract interiority,"[42] as an "original" who persisted in "concentration on his deep particularity, which proved incapable of any form of universality, whether of the expansion of thinking reason or of taste."[43]

In saying this Hegel does not do justice to Hamann, in whose experience, speaking, and thinking the pure universality both of historical-philosophical and of personalistic categories is burst.

> I am convinced that every soul is a theatre of such great miracles as the history of creation and the entire Holy Scriptures includes. The course of the life of every Christian is comprehended in the daily work of God, in God's covenants with people, in transgression, warning, revelation, miraculous preservation, etc. For a Christian, who has passed from the death of sin into a new life, can the preservation of Jonah, the raising of Lazarus, the healing of a cripple, etc. appear to be greater miracles? Does not our Savior himself say: Which is easier, to forgive sins or to say: take up your bed and walk?[44]

Narrated histories offer possibilities for identification. Suddenly I see myself in the narrated history and hear it as my own. *Mutato nomine de*

---

41. "Fragments," in Smith, 166 (*Brocken* §3, in N I, 303, 11-18).
42. *Hegel on Hamann*, 25 (compare above Introduction, note 3).
43. *Hegel on Hamann*, 6.
44. "Betrachtungen zu Kirchenliedern," in N I, 297, 25-35.

te fabula narratur — a line from Horace, is especially important for Hamann's dealing with the Bible.[45]

Hamann shares the basic anthropological definition of the human as a being entangled in history. What is decisive, however, is how a comprehensive perspective results — "how the individual histories fuse into a comprehensive history of the one entangled."[46] At issue is the original motif that organizes the store of images and arranges not only what involves knowledge and activity, but extends deeper and wider, concerns us initially and chiefly in the images that can consciously or unconsciously guide our behavior, determine or alter the direction of our will. What is decisive is the arrangement of our store of images and in it the strength and direction of affects and passions.

With the precise definition of this primary motif we encounter the difference between general linguistic theory and anthropology on the one hand and Christian theology on the other. Theology is such by the fact that it reflects on the human store of images in the context of that event in which a new person emerges from the old. It reflects on the death of the old and the life of the new being created by the gospel as the promise of life.

Hamann[47] heard as his own the story of fratricide in the biblical original history, the story of Cain and Abel, the story beyond Eden, since together with the accusing and absolving nearness of God he learned that he was such a person as is withdrawn and hidden from himself in a twofold way, in the hiddenness of the sinner and the hiddenness of the one justified.

The hiddenness of the sinner is the hiddenness of the one ignorant of self at its core. This ignorance of self is not a neutral state of not knowing. It rumbles. Hamann experiences it as "inner unrest," "from which I was long ailing in my life, a lack of peace and an incapacity to endure myself."[48] Like Cain he is "a fugitive and restless" (Gen. 4:12): "I could enjoy nothing," he writes in his *Thoughts about My Life-Story,* "was

---

45. Horace: *Satires* I/1, 69ff. *("quid rides? Mutato nomine de te fabula narratur")* combined with 2 Samuel 12:7: "So why do you laugh? With the name changed the story is told about you!" (ZH I, 396, 27 to Lindner; 1759).

46. Schapp, *In Geschichten verstrickt,* 128 (see note 26).

47. For the following, cf. "Thoughts about My Life," in Smith, 153-54 (N II, 40, 25–41, 30) and furthermore "Biblische Betrachtungen," in N I, 76, 7-26; 78, 4-27.

48. "Gedanken über meinen Lebenslauf," in N II, 23, 30-32; 27, 25. Cf. H IV, 301, 24–302, 2 (to Herder; 1781): "anxiety in the world," "homesickness," "impertinent unrest."

constrained on every hand and anxious for myself, deep in thought without thinking, unsteady and unhappy like a refugee with a bad conscience."[49] I "distracted myself as much as possible, all for nothing. The worm does not die, as every sinner should be terrified without thinking of the fire which does not go out. This alone is sufficient punishment and torment."[50]

The hiddenness before the self of the justified is quite different from the hiddenness before the self of the sinner. Justification does not take place in such a way, for example, that one would now be so thoroughly transparent to oneself as to freely connect with everything that had earlier driven one under the servitude of sin, so that now one could finally tell one's own life-story (with a happy ending), in which deliverance from sin would be a decisive event but still only one event among others. As truly as one is retrieved from the hiddenness of the sinner in allowing oneself to be "discovered"[51] by the accusing voice of the law, one moves from agonizing alienation into the joyous alienation of the *iustitia aliena* (alien righteousness). One emerges from unbearable hiddenness into a hiddenness and safety that bear one up. What results for the life of the justified is the liberating consequence that I am not thrown back on my liberated I and am forced in an objectifying self-assurance to recall a salvation received.

In either case, in judgment as well as under grace, the human is so hidden before the self with the nearness of the accusing and absolving God that one can neither speak nor hear oneself and God. One must be represented. So Hamann hears another who represents and replaces him. He hears an "advocate," a "mediator," "without whom" we are "incapable of rightly fearing or rightly loving God."[52]

The "voice from the depth" of his heart, which Hamann hears "sigh-

---

49. "Gedanken über meinen Lebenslauf," in N II, 31, 12-15. Cf. "Thoughts about My Life," in Smith, 153 (41, 6f.) ["which made Cain a wanderer and a fugitive"].

50. "Gedanken über meinen Lebenslauf," in N II, 31, 40–32, 3; Mark 9:44, 46, and 48 (Isaiah 66:24) is taken up. Cf. S. Kierkegaard, *The Sickness unto Death*, trans. Howard and Edna Hong (Princeton: Princeton University Press, 1980), 17ff. In telling of his career as the history of the hiddenness of one who has no understanding of self at its core, and up to the late texts (cf. especially H IV, 301f.; note 48), Hamann is the one who prepares the way for Kierkegaard's analyses.

51. Cf. with the texts named in note 47, N II, 42, 19.

52. "Thoughts about My Life," in Smith, 153 (N II, 40, 35-37). Cf. "Biblische Betrachtungen," in N I, 76, 19-26; "Betrachtungen zu Kirchenliedern," in N I, 294, 3-5.

ing and wailing," is the voice of lament and accusation. It is the voice of his "brother," his neighbor, his fellow human, from whom he has separated himself and whom, separated from himself, he has killed by this separation. And simultaneously it is the voice of the God from whom he has separated himself by his disassociation from the brother. Along with fratricide he is convicted of the murder of God,[53] yet "this God himself has become his neighbor and his neighbor's neighbor in the strictest sense," "so that we all would have a good reason for loving God and our neighbor."[54]

The gospel, as the word that is "very near to you" (Deut. 30:11-14; Rom. 10:5-13) and creates faith, gives us who "cannot estimate" the "abyss" of our hearts and their chaotic "emptiness" and "darkness"[55] the basis for loving God and our neighbor. "Faith convinces us that nothing but a God who is love can assure us, make us righteous, and accept us."[56] Hamann testifies to the "God, who is love," as the One who is nearer to him than he is to himself, who has "anticipated his desires" and "exceeded them."[57] "All that we lack, even more than we can ask for and hope and desire, is given us in him."[58] "As nature beforehand prepared and anticipated everything that the voice of our bodily needs could have required of the Creator, so grace has slaughtered and judged for us, and we have no need other than to follow its call, to share in its Lord's Supper, for the preparation of which it rose earlier, earlier than we were conscious of our existence and our future hunger or of its prevenient love. Indeed, to allow us to share in this symposia we were awakened from the bosom of night into life."[59]

---

53. "Thoughts about My Life," in Smith, 153 (N II, 41, 8-10): "I could no longer conceal from my God that I was the fratricide, the murderer of his only begotten Son."

54. "Fragments," in Smith, 165 (*Brocken* §1 in N I, 302, 29-31) (translation altered). Cf. "Biblische Betrachtungen," in N I, 71, 30-34; 211, 4–213, 25; "Betrachtungen zu Kirchenlieder," in N I, 291-97.

55. "Biblische Betrachtungen," in N I, 75, 37–76, 6; 78, 6.

56. "Betrachtungen zu Kirchenlieder," in N I, 294, 7-9.

57. "Betrachtungen zu Kirchenlieder," in N I, 295, 29f.

58. "Betrachtungen zu Kirchenlieder," in N I, 295, 31-33.

59. "Betrachtungen zu Kirchenlieder," in N I, 294, 13-21.

God as the Author of My Life History

To hear a history in the Bible as my own and in so doing to become a new being is not an achievement of application on the part of the I that arbitrarily and on its own interprets itself and its life by understanding another history, an understanding that also in the other arrives only at self. If the truth lay here, then, as Novalis, the pupil of Fichte, says, even in "self-emptying . . . toward the outside" the "highest task of formation *(Bildung)*" would be to "take possession of its transcendental self, to be the I of its I."[60] But I do not interpret myself. I am interpreted. This is the decisive thing Hamann clearly confesses: "I proceed through sighs, which are represented before God through an interpreter, which is faithful to and worthy of him, in reading the divine word and relishing its succor, of which the same has been written, as receiving the single way to understand this scripture."[61]

We must make clear what epistemology follows from this process and state of affairs. To know, or more precisely, to be known, is from the first a linguistic event. That I do not know, but rather am known, as Paul emphasizes,[62] is not only to be taken theoretically but above all linguistically and sensuously, and in Hamann always has sexual connotations, corresponding to the Hebraic word for "knowing" (cf. Gen. 4:1: "Now the man knew his wife Eve, and she conceived").

To understand the Bible in such fashion that I myself am interpreted by it and changed, made a new person, is the work of God. So God as Interpreter of a life history remains its Author, which he is from the first.

If God as "Author" is from the first the One who speaks through the creature, more precisely, through the humiliation and emptying of the Son, then as "Author" and "Father" — in Hamann authorship is always combined with fatherhood[63] — he is also humble.

This has fundamental significance for the dispute between theology and philosophy over the concept of God. Hamann rejects the metaphysical and theistic predicate for God as "Originator" and replaces it with the

---

60. Novalis, "Vermischte Bemerkungen," in Novalis, *Schriften, Die Werke Friedrich von Hardenbergs,* ed. P. Kluckhohn and R. Samuel, vol. 2 (Stuttgart: Kohlhammer, 1960) (numbered by the editor as fragments 24 and 28).

61. "Thoughts about My Life," in Smith, 154 (N II, 41, 16-20) (translation altered). Naturally, Romans 8:26 has been incorporated here.

62. Galatians 4:9; cf. 1 Corinthians 8:2f.; 1 Corinthians 13:12; Philippians 3:12.

63. Cf. for example ZH III, 98, 28-30 (to Herder; 1774).

title of the actively speaking "Author." A limiting concept becomes a vocative that replies to the One who addresses the creature through the creature. Accordingly, the relation between God and the world is no longer conceived within the scheme of causality as in Schleiermacher and other transcendental philosophical and transcendental-theological efforts.

On the basis of the "word that is very near" as a "word of omnipotence and love,"[64] God the Creator is not to be spoken of without refraction in the metaphor of the dictator, and the creative word is not to be spoken of without refraction in analogy to the command of a generalissimo. For this makes for speedy trial, leaves no time for hearing and understanding, but demands quick, abrupt obedience. Psalm 33:9 and the corresponding image from the Priestly narrative of creation (Gen. 1:3: "Then God said: 'Let there be . . . !' and there was") are thus not to be seen in isolation. For the power of the creative word is the power of love that takes and allows for time. A "Fatherhood" of God conceived as such "authorship" of the "Poet" is recognized in the address of the Lord's Prayer. That is, the cosmological and soteriological understandings of the fatherhood of God coinhere.

The history woven together and led by the Father and Author addressed in prayer is my true life-story and also my history with God. He leads me, as Hamann said, into the hell of self-knowledge and out of it again.[65]

This true life-story does not occur above, below, or only in the background of my actual life history and its "tiniest coincidences," "twists and turns."[66] It occurs in and with it and yet is not identical with my own judgment about myself or with others' judgment about me, with the judgment of conscience established by the group. My true life-story is not identical with that balancing act between individuality and sociality. It does not disappear, but is embraced by the unconditional

---

64. "Betrachtungen zu Kirchenlieder," in N I, 291, 32f.

65. That God kills and makes alive, leads into hell and out of it again (1 Sam. 2:6; cf. Deut. 32:39; Ps. 71:20), experienced and often witnessed to by Luther, is also determinative for Hamann's career: "nothing but the descent into the hell of self-knowledge prepares our way to deification" ("Kreuzzüge des Philologen," in N II, 164, 17f.). Cf. H VII, 163, 20-23 (cf. below note 73).

66. "Gedanken über meinen Lebenslauf," in N II, 45, 26-28 in relation to 45, 9–46, 14. Cf. "Biblische Betrachtungen," in N I, 36, 35–37, 11; 38, 7-22; 53, 12-25. By contrast Hegel: "trivial faith in providence" (see *Lectures on the Philosophy of World History: Introduction,* trans. H. B. Nisbet [Cambridge: Cambridge University Press, 1998], 36).

justifying word of God, judged and conserved and saved in it. In answer to such a word Bonhoeffer prays: "Whoever I am, Thou knowest, O God, I am thine!" And for Hamann God is the one who interprets and understands him and therein can verify, does verify and make true his existence which he cannot make true himself. In his *Thoughts about My Life-Story* he tells of the God who encounters him in the Bible as the friend who understands him: "In the tumult of the passions which overwhelmed me . . . I continually prayed to God for a friend. . . . A friend, who could supply the key to my heart, the clue and thread to lead me out of my labyrinth, was a wish I often had, without properly understanding or seeing its content. Praise God, I found this friend in my heart, who crept in there at the time when I felt most heavily its emptiness and darkness and wildness."[67]

This confession remains determinative till the end of Hamann's life. In 1787 he writes to Jacobi from his sickbed: "With all my head-splitting I'm in the same boat with Sancho Panza, that I finally must content myself with his *Epiphonem* [exclamation]: God understands me!"[68]

Whoever judges this from the outside, as a sociologist of religion of the Luhmann stripe (for example Hermann Lübbe), will see in it the basic act of mastering contingency; or, as a psychologist, will see it as a self-stabilization reached in an especially clever way, even though self-knowledge is confessed as a descent into hell. This should not seem strange. In the encounter with other gods and viewpoints, the experience of faith and its language cannot avoid the conflict of interpretations. Hamann came into such a conflict soon after his return from London, when his old Königsberg friends Kant and Berens saw in him an "enthusiast" ("Schwärmer")[69] and risked everything to make him a rational man again, a useful member of bourgeois society. Hamann did not submit to this socially established counsel of conscience, and as a result of the change of 1758 became and remained spiritually as free and agile a person as scarcely any other.

---

67. "Thoughts about My Life," in Smith, 152 (N II, 39, 31–40, 20). Cf. Paul Gerhardt's hymn cited by Hamann at the end of his "Thoughts about My Life," "*Ich weiss, mein Gott . . . ,*" Stanza 5: "*Sei du mein Freund . . .*" (N II, 44, 37), but above all the meditation of the hymnary on the friendship of God, "*Mein Geliebter ist mein,*" N I, 283-91. In the eighteenth century the metaphor "friend" is obvious.

68. H VII, 135, 17-19 (to Jacobi; 1787). Cf. even the letter from Bode to Hamann: ZH III, 65, 13f. (1773).

69. ZH I, 301, 28 (to his brother; 1759).

The Bible as Historical A Priori

What was established about the original motif of Hamann the journalist and author has paradigmatic significance for every understanding of self, world, and God. And whoever may not agree with the train of what is said will in any case not be able to avoid a debate with the world of the text that has just emerged, and its original motif. For in its problematic ambivalence the Western history of monarchical reason and its violence are clear to everyone, at least since the ecological crisis. For the sake of survival alone we are forced to think and to live out alternatives. Hamann thought and lived out his alternative, not because he exited — we ought not be deceived by an existence that in many respects was not overly bourgeois — but because he entered, was a contemporary to the core, and in his metacritical attempts, i.e., attempts at retesting, did not avoid dissent, but precisely through it experienced resistance and rejection and suffered under it.

In "obedience to the cross in aesthetic discipleship,"[70] to use Hamann's expression, I recognize that in my life and thought I cannot proceed from a universal openness in which universal incurvation, that is, sin (cf. Rom. 11:32; Gal. 3:22), is always overcome. Precisely this is the departure for every transcendental-philosophical and transcendental-theological thought, in Kant and subsequently, for example, in Schleiermacher, Tillich, Pannenberg, or Rahner. A transcendental thought according to which the essence of humanity consists in its openness to the world and the self-mediation of God, which in turn presupposes humanity's openness and receptivity, proves to be harmless, or put more pointedly, illusionary. The only thought that is without illusion is the kind that does not overplay the opposition between sin and grace and seeks to find and cultivate no a priori, not even a logical a priori, before and behind, in and under this opposition. If theology, no longer understood as a single but as a universal discipline, intends briefly to name its object and theme, then in terms of the original motif of the journalist and author Hamann it can only speak with Luther of the justifying God and of the human being as a justified sinner.[71] This definition of the object and theme of theology is authoritative and decisive for Hamann's flying

---

70. Apparatus in N III, 459.

71. Cf. Hamann on the Epistle to the Romans, especially Romans 1 and 2: "Biblische Betrachtungen," in N I, 226-30, especially 229, 37–230, 5.

leaves. It briefly states in a formal way what moves him and what makes up the thematic tension and design of his staging of scenes, his collages.

Hamann hid his original motif almost totally from the literary public. He did so in methodical, systematic disguise and alienation, and for the reason already named, in order to allow the reader distance from the author and thus freedom for independent judgment. He often did so from a love of hide and seek. Play and seriousness are mixed in the humor of one who is aware of God's eternity in the face of one's own nothingness and, touched by God's eternity, experiences one's own nothingness.[72] Part of the element of seriousness in this humor is that Hamann wanted to make agreement among pious readers as difficult as rejection among others. So in his flying leaves the journalist and author has allowed his original motif to have only indirect effect. The incognito was intentional; it belonged to the strategic total plan that Hamann nurtured and pursued throughout, as did Kierkegaard later in his "indirect communication of existence."

If the Christian faith, as Hamann correctly and impressively says, is "not communicable like a product but is heaven and hell in us,"[73] then in any event for the literary public it can only be indirectly shared. But all the more noteworthy are those documents concerning the life-change in London in 1758, not intended for the public and not revealing the original motif indirectly but directly, in the form of *confessio*, the confession of one's sins and praise of the justifying God. The form of this dialogue with God and the monologue occurring in it — "I . . . spoken with God and myself. I have justified God with regard to my life, and I have accused myself"[74] — is not only characteristic of the *Thoughts about My life*, but of the *Biblical Meditations*, which often move in the form of a prayer.[75]

This happens informally in the *Biblical Meditations*. With respect to form, along with the *Thoughts about My Life*, the *Meditations on*

---

72. Kierkegaard called Hamann the "greatest humorist of Christianity." Cf. M. Seils, ed., *Johann Georg Hamann. Eine Auswahl aus seinen Schriften. Entkleidung und Verklärung* (Wuppertal: Brockhaus, 1987), 511 (afterword); on the subject cf. L. Steiger, "Humor," in *Theologische Realenzyklopädie* (Berlin: De Gruyter, 1986), vol. 15, 698-700, as well as N I, 70, 29ff.

73. H VII, 176, 6-8 (to Jacobi; 1787). Cf. above note 65.

74. "Thoughts about My Life," in Smith, 155 (N II, 42, 17-19).

75. "Biblical Reflections," in Smith, 129 31, 138 (N I, 8, 1-6; 63, 5–64, 2; 64, 19f. and 36f.); "Biblical Reflections," in Smith, 129 (N I, 70, 24ff.); cf. N I, 76.

Church Songs (Betrachtungen zu Kirchenliedern) as well as the *Prayer (Gebet)*[76] and the *Fragments,* they can be compared to Augustine's *Confessions.* In their theological and philosophical significance, for example, as it relates to the understanding of the time received in prayer, before God,[77] they are equal in stature.

Despite the aforesaid commonality with Augustine, Hamann's original motif yields a remarkably different total orientation of the relationship between God, the world, and the self. If in Augustine relationship to the world has finally only negative significance for the relationship between God and the self, as is true also for Kierkegaard, and if in deciding anything Augustine longed to know nothing but God and the soul, was thus concerned only with detachment from the world, Hamann by contrast was concerned precisely with turning toward the world, with a new "aesthetics" understood as perception of the world in the most comprehensive sense, including the moral, the physical, and what we today understand in a limited sense as the aesthetic. Not least in this respect Hamann is a Lutheran and, like Luther, is defined by the Old Testament. We find in Hamann a high esteem for the Old Testament, an esteem offensive to his contemporaries, not least to Kant.

For Hamann the Old and New Testaments heard and read, vitally transmitted, form the irreversible condition of the possibility of understanding the world and self in the communicative fellowship of justified sinners, thus of those who had driven their refusal to communicate to the ultimate end of fratricide and deicide, and thus cut themselves off from life and destroyed themselves — and only through a mediator, a representative, an advocate, were miraculously called from death into new life. Insofar as the Bible forms the a priori, thoroughly accidental, but a posteriori necessary condition for understanding self and world, one can speak of it as a historical a priori.

According to Hamann, the voice of the law that kills and of the gospel that makes alive, the voice that another has for us cannot be abstracted from the letters of the transmitted scriptures.[78] It is not something that would underlie everything and could possibly be given validity in existential interpretation. The voice is not without the letters,

---

76. "Betrachtungen zu Kirchenlieder," in N I, 291-97.

77. For example, "Biblical Reflections," in Smith, 129 (N I, 70, 24ff.). Cf. below chapter 12, "Created Time," notes 30-37.

78. Compare ZH II, 9, 32-34 (to his brother; 1760).

just as the ear is not without the eyes, hearing is not without seeing, and time is not without space. "The Holy Scriptures should be our dictionary, our linguistics, on which all concepts and speech of Christians are based and of which they would consist and be combined."[79] "Let the Bible be your daily bread," he writes to his brother, "take and eat."[80] He emphasizes that "nothing else but this book stills my hunger, so that I have swallowed it like John and tasted its sweetness and bitterness."[81] Here Hamann cites the Book of Revelation (10:8-11) and Ezekiel (3:1-3). The prophet receives a scroll to eat; he eats it, in order totally to incorporate the heard and read word.

Whoever like Hamann incorporates the book of the Bible is set in a relationship with nature and history that cannot be conceived more widely or deeply. What is implied here respecting Hamann's original motif is already made explicit in the *Biblical Meditations:* "The knowledge of nature and history are the two parts on which the true religion rests. Disbelief and superstition are grounded in a shallow physics and a shallow history."[82]

The implicit criticism to which Hamann is forced and given license by his original motif has validity in his knowledge of the situation, well aware of what moves his contemporaries. With his crystal-clear understanding of the traditions of modern reason Hamann has keenly recognized the dialectic of the Enlightenment, as after him perhaps only the critical theory of Horkheimer and Adorno recognized it. Till now, the ecological crisis has found no sharper anamnesis and diagnosis than with Hamann.

---

79. "Biblische Betrachtungen," in N I, 243, 18-20.
80. ZH I, 401, 22f. (to his brother; 1759).
81. ZH I, 305, 6-8 (to Lindner; 1759).
82. "Biblical Reflections," in Smith, 120 (N I, 8, 37–9, 21; cited: 9, 13-16).

Chapter 4

The Modern Concept of Nature in Crisis

"What Homer was to the ancient Sophists . . . the holy books are for me."[1] Hamann allows the textual world of the biblical writings such definitive character that he does not exclude them from his world or his contemporaries, does not make them a sacred precinct, but allows them to disclose the decisive viewpoint for a comprehensive perception of the world. The Bible does not exclude everything else but unlocks and discloses everything else. Hamann regards it as a great prejudice to limit God's action as witnessed to in the biblical writings to the history of Israel, and understands "the entire history of the Jewish people" as "a living . . . primer of all historical literature in heaven, on and under the earth."[2] In this history God has intended "to explain . . . to make meaningful to us" paradigmatically "the hiddenness, the method, and the laws of his wisdom and love" and "left to us the application of this to our own life and to other objects, peoples, and events."[3] In this application left to us, all the individual vitality and facility can now have effect. Admittedly, it is not free-floating and self-sufficient, but owes its constitution and total orientation to the predetermined and encountered original motif which, as has become clear, in contrast to every philosophical principle does not represent an inflexible, monarchic unity but

1. H V, 314, 21f. (to Jacobi; 1785).
2. "Golgatha and Scheblimini," in Haynes, 192 (N III, 311, 6-8); cf. below chapter 8, "History and Reason," note 72. In addition: "Biblische Betrachtungen," in N I, 24, 3.
3. "Fragments," in Smith, 78 (N I, 303, 14-18).

a context best reflected on in a poetological way. The characteristic predicates for God in Hamann's flying leaves are therefore Writer, Poet, Author, Art Critic, Reviewer, the Final Judge.

Hence, it is the poetological viewpoint that plays the definitive role in Hamann's criticism of the modern understanding of nature and history. Nothing happens without the poetic power of imagination, without the threads of a context that this poetic power finds and invents. In every instance poetry must be written: contexts must be spun. "Whoever does not believe Moses and the prophets," as it reads in the Introduction to the *Socratic Memorabilia*, "always becomes a poet, against his knowledge and his will, like Buffon on the history of creation and Montesquieu on the history of the Roman Empire."[4] Even in Descartes or in Kant, Hamann sees a poet. In any case, he sees in them authors who write what they have read, and thus indicate how they have read and judged. It is not "the" pure reason that comes to an understanding of itself in the *Critique of Pure Reason*, but Immanuel Kant from Königsberg who writes and evaluates. Analyzing and synthesizing is individual hearing and reading, individual responding and writing.

The philosophers, however, fail to recognize this characteristic of their own activity. They want to be pure philosophers and not authors, least of all poets, since according to Plato, poets lie. This means they want to be independent of what no poet is independent of, the sensuous and accidental. A timeless validity is claimed for the truth conceived, just as, according to Hamann's provocative remark, some see the laws discovered by Galileo and Newton "transfigured into eternal laws of nature," instead of taking them as "impromptus" of human language, as improvisations, ideas, as human acts and inventive answers, which have their limited time and scope.[5]

The timelessness of truth laid claim to is the chimerical product of an abstraction and of a purism characteristic of modern Rationalism, and in fact was strongly criticized by Hamann and rejected as "mysticism." "Since our philosophers tightly shut their eyes, so as not to be able to read distractions at the cost of nature, . . . it has rained castles in the air and systems from the sky."[6]

Without expressly citing it, Hamann is referring to the basic text of

---

4. "Socratic Memorabilia," in Dickson, 382 (N II, 64, 15-18) (translation altered).
5. "Zwei Scherflein zur neuesten Deutschen Literatur," in N III, 240, 1-3.
6. "Fünf Hirtenbriefe," in N II, 365, 3-6.

modern thought and to the world-transforming science and technology reflected in it. He is referring to the *Meditations* of Descartes that apply to metaphysics, to philosophy, insofar as it deals with the First, the Principle, the *archē*, in which are demonstrated the existence of God and the separation of the human body and soul. The beginning of Descartes' Third Meditation, which Hamann doubtless has in mind, reads:

> I will now shut my eyes, stop my ears, and withdraw all my senses. I will eliminate from my thoughts all images of bodily things, or rather, since this is hardly possible, I will regard all such images as vacuous, false and worthless. I will converse with myself and scrutinize myself more deeply; and in this way I will attempt to achieve, little by little, a more intimate knowledge of myself. I am a thing that thinks: that is, a thing that doubts, affirms, denies, understands little, is ignorant of many things, is willing, is unwilling, and also which imagines and has sensory perceptions; for as I have noted before, even though the objects of my sensory experience and imagination may have no existence outside me, nonetheless the modes of thinking which I refer to as cases of sensory perception and imagination, in so far as they are simply modes of thinking, do exist within me — of that I am certain.[7]

Like Descartes, Hegel states that one only begins to think who has lost hearing and sight.[8] On the other hand, from Hamann's original motif it follows that "as Nature is given to us to open our eyes, so history to open our ears."[9] And, though the senses "may ever so deceive" and history "be ever so simple: I prefer them to all the castles in the air — only no purified, disengaged, and empty words — which I avoid like deep water and slippery ice."[10] Experience of the senses and history. This is the foundation and base.[11]

Whoever like Hamann does not undervalue sin knows that what nature and history have to say to us is not seen and heard by us.

7. Descartes, "Meditations on First Philosophy," in *Classics of Philosophy*, vol. 2, *Modern and Contemporary*, ed. Louis P. Pojman (New York: Oxford, 1998), 471.

8. G. F. W. Hegel, *The Phenomenology of Mind*, trans. J. B. Baillie, 2nd ed. (London: Allen & Unwin, 1931), p. 180.

9. "Socratic Memorabilia," in Dickson, 382 (N II, 64, 12f.).

10. H V, 265, 36–266, 2 (to Jacobi; 1784).

11. H V, 265, 34-36.

The Book of Nature and of History

In paragraph 8 of his *Fragments* Hamann writes that "the book of nature and the book of history are nothing but ciphers, hidden signs, which need the same key as unlocks Holy Scripture, and is the point of its inspiration."[12]

Hamann takes up the ancient metaphor of the *liber naturae* (the book of nature) and parallel to it speaks of the "book of history,"[13] presumably on his own. Neither text is self-revelatory. They are as it were "sealed with seven seals" (Revelation 5) and must first be opened. But the key is not simply the book of the Bible on the basis of which the metaphor of the "book of nature" had been formed. The key is what for its part first "interprets" "the Holy Scriptures" and "is the point of its inspiration." It is the "divine word" itself. This in turn creates its breadth and interpretation in nature and history.

"Nature and history are . . . the two great commentaries on the divine word, and this word is the only key to unlock a knowledge of both."[14]

The text of the "divine word" leads to commentary. But its criterion remains the text itself. It is the "key." In this way Hamann conceives the *breadth* of God's word in relation to its *specificity*. At the same time he sees this relationship as attentive to the distinction between natural and revealed religion.

"What does the difference between natural and revealed knowledge mean? If I understand it aright, the difference is no more than that between the eye of a man who sees a picture without understanding the least thing about the painting or drawing or the story that is represented, and the eye of a painter," who sees and recognizes it.[15]

The fact that and the way in which Hamann engages the problem of natural theology (the "distinction between natural and revealed religion") is striking. His simile of the painting and the eye that on the one hand sees but does not recognize and on the other sees and recognizes,

---

12. "Fragments," in Smith, 172 (N I, 308, 34-36).

13. On Hamann's transfer of the book metaphor from nature to history cf. for example "Socratic Memorabilia," in Dickson, 383 (N II, 65, 10f.). Accordingly "the whole of history is . . . like nature a sealed book." "Nature" as a "sealed book" in "Biblische Betrachtungen," in N I, 148, 19f.

14. "Fragments," in Smith, 166 (N I, 303, 35-37).

15. "Fragments," in Smith, 166 (N I, 303, 38–304, 4).

indicates that God reveals himself through everything worldly, that he speaks to us through nature and history, allows himself to be known in the works of his creation (Rom. 1:19f.). It is not true that there would be nothing to see! But the human does not have the eye for what is to be seen. Not that there would be nothing to hear. The world is not mute! "The heavens declare the glory of God" (Ps. 19:2). But the human ear is stopped. It must be opened. A miracle of salvation must first take place. Only in this way can nature be heard as creation.

Since Hamann clearly establishes that the book of nature and the book of history do not have the key to understanding in themselves and are not to be known from themselves, he disagrees with his enlightened contemporaries who, despite the earthquake in Lisbon (1755) in 1758, the year the *Fragments* were composed, were still greatly influenced by the Leibniz-Wolffian Philosophy.

The disagreement can be made clear from a few sentences of Christian Wolff's *Vernünftige Gedanken von Gott, der Welt und der Seele des Menschen . . .* (Rational Thoughts on God, the World and the Human Soul . . .).[16] "We must have regard . . . for what happens in the world . . . so that we can . . . devise rules from it as to what God may want."[17] For it "is clear, that God does not reveal what we are able to know through reason,"[18] and conversely "what God is supposed to have revealed cannot be contrary to the truths of reason."[19] The most illuminating proposition within this system can be formulated thusly: "Because God knew everything that can result from the nature of things and only for this reason brought them forth, the necessary consequences of the nature of things are God's intentions."[20] The Romantics, consequently, experience nature in an immediate way as the revelation of God. In his *Herzensergiessungen* Wackenroder confesses, "Since my early youth, when I learned to know the God of humans from the ancient holy books of our religion, nature was always for me the most basic and clearest book that explains his nature and attributes."[21]

---

16. Christian Wolff, *Vernünftige Gedanken von GOTT, der Welt und der Seele des Menschen, Auch allen Dingen überhaupt/Den Liebhabern der Wahrheit mitgeteilet* (Hildesheim: Olms, ⁵1733).

17. Wolff, *Vernünftige Gedanken von GOTT*, §1007.

18. Wolff, *Vernünftige Gedanken von GOTT*, §1012.

19. Wolff, *Vernünftige Gedanken von GOTT*, §1014.

20. Wolff, *Vernünftige Gedanken von GOTT*, §1028.

21. W. H. Wackenroder, *Herzensergiessungen eines kunstliebenden Klosterbruders*

What Wolff says of the "natural" world Ranke will say of the "historical" world, once talk of the "book of history" had become universal: "The book of history lies open. We can know how nations become great, how they perish," for "God has not left us without a witness."[22] In giving a historical-theological basis for the legibility of the book of history, Ranke reaches back to the Stoic traditions reworked in Acts 14:17, laying claim to them as transferred from the natural to the historical world. The historicizing of the world brought about by Judaism and Christianity is associated with the Stoic certainty of reason. History is recognizable in its coherence and meaning. To this corresponds the conviction, represented in variegated shape in the nineteenth and twentieth centuries and with wide-reaching political effect, "that it is really history itself which speaks."[23]

Hamann contradicts this type of natural theology of a Ranke and Wolff, but not in such a way as to fall into a biblicistic anxiety and narrowness in which one shuts oneself off from the world. Rather, because everything worldly is disclosed to me I may open myself to it.

Of what sort is this disclosure and freedom? Where does it come from and how is it encountered? With these questions we are inquiring after the key to the breadth, to the great "book of nature and history," to the "divine word."

The World as Text

Inquiring after the "divine word," we can also avoid a possible misunderstanding of the book metaphor and reference to the world as "text."[24] With his book metaphor Hamann is not concerned with what is written in terms of letters rigidly fixed, with an objectifiable positivity, but with something living and animate, with an event of communica-

---

(Berlin: J. F. Unger, 1797); section "Von zwei wunderbaren Sprachen": Natur und Kunst, 1904, 83.

22. L. Ranke, *Historisch-Politische Zeitschrift*, 1832, I, 375; cited by R. Koselleck, *Historia Magistra Vitae*, in *Vergangene Zukunft. Zur Semantik geschichtlicher Zeiten* (Frankfurt am Main: Suhrkamp, 1979) (38-66) 55, note 54.

23. H. Luden, *Handbuch der Staatsweisheit oder der Politik* (Jena: Frommann, 1811), VIII.

24. "Nature is a book, a letter, a story . . . or however you want to call it"; it is necessary to "interpret" it (ZH I, 450, 12f., 17f.; to Kant; 1759).

tion, with "so intimate a relation to one another . . . as author, book, and reader": "God, nature, and reason have such an intimate relation to each other as light, eye, and everything that light reveals to it . . . or as author, book, and reader. But in what lies the puzzle of a book? In its language or in its content? In the plan of the author or in the spirit of the interpreter?"[25]

These questions in a letter to Jacobi set a play in motion in which an entire hermeneutic could be developed that would concern nature and history, and at the same time would be an ontology. How does the "content," the substance that comes to its own in "language," relate to the subject it appropriates? Is language, understood as speaking, as a speech act, to be accentuated and thought of more after the aspect of substance and its positivity or more after the aspect of the subject that accepts it, hears it in freedom? Or does "language," the event of communication as such, decide the issue, so that from it questions about the "author's plan" or the "interpreter's spirit" prove to be misdirected and are resolved in order to avoid these alternatives because, to speak with Hölderlin, "we are a conversation"?[26]

Within the given framework these questions can only be put, but not further fleshed out. It was merely to point to a possible misunderstanding of the book metaphor, a metaphor that should be dismissed when we inquire after the key to the book of nature and history. By "book," an event of communication is spoken of in which such intimate relationships are at play as between "author, book, and reader." The question of the "key" is that of the failure or success of communication. If what is at issue is the book of nature and history, then our interest is directed to the type of the perception of the natural and historical world, to the experience of "world."

For theology, "world" is a theme particularly in the doctrine of creation. Along with our inquiry after the key to the book of nature and history, and our attention to Hamann's diagnosis of the crises of the modern concept of nature in what follows, we are searching for the basic features of a Christian doctrine of creation. For this purpose, we will keep essentially to Hamann's *Aesthetic in nuce* (1762),[27] till now only a

---

25. H V, 272, 14-18 (to Jacobi; 1784).

26. F. Hölderlin, "a reconciler whom you never believed . . . ," third draft in Hölderlin, *Sämtliche Werke*, ed. F. Beissner, vol. 2/1 (Stuttgart: W. Kohlhammer, 1951), 137, 50.

27. "Aesthetica in nuce," in Haynes, 60-95 (N II, 195-217).

classical text in German Studies but one that deserves to be a classical text in theology as well.

"*Speak, that I may see you!* — This wish was fulfilled by creation which is a speech to creatures through creatures."[28]

As the first step in a doctrine of creation, this argumentation is offensive. In any case it contradicts the customary logic and idea according to which there is at first nothing at all and then God creates everything from nothing. This "chronological," "chronometrical"[29] consequence seems ironclad to the one who does not allow the metaphysical question about something like a primal beginning to be ruled out — by Marx, for example, who sees in it the question of the one who reflects on it out of his actual situation and in this way forgets it.

However, Hamann contradicts the above-mentioned logic differently than Marx. If Marx insists on the "self-engendering act of the human,"[30] thus on an absolute relationship to self, Hamann is concerned with an exchange of words between God and human beings. His setting of the scene for this exchange can be called anachronistic. It occurs in a peculiar inversion. The creature says to God: "Speak, that I may see you!"[31] and God fulfills the desire. But this is already a false interpretation. For the exchange means that this desire *was* fulfilled. It was fulfilled before it could be spoken. God already anticipated my desire.[32] The change of tense indicates that we are dealing with a reconstruction, just as the character of reconstruction belongs to every narrative of creation.

The Priestly and Yahwist narratives of creation (Genesis 1 and 2) are in the third person and appear to maintain strict objectivity. In the Psalms of creation, the second person is used in addition to the third. In the second person they appeal to God; they speak in answer and expectantly "look to you" (Ps. 104:27). Hamann goes still further and speaks in summons,

28. "Aesthetica in nuce," in Haynes, 65 (N II, 198, 28f.).

29. Cf. below chapter 12, "Created Time," especially notes 59-67.

30. Karl Marx, "Critique of Hegel's Dialectic and General Philosophy," in *Karl Marx: Selected Writings*, ed. David McLellan (Oxford: Oxford University Press, 1970), 108.

31. According to Erasmus, *Apophthegmata* III, 70, a word of Socrates. Cf. S. A. Jørgensen (cf. above chapter 2, "Style and Form," note 2), 86 (on the passage). The apophthegm stems from Lucius Apuleius of Madaura: A. Schöne, *Aufklärung aus dem Geist der Experimentalphysik*, second edition (München: Beck, 1983), 167, note 16, as well as M. Fauser, "Rede, dass ich Dich sehe," *Carl Gustav Jochmann und die Rhetorik im Vormärz* (*Germanistische Texte und Studien* 26) (Hildesheim: Olms, 1986), 110-24.

32. "Biblische Betrachtungen," in N I, 291-97: "God had anticipated his desires, had exceeded same."

downright blasphemously. But the Creator allows being summoned in this way. The one who humbles himself in the question searching for the man, "Adam, where are you?" and thus denying his omniscience "descends to the blindness of Adam,"[33] allows himself to be summoned by Adam: "Speak that I may see you!" God has already anticipated this summons by his address.[34] He has anticipated it in a worldly and human way.

Put in a lapidary way, "creation" is "address to the creature through the creature." The conciseness and expressiveness of this formula citing Psalm 19[35] can scarcely be overestimated. It is the terse formula of a Christian doctrine of creation as such. We will consider it first of all as a response to the summons, then in its two striking prepositions "to" and "through," and their relation to each other.

That God makes himself visible only by allowing himself to be heard,[36] indicates his freedom and agility. Since the invisibility of God[37] remains intact, his freedom is acknowledged. God will not let himself be reduced to an image to be dealt with in orderly fashion and his dwelling and place of encounter pointed out to him. "No one has ever seen God" (John 1:18a).

God cannot be recognized, seen, but indeed can be heard as address to me. The fact that creation as God's address is not only issued "to" the creature but also "through" the creature indicates the worldly mediation of this address. "No one has ever *seen* God." But: "the only begotten Son, who is in the bosom of the Father: he has *told* us of him, exegeted him" (John 1:18b). In the mediation effected by Jesus Christ, the "exegete" of God, nature and history speak as creation. Jesus Christ is mediator of creation.

We assert that the first point of Hamann's formula, decisive for its meaning, is that creation is "address." Thus God the Creator does not appear primarily to the eye but to the ear, and indeed in such a way that one sees him through the creature.[38]

---

33. "Biblische Betrachtungen," in N I, 19, 5-8.

34. Cf. "Biblische Betrachtungen," in N I, 64, 27f.

35. "Aesthetica in nuce," in Haynes, 65 (N II, 198, 30-32) and "Biblical Reflections," in Smith, 120 (N I, 9, 40f.); 127, 26.

36. "Biblische Betrachtungen," in N I, 64, 27f. ("you saw a voice").

37. "Aesthetica in nuce," in N II, 198, 5f. Cf. "New Apology for the Letter h by itself," in Haynes, 157 (N III, 100, 34f.); but especially "New Apology for the Letter h by itself," in Haynes, 159-63 (N III, 103-107). Cf. Hamann on Deuteronomy 4:1 in "Biblical Reflections," in Smith, 128-29 (N I, 64, 3-18).

38. Cf. below chapter 12, "Created Time," especially notes 33-35.

Next to the noun "address," which clearly betrays its origin from the verb, appear the two prepositions, striking in their parallelization.

The preposition "to" symbolizes a relation but also indicates a distinction. Whoever perceives the relation and the distinction notes that it allows for distance. Its discovery is the basis for surprise and astonishment. Since something like "nature" or "world" does not persist by itself; since it does not talk to itself on its own, but an address occurs (and with it, with that unconditioned "call" — Romans 4:17 — "creation" enters the conversation), and since an address goes out "to" the creature, something other than world can first be heard, then find an answer; and finally also be thought.

It is equally important that the addressee is at the same time its mediator; therefore world is addressed *through* world, but in being addressed becomes free of itself.

The two prepositions mark the decisive theological point: God speaks in a worldly way, *through* the creature, but in such fashion that this address indicates it is an address *to* the creature. In this way the creature addressed is distinguished from the One who addresses it through the creature.

It is better to speak of the mutual interweaving of God's freedom and love than of his transcendence from and immanence in the world. In his freedom God enjoys distance from the world by taking it to himself to address it, and in such address to set another over against himself (address *to* the creature). In his love he is so related to the world that he not only relates to it but enters it and chooses a creature as a mediator of creation (address *through* the creature).

Only the two propositions together render theological talk about creation true. The preposition "to" accents God's *freedom* in his love; the preposition "through" accents the embodiment of his freedom, *love*.

God's free love for the world means that God will not be apart from the creature. This is something fundamentally different from saying, perhaps with Hegel, he *can* not be without the creature. "Without the world God is not God."[39] According to Hegel God needs the world as his other in order to come to himself. His journey through world history is necessary to his becoming a subject. While in this way the necessity of the incarnation is to be speculatively proved, God's freedom is contested.

---

39. Hegel, *Lectures on the Philosophy of Religion*, vol. 1, *Introduction and the Concept of Religion*, ed. Peter Hodgson (Berkeley: University of California Press, 1984), 308.

Creation is "address." Whoever speaks, speaks to another, takes time and gives time for the other, time for hearing and responding. The Creator as Speaker has time for us and gives time for us. He allows time for himself and us by talking to us, and, to borrow from the title of Kleist's famous essay, in speaking he gradually produces his ideas of creation. The medium and the process of the address are essential to it. "The recitation makes the point as often as clothes make the man. Every subject is an invisible embryo, whose concept and content must first come into the world, so to speak, and become evident through speaking. Hence that jocular saw of the wise man: Speak that I may see you."[40] If God allows himself time by speaking, then more than ever he allows himself time, indeed, enters into time when addressing the creature *through* the creature. God's address to the creature is not without a creaturely and temporal medium.[41] According to Luther "the almighty God did not create the world in a snap but took time and leisure with it and carried on with it just as he now makes a child. . . ."[42] Hamann emphasizes that "it pleased" God "to create in six days that which his will could just as well have realized in a single instant of time."[43]

Looking ahead it was already stated that the formula of creation as the "address to the creature through the creature" does not denote a worldly mediation in general but from the outset is meant to be a Christological definition. This follows from the total context of the *Aesthetica in nuce* as well as from other Hamann texts. With respect to the subject the Christological point of the formula totally agrees with Luther's provocative thesis in the disputation *On the Divinity and Humanity of Christ* (1540): There, in Christ, the Creator and creature are one and the same *(Ibi creator et creatura unus et idem est)*.[44]

The identity of Creator and creature does not simply apply as such. That would lead to the *"deus sive natura"* (God as nature) of Spinoza. Rather, it constitutes the being of Jesus Christ, and again this being in its

---

40. "Über das Spinozabüchlein Friedrich Heinrich Jacobis," in N IV, 456, 16-19; Cf. above note 31.

41. "Biblical Reflections," in Smith, 124 (N I, 12, 39f.; 15, 16f.).

42. WA 24, 25, 25-27.

43. "Biblical Reflections," in Smith, 121 (N I, 10, 31f.).

44. WA 39/II (92-121) 105, 6f. Cf. O. Bayer and B. Gleede, eds., *Creator est Creatura: Luthers Christologie als Lehre von der Idiomenkommunikation* (Theologische Bibliothek Toepelmann 138) (Berlin/New York: De Gruyter, 2007).

concretions that cannot, as with Hegel, be abstracted by sleight of hand into universal definitions of the world and its history.

The Ruined Language of Nature

Nature and history do not speak unambiguously — no longer and not yet again. But if they no longer clearly witness to their Creator, they do not witness to him at all. If they do not speak clearly of him, then in a certain sense they do not speak of him at all. For sin has corrupted the original world, original nature and its language, reduced them to confused speaking or silence, to confused speaking and at the same time to silence.

"The fault may lie where it will (outside or in us): all we have left in nature for our use are jumbled verses and *disiecti membra poetae*" (scattered poetic members).[45] Whether evil comes upon us as destiny or whether we ourselves are responsible for it is not discussed here. Whatever the case may be, the result is the dismembering of the language of nature. We encounter only a dismembered and confused text, "Turbatverse" (jumbled verses), shards that no longer allow for guessing at an original whole, to say nothing of recognizing it.

A parallel section in the *Aesthetica in nuce* more sharply emphasizes that the text of the books of nature and history is fundamentally ruined and can no longer be read and understood. It also shows how it can be seen at all that and why the book of nature and history has become illegible and that the creation, the address to the creature through the creature, is no longer heard.

God's Nearness and Distance

The book of creation contains examples of general concepts which GOD wished to reveal to creatures through creation. The books of the covenant contain examples of secret articles which GOD

---

45. "Aesthetica in nuce," in Haynes, 65 (N II, 198, 32–199, 1). This uses a quotation from Horace, Satire I, 4, 62 in *Horace, Satires, Epistles and Ars Poetica*, trans. H. Rushton Fairclough, Loeb Classical Library (Cambridge, MA: Harvard University Press, 1970), 53, in such a way that God himself, the "Poet" (N II, 206, 20f.; cf. N I, 5: "God an author!") appears dismembered.

wished to reveal to man through man. The unity of the Author is mirrored even in the dialect of his works — in all of them a tone of immeasurable height and depth! A proof of the most splendid majesty and of total self-emptying! A miracle of such infinite stillness that makes GOD equal to the nothing, so that in all conscience one would have to deny his existence, or else be a beast. But at the same time a miracle of such infinite power, which fills all in all, that we cannot escape his intense solicitation![46]

The "book of creation" (now not "book of nature") and the "books of the covenant," thus covenant and creation, are parallel. In essence, the two prepositions "to" and "through" recur. The second time "through" is in the lead. Again, corresponding to "guilt" in the parallel section and to dismemberment and confusion as its result,[47] there is immediate reference to the ruination of the original language of creation: The "unity of the Originator," the speaking Author, in his "height" and "depth," his "majesty," and "emptying," one act, in which Creator and creature are mutually enfolded and disclosed to each other, is ruptured in the extreme, "in the dialect," in the word and the voice, in "his works," in a sound so immeasurably high that it can no longer be heard and in a tone so immeasurably deep it too can no longer be heard.

As Psalm 19 emphatically speaks of creation's pouring forth speech (19:2ff. and 5a), but in sharp contrast to that of its inaudibility, so Hamann in a paradoxical way contrasts speaking that is audible and unheard, and as unheard has become inaudible.

The quotation (Ps. 73:21ff.) that Hamann himself cites points by itself and its context to the experience of the limit between faith under attack that laments and a godlessness that is mute. God moves so far away, hides himself so deeply, that the lament directed to God, "Where are you, my God?" becomes the question of the godless directed to myself and universally: "Where then is God? Does God even exist?" If what occurs here is the move from an attack on the believer to the godlessness of the unbeliever, then this godlessness is heightened. I become mute and not only no longer call to God, but no longer ask myself and others about him. In this I am like a beast that does not ask about God at all. This growing mute, often given utmost reflection and resigned like the

---

46. "Aesthetica in nuce," in Haynes, 75 (N II, 204, 4-14) (translation altered).
47. "Aesthetica in nuce," in Haynes, 65 (N II, 198, 32ff.).

muteness of the "fool" (Ps. 73:22a), naïve and huddling, is something fundamentally different from the laments of Job and more likely characterize our present situation. On the one hand God is so frightfully distant that to me he becomes "equal to the nothing." As in the event of Auschwitz he is so hidden "that in all conscience one would have to deny his existence" and with moral resolve become an atheist. In such "a tone of immeasurable height and depth" God is inaccessibly distant from me.

If this has do with "the weakness of those who can see no God," on the other hand it has to do with "the coal-blackness of those who are burned by him."[48] Viewed from this obverse side God is so frightfully close to me "that we cannot escape his intense solicitation," his innermost activity toward me. Since he is closer to me than I am to myself, but in such nearness hides himself from me, he is frightfully and cruelly intrusive, active, threatens, "burns," and kills me. This hidden and consuming nearness of God is not only attested in the Book of Job (for example 13, 15, 24f.), Jeremiah (20:7-9; 23:23f., 29), and indirectly in Psalm 139, but also in the response to these texts. In various ways, the hidden and consuming nearness of God has been lamented, confessed, and cursed in Luther,[49] Hamann,[50] and Tilmann Moser.[51] Then again, such inaudible "hearing" of the immeasurably deep "tone" voices the experience of a limit. It is the limit between confession of the seriousness of God's love that consumes sin and the curse of God that will hold God at arm's length.

Hamann's reference to the inaccessibly distant and, as stressed, "at the same time" intrusively near God, to his hidden distance and nearness, is not a "hymnic celebration" of "the oneness of God in the contradictoriness of his works."[52] But it is not intelligible without assuming a Christological background, given emphasis in terms of the *communicatio idiomatum,* a unified background to be sure, but in its unity cannot be conceived in theoretical-speculative fashion, can only be believed.

---

48. H V, 329, (12-15), 14f. (to Jacobi; 1785).

49. LW 31, 129-30 (WA I, 557, 33–558, 18 (1518); cf. WA I, 540, 8-30.

50. "Thoughts about My Life," in Smith, 153 (N II, 41, 1-10); "Biblische Betrachtungen," in N I, 76, 7-26; 78, 4-27.

51. T. Moser, *Gottesvergiftung* (Frankfurt am Main: Suhrkamp, 1976). Cf. O. Bayer, "Ichfindung als Gottesfluch," in Bayer, *Gott als Autor: Zu einer poietologischen Theologie* (Tübingen: Mohr-Siebeck, 1999), 65-72.

52. M. Küsters, *Inhaltsanalyse von J. G. Hamanns Aesthetica in nuce,* Diss. 1936, 33f.

In Jesus Christ there interpenetrate in one and the same person — that is, in the event named Jesus Christ — the divine and human nature, the majesty and emptying, the height and depth. Two movements that appear contrary to usual understanding are mutually integrated. They are identical with "the cross-wise relation between the deepest humiliation and most sublime exaltation of the two distinct natures."[53] If Hamann speaks of the "unity of the Author," of the unity of God, then it is to be understood in terms of this *communicatio idiomatum,* the "master-key of all of our knowledge,"[54] not, however, in a theoretical and speculative way, since the "Author" is the Speaker.

On the basis of the "unity of the Author" so understood, the nihilistic experience of the cold distance and the searing nearness can be identified and read as a mirror writing[55] of the God who is mercifully close and omnipotent in his love. The point is that only this unity that can be heard and believed in the face of attack allows or requires speaking of that distance and nearness as the nearness and distance of God.

The threatening and killing distance and nearness of God are expressed in the confusion of voices and muteness of the world. They are, as Nietzsche says, "a thousand wastes, silent, cold."[56] Nature and history are either alarmingly mute or alarmingly ambiguous, alarmingly silent or alarmingly eloquent; they are both "at the same time." The word of their Author that creates certainty, the "unity of the Author," is "heard" as fractured. Because its language no longer speaks clearly and for that reason makes certain, it has "died out." It has no greater need than to be awakened from the dead.[57]

Tyrannizing and Redivinizing Nature

If Luther's and Hamann's thesis of the Christological identity of Creator and creature is to result in a doctrine of creation, then according to what became clear concerning the book of nature and history as having be-

---

53. "Ein fliegender Brief," in N III, 407, 1-3.

54. "The Knight of the Rose-Cross," in Haynes, 99 (N III, 27, 13).

55. "Aesthetica in nuce," in Haynes, 75 (N II, 199, 8f.).

56. Nietzsche, *"Der Freigeist,"* Part I, stanza 3 in *Werke, Kritische Gesamtausgabe,* ed. G. Colli and M. Montinari (Berlin: De Gruyter, 1974), VIII-3, 37 (from the Autumn fragment remains, 1884); KGW VII-3, 28 [64].

57. "Aesthetica in nuce," in Haynes, 85 (N II, 211, 5f.).

come illegible, indeed of its language as having "died out," the formula of creation as "address" can only apply when there is also reference to human guilt that renders it inaudible. Otherwise, speaking of creation becomes oblivious of the situation and speculatively overplays our actual situation.

Human guilt that dismembers the book of nature and history into "jumbled verses" ("Turbatverse") is not maintained in the abstract by Hamann. He speaks of it concretely in his diagnosis of the modern world. He points to the dialectic of the Enlightenment in which the dominance of instrumental reason and its attempt at reifying and objectifying invites to a Romantic counterblow in a redivinizing of nature, to the point of deifying it anew. In this way he counters the "Virtuosos of the present aeon, upon which the LORD GOD caused a deep sleep to fall,"[58] in a numbing and blinding[59] that consists in their wanting to be imitators of "Nature the beautiful,"[60] but in fact have become its "worst enemies."[61]

> Every creature will alternately become your sacrifice and your idol.
> — Subject against its will — but in hope, it groans beneath your yoke or at your vain conduct; it does its best to escape your tyranny, and longs even in the most passionate embrace for that freedom with which the beasts paid Adam homage, when GOD brought them unto man to see what he would call them; for whatsoever man would call them, that was the name thereof.[62]

That *every creature alternately* becomes *sacrifice and idol* is a diagnosis long unsurpassed in brevity and conciseness and interprets the modern world through the Pauline understanding of sin (Rom. 1:18-32). The doctrine of sin as analysis of the age! The Creator is the Judge; Hamann sees himself and his time in light of the judgment that punishes sin. Only through the judgment can nature be perceived as creation.[63]

---

58. "Aesthetica in nuce," in Haynes, 68 (N II, 200, 17f.).

59. Along with Genesis 2:21-23, Isaiah 29:10 and Job 12:24 may be in mind.

60. "Aesthetica in nuce," in Haynes, 77 (N II, 205, 20f.).

61. "Aesthetica in nuce," in Haynes, 81 (N II, 208, 17).

62. "Aesthetica in nuce," in Haynes, 78 (N II, 206, 25-31).

63. "Aesthetica in nuce," in Haynes, 95 (N II, 217, 15-19); Haynes, 62 (197, 10f. [compare Matt. 3:12]); "Aesthetica in nuce," in Haynes, 78 (206, 20f.); "Aesthetica in nuce," in Haynes, 79 (207, 10f. [Mal. 3:2 is to be compared with Matt. 3:12]); 213f.

In its first point ("sacrifice"), the proposition that "every creature alternately becomes your sacrifice and idol" is related to the separation of subject and object as classically formulated in Descartes' philosophy. In this separation the subject becomes worldless and in precise accord with this the world made pure object is spiritless, reified. Nature and spirit break apart. "Nature" become a *res extensa* (an extended thing), comes into question only as an object of quantifying investigation. Everything else is screened off in the interrogation of the experiment in which the human as judge puts questions to nature, does not listen to it as a student[64] or serve it as a "trustee" *("Pflichtträger")*. Such a one "has least of all an exclusive right to and hateful monopoly over his abilities, neither to the products thereof, nor to the sterile mule of his industry and the sadder bastards of his usurping acts of violence over the creature made subject, against its will, to his vanity."[65] As word of God, nature is totally silenced. It is no longer the medium by which God speaks to humans. The book of nature as the book of creation becomes illegible. God is no longer heard in it. The philosophical, above all, the Cartesian "tradition" ("Masorah"), has done this: "Behold! The large and small Masorah of philosophy has overwhelmed the text of nature, like the Great Flood."[66]

The frightfulness that has happened and is still occurring was first keenly recognized by Pascal. In view of nature perceived scientifically and technologically in Cartesian fashion as *res extensa,* and in view of the effects of this perception he reasons as follows: *"La nature est telle, qu'elle marque partout un Dieu perdu, et dans l'homme, et hors de l'homme, et une nature corrompue."*[67] (Nature is such that it points everywhere to a God who is lost, both within and outside of man, and a corrupted nature.)

Understandably one sought to encounter this ruin of nature and in it the loss of God that makes him "equal to the nothing"[68] with a natural

---

64. Kant, *Critique of Pure Reason,* trans. Norman Kemp Smith (New York: St. Martin's, 1929), B XIII f., p. 20.

65. "Golgatha and Scheblimini," in Haynes, 173-74 (N III, 298, 37f.); cf. Romans 8:20. Cf. below chapter 10, "Natural Right and Social Life."

66. "Aesthetica in nuce," in Haynes, 80 (N II, 207, 21f.; Cf. *"Konxompax,"* in N III, 221, 5ff.

67. Pascal, *Pensées,* trans. Henri Levi (Oxford: Oxford University Press, 1999), #441, p. 173.

68. "Aesthetica in nuce," in Haynes, 75 (N II, 204, 11).

philosophy that redivinizes nature. Deadening reification and deifying exuberance condition each other "reciprocally." In defense against a reduction of nature to a *res extensa*, to a spiritless matter, an alter ego is looked for in nature, a partner, a hearing and understanding counterpart, a spirit-laden living matter, a nature as mother who "makes all things in [herself] and through [herself]," as Goethe put it, incorporating Spinoza in his *Sorrows of the Young Werther.*[69] As in Nature-romanticism one seeks the person who "merges into the all of nature" or "for that feeling which sinks us into the fullness of nature."[70] Now one seeks to balance that loss endured by the "tyrannizing" of nature, in which the creature becomes a "sacrifice," by the most passionate embracing of nature. The creature thereby becomes an "idol."

In such idolatry, becoming stronger now in view of the ecological crisis, the distance that belongs to the humanity of the human is lost. The freedom is forfeited that Adam allowed the beasts and all of nature by finding and inventing their "names" and in so doing enjoyed his fellow creatures, assimilated them in singing and versifying, and involved himself in an ordering and ordered association with them.

With regard to the human's free activity, in his debate with Herder's anthropology of the "*critical* and *archontic* dignity of a *political animal*," yet to be described in detail, Hamann speaks of the fact that "the true character of our nature consists in the judicial and administrative dignity of a political animal."[71]

Corresponding to the Greek word *krinein,* the critical activity essential to the human being consists in drawing distinctions, classifying differences and thus mastering them. In this way is indicated the correlation between the critical and the archontic. Both together form the chief element of the logos, the *ratio*. In its "critical and archontic dignity" the human is an *animal rationale,* a rational essence.

The perversion of the human's use of reason does not indicate the need for a flight from it but for its liberation and renewal. But even renewed reason sets the human at a distance to the environment and always includes processes that render nature an object. The human's "judicial and administrative dignity" must not be misused through tyranny any more than it should be lost through subjugation. The freedom

---

69. Goethe, *The Sorrows of Young Werther* (London: Penguin Classics, 1989), p. 66.

70. Heinrich Steffens, *Anthropologie* (Breslau: Max, 1822), vol. i, 14f.

71. Cf. below chapter 6, "Criticism and Politics," notes 29-31.

promised to Adam, in which he encounters his fellow creatures so that they in turn "pay homage" to him in freedom, holds him within a context of life and world in which play is simultaneously work and work simultaneously play.

However, such free and open relationship to one's fellow creatures is only a matter of a freedom promised, for which the world waits, for which it "groans" (Rom. 8:19-23).[72] For Hamann, the eschatological hope in world-consummation is combined with the promise given beforehand, with the "address to the creature through the creature." Elsewhere he reverses the process and weaves into the creation narrative the text of Romans 8:18-25.[73] In the *Aesthetica in nuce* the surprising tracing of Romans 8 back to Genesis 2 ("according to the same freedom by which the animals paid homage to Adam") prevents absorption of the doctrine of creation by eschatology. As if, as Ernst Bloch supposes, the "true Genesis . . ." were "not at the beginning but at the end."[74]

The creation as "address to the creature through the creature" occurs at the beginning, not in a pantheistically diffuse but in a Christologically defined way. That "Creator and creature are one and the same" can only be said in reference to the mediatorship of Jesus Christ in creation, of his existence in the "majesty in his form of a servant."[75] But, the being of Jesus Christ as communicative being is "speaking." Hamann gives this special stress at the end of the *Aesthetica in nuce*. Strikingly enough, he cites the beginning of the Epistle to the Hebrews (1:1-4). By way of an extensive paraphrase the passage emerges in its creation-theological significance, and appears more deeply than usual as a parallel to John's prologue and its Christological theology of creation: "After God had exhausted himself of speaking to us through nature and Scripture, through created things and prophets, through reasonings and figures, through poets and seers, and grown short of breath, he spoke unto us at last in the evening of day through his Son — yesterday and today! — until the promise of his coming, no longer in the form of a servant, shall be fulfilled."[76]

72. "Aesthetica in nuce," in Haynes, 78 (N II, 206, 28).

73. "The Last Will and Testament of the Knight of the Rose-Cross," in Haynes, 107-9 (N III, 31, 27–32, 31) (insertion 32, 15-21).

74. Bloch, *Principle of Hope*, vol. 3, trans. Neville Plaice, Stephen Plaice, and Paul Knight (Cambridge, MA: MIT Press, 1995), 1375.

75. "Aesthetica in nuce," in Haynes, 87 (N II, 212, 11).

76. "Aesthetica in nuce," in Haynes, 89 (N II, 213, 6-11) (translation altered).

The "promise of his future" will be fulfilled in the "day of the Lord," in which "this very last tear . . . God with his own hand will wipe away . . ." (Rev. 7:17; 21:4).[77]

Still, hope does not reach toward the eschaton without returning to the present place at which it becomes speech in an unmistakable way, to the place that serves to "preach the Lord's death" (1 Cor. 11:26),[78] to the Lord's Supper. The Lord's Supper is the place in which the emerged elements of Hamann's understanding of creation are gathered paradigmatically. Here the truth of the being of Jesus Christ, the community and the unity of Creator and creature, are disclosed in the concrete. As he is encountered in the Lord's Supper, Jesus Christ is the "image of the invisible God" (Col. 1:15).[79] The more vitally he communicates himself, the more able we are "to see and taste his loving-kindness in creatures, observe it and grasp it with our hands."[80]

In the *Aesthetica in nuce* Hamann has continually emphasized in a paradigmatic way the confession of God the Creator in its critical relation to the great problems of the modern world, in a keenly realized companionship with his time.

---

77. "Aesthetica in nuce," in Haynes, 90 (N II, 213, 18–214, 10) (translation altered).

78. "Aesthetica in nuce," in Haynes, 90 (N II, 214, 11f.).

79. "Aesthetica in nuce," in Haynes, 79 (N II, 207, 2f.).

80. "Aesthetica in nuce," in Haynes, 79 (N II, 207, 3-5). Besides Psalm 34:9 (= 1 Peter 2:3), Titus 3:4 (*"Leutseligkeit"*; in Latin: *"humanitas"*) and 1 John 1:1 are cited.

Chapter 5

Freedom as a Fundamental Concept of Anthropology

(Herder–Hamann)

Hamann's flying leaves are occupied throughout with the motif of "freedom." Given the original motif, this too is understandable. By being set free from sin the human is again restored to critical and archontic dignity, to the freedom and responsibility granted with the creation. In fact, freedom becomes a separate theme in Hamann's response to the *Treatise on the Origin of Language,* with which his pupil and friend Johann Gottfried Herder had answered the prize question put by the Royal Academy of Sciences in Berlin in 1769.[1] In Herder's translation, this question, formulated in French, understood in Berlin of that era, reads: "Have humans, left to their natural capabilities, been able to invent language?"

Herder was awarded the prize for this essay and published it in 1772. Hamann reviewed it in the same year in the *Königsbergsche Gelehrte und Politische Zeitungen*[2] and in irony dispatched his own review shortly thereafter in the same journal[3] — a typical Hamannian act of parody.

Even this was not enough. The piece appears pseudonymously, as all Hamann's flying leaves: *The Last Will and Testament of the Knight of the Rose-Cross, Concerning the Divine and Human Origin of Language.*[4] It rejects the disjunction, whether divine or human. This is al-

1. *Treatise on the Origin of Language,* in *Philosophical Writings,* trans. and ed. Michael N. Forster (Cambridge: Cambridge University Press, 2002), 65-164.
2. "Königsbergsche Gelehrte und politische Zeitungen," in N III, 17-19.
3. "Königsbergsche Gelehrte und politische Zeitungen," in N III, 17-19.
4. "The Last Will and Testament of the Knight of the Rose-Cross," in Haynes, 96-110

ready clear from the title. As such it reveals Hamann's own solution to the prize question. The other piece within the same cycle, *Philological Ideas and Doubts about an Academic Prize Essay,*[5] *Drafted by the Magus of the North in October 1772,*[6] just as the one attached to it and addressed to the king, thus in French and titled *To the Solomon of Prussia,*[7] finds no publisher because of this second, cheeky section.

This leaves Hamann no rest. He courts a publisher for his dual piece[8] along with two others and, while the dual piece remains unpublished in his lifetime, he is able to publish one of the others. The *Selbstgespräch eines Autors* ("Soliloquy of an Author")[9] appearing in January 1773 concludes the series of the six writings that form something of a circle around Herder's *Treatise on the Origin of Language.*

The concept of "freedom" may be taken to be the key concept in these writings. It unlocks Hamann's anthropology. Though this may immediately be seen in a certain sense, it is not at all obvious what the theme of Herder's writing on the origin of language has to do with anthropology. In any case, the theme of language appears to deal with only one aspect of anthropology.

Actually, the situation is quite different. If what Hamann emphasizes along with Luther is true, namely, that the human differs from other creatures "through speech," through language, then the question of the peculiarity of human language has to do with the peculiarity of the human itself.[10] Even in modern anthropological research the question of language is front and center. In his work *Man: His Nature and Place in the World,*[11] Arnold Gehlen has made explicit and extensive reference to Herder as his predecessor: "Philosophical anthropology has not pro-

---

(N III, 25-33) (1770: predated, appeared in 1772 without data of place and publisher, with Kanter in Königsberg: N III, 419).

5. "Philological Ideas and Doubts about an Academic Prize Essay," in Haynes, 111-36 (N III, 35-53).

6. "Philological Ideas and Doubts about an Academic Prize Essay," in Haynes, 111 (N III, 35 [Title Page]).

7. "To the Solomon of Prussia," in Haynes, 137-45 (N III, 55-60).

8. Cf. "An den geheimen Ausschuß," in N III, 64, 1-4.

9. The writing "An den geheimen Ausschuß" (N III, 61-65) does not appear (to be inferred from N III, 429). "Selbstgespräch eines Autors": N III, 67-79.

10. "Golgatha and Scheblimini," in Haynes, 177 (N III, 301, 24.40). Cf. "Königsbergsche Zeitungen," in N IV, 425, 40; cf. above chapter 1, "Life and Work," note 38.

11. Gehlen, *Man: His Nature and Place in the World,* trans. Clare McMillan and Karl Pillemer (New York: Columbia University Press, 1988), 73-76.

gressed significantly since Herder. His is in essence the same approach I wish to develop using the tools of modern science. Indeed, philosophical anthropology does not need to progress any further, for this is the truth."[12]

Herder saw the human in the reduction of its instinct and its lack of specialization as a creature of need and thereby destined to formation, to work, as Marx emphasizes. For both Herder and Gehlen the problem of language is at the center of attention. In it the knot is tied; in it is shown in a peculiar way that and how the human as a natural creature is a creature of culture.

Gehlen subsumes knowledge from the behavioral sciences, anatomy, physiology, and psychology, epistemology, linguistics, and sociology under the point of view of "action," and accordingly shows that language is not one theme among other anthropological themes and that concentration on it is not an illicit and untenable reduction of complex anthropological subject matter, but rather its center. The relevance of our theme is obvious. But it does not spare us from noting the specific formulation of the question in the eighteenth century, as Hamann, the radical enlightener, articulates it in opposition to Herder.

Herder's *Treatise on the Origin of Language*

The prize question put by the Berlin Academy of Sciences in 1769 read: "*En supposant les hommes abandonnés à leur facultés naturelles, sont-ils en état d'inventer le langage? Et par quels moyens parviendront-ils à cette invention? On demande une hypothèse qui explique la chose clairement et qui satisfait à toutes les difficultés . . .*"[13] Herder's work is structured in accordance with these questions. The first sentence heads the most important and comprehensive section:[14] "Were human beings, left to their natural abilities, able to invent language for themselves?" The second section is titled, "In what way have humans most suitably been able and obliged to invent language?"[15]

---

12. Gehlen, *Man: His Nature and Place in the World*, 75-76.

13. "In assuming humans left to their natural capacities, are they in position to invent language? And by what means will they arrive at this invention? A hypothesis is required which clearly explains the matter and satisfies all the difficulties."

14. Herder, *Treatise*, 65.

15. Herder, *Treatise*, 81.

Along with presenting clearly the matter, to answer the prize question concrete difficulties were to be considered. These lay in the fact that two members of the Royal Academy in Berlin were at loggerheads over whether language is of divine or human origin. They were the President of the Academy, Maupertuis, and another member, Johann Peter Süssmilch. In the context of his sensualist approach of 1754 Maupertuis represented the convention theory, that is, that language came about by humans having reached an agreement to denote this or that thing and idea with this or that sound. By contrast, in 1756, Süssmilch, a former pastor, by way of church registries having become a population statistician and a national economist put before the Academy the attempt to prove "that the first language did not receive its origin from humans but solely from the Creator."[16]

In his *Treatise*, Herder seeks to remove the aporia resulting from the opposition between the theses of Süssmilch and Maupertuis. He will not agree with either of them but wants to hold to the element of truth in the argument of both. He does so by first taking up the thesis of the sensualist Condillac, who in his *Essai sur l'origine des connaissances humaines* (1746) as well as in his *Traité des sensations* (1754), maintained the animal origin of language, that is, that human language developed from animal language. In relation to this Herder pithily begins his treatise with the following thesis: "Already as an animal the human being has language."[17]

Human and Animal

For Herder, in contrast to Condillac, human language, just as the humanity of the human at all, does not derive from a continuous development of what the human shares with other forms of life. Herder, later most often taken to be merely a theoretician of evolution, did not argue with this in mind. According to Herder, the human is not quantitatively but qualitatively distinguished from the animals, not by "degrees," but by "kind." Herder does not simply assert this; the human as natural creature is not simply opposed to the human as rational being. Rather, for him, the human as a natural being is a rational being. This, as

16. Cf. the afterword by D. Irmscher in Herder, *Abhandlung über den Ursprung der Sprache* (Stuttgart: Reclam, 1966), RUB 8729; "Treatise," 139.

17. Herder, "Treatise," 65.

Hamann unerringly makes the cardinal point of his criticism, results from the universal economy of animal life.[18] Herder sets his argument in motion by inquiring after the difference between human and beast: "And since human beings are the only linguistic creatures that we know, and are distinguished from all the animals precisely by language, where would the path of investigation begin more securely than with experiences concerning the difference between animals and human beings? *Condillac* and *Rousseau* inevitably erred concerning the origin of language because . . . the former made animals into human beings, and the latter made human beings into animals."[19]

Thus it is necessary to distinguish between the human and the animal, not to be involved in establishing quantities in the area of the transition from beast to human. In comparison with the beasts the human is constitutionally weak. But in this weakness lies the human's strength. Compensation for this lack constitutes the human's uniqueness, the "character of his species."[20]

Unlike those of the animals, human senses are unspecialized, "not sharpened for a single thing."[21] Accordingly, the human has no uniform and narrow "sphere" such as the beast confined to its ecological niche. However, in contrast to the beast, the human's environment is not simply extended. Thus, in the area of transition between beast and human we cannot proceed comparatively. It is not a matter of more or less. For the humanity of the human, not quantity but quality is determinative. "For with the human being the scene changes completely"; "his whole soul, the whole economy of his nature, was changed." Herder seeks to show "that the human species does not stand above the animals in levels of more or less, but in kind."[22]

Ultimately, this thesis of the "peculiar character of humanity" in contrast to the beast must be proved at the point of the problem of language. Herder appropriately writes that the human comes into the world with a cry, and in this respect is not mute, but by no means brings along with it a language that distinguishes it as such from the beast. In this sense the human is "born dumb."[23]

18. Herder, "Treatise," 82. At this point Hamann begins his criticism.
19. Herder, "Treatise," 77.
20. Herder, "Treatise," 81.
21. Herder, "Treatise," 79.
22. For the quotations in this sentence, cf. Herder, "Treatise," 80; 84; 81.
23. Herder, "Treatise," 81.

Language as Compensation

With the observation that the human is born dumb Herder breaks off in mid-sentence and seeks indirectly to answer the question of the origin of language. He points to the fact that in contrast to the beasts the deficiencies ascertainable among humans provoke "compensation." In order to stay alive the human must compensate for the lack of specialization of organs as well as equalize the lack of the security and specificity of instinct. To quote Nietzsche, in and with its indeterminacy and uncertainty as the "not yet finished and fixed beast"[24] the human has by this fact "the advantage of freedom" and by it a "further prospect," a totally other field of vision. By means of its biological gaps and deficiencies the human achieves "free space," elbow room. Thus its thinking and acting are "not an immediate work of nature, but precisely because of this it can become its own work," must in fact become its own work, its own achievement. "No longer an infallible machine in the hands of nature, he becomes his own end and goal of culture," that is, of the culture not only of the external nature that surrounds it but also of the inner nature which the human is itself in its needs, drives, and passions. Because it must not react like a tick on a warm-blooded animal the human is "his own end and goal of nature."[25]

The human is thus the being that, as biologically deficient, by its very nature is both obligated as well as liberated, set free for culture. The human is the "first one liberated in the creation," as Herder will state later.[26]

"In comparison with the animals," the human, this "thinking being," the *"animal rationale,"* has "the space to express its force more freely, and this state of affairs is called rationality." Equivalent to the Platonic *sophrosyne,* Herder calls it "awareness."[27]

---

24. Friedrich Nietzsche, *Jenseits von Gut und Böse, Werke in Drei Bänden* (Darmstadt: Wissenschaftliche Buchgesellschaft, 1966), 623. The Zimmern translation reads: "the animal not yet properly adapted to his environment," *Beyond Good and Evil* (New York: Russell & Russell, 1964), 82.

25. All the citations in this section are in Herder, "Treatise," 82 (except for "gaps and shortcomings," 81) (translation altered).

26. Herder, "Ideas on the Philosophy of History," First Section in *Sämtliche Werke* (Riga; Leipzig: Johann Friedrich Hartknoch, 1784), 13:146.

27. Herder, "Treatise," 86 (all citations in this section).

Awareness as the Fundamental Concept of Herder's Anthropology

The central word in the entire writing on the origin of language is "awareness." If the human is "not an animal moderated by instinct" but "by reason," then "in virtue of the freely effective positive force of his soul" it must be a "creature of awareness."[28] According to Herder, by virtue of its awareness the human is not to be quantitatively but qualitatively distinguished from the animals, not by degree but by kind.

Now, this "awareness" is not, as a longstanding and sturdy philosophical tradition will have it, one capacity of soul among others, but "the total determination" of the human's "thinking force in relation to [its] sensuality and drives."[29] It is "no compartmentalized, separately effective force but an orientation of all forces peculiar to its species."[30]

After this detour Herder returns to an argument he initially broke off respecting the origin of language in order to answer it with a thesis which, however, did not enjoy the incense of agreement with Hamann but rather evoked doubt.[31] The thesis read: "The human being, put in the condition of awareness which is his very own, with this awareness (reflection) operating freely for the first time, invented language."[32]

For language Herder must assume awareness: "A creature taking awareness invented language!"[33] On the other hand he emphasizes that "even the first, lowest application of reason was not able to occur without language."[34] But this in no way corroborates Süssmilch's thesis about the divine origin of language, a thesis that Herder disputes. Herder continues:

> But when he now infers that no human being can have invented language for himself because reason is already required for the invention of language, so that language would have already had to be present before it was present, then I stop the eternal spinning top, consider it rightly, and now it says something completely different: *ratio et oratio!* [Cicero] If no reason was possible for the hu-

28. Herder, "Treatise," 85 (translation altered).
29. Herder, "Treatise," 84.
30. Herder, "Treatise," 85.
31. "Philological Ideas and Doubts," in Haynes, 119 (N III, 41, 19f.)
32. Herder, "Treatise," 87.
33. Herder, "Treatise," 90.
34. Herder, "Treatise," 91.

man being without language, good!, then the invention of the latter is as natural, as old, as original, as characteristic for the human being as the use of the former.[35]

Does Herder actually succeed in stopping the "eternal spinning top" of the mutual relation of language and reason? On the one hand he wants to "stop" the eternal spinning top. On the other he himself sees that "I can of course just as well turn it against him as he can against me — and the thing revolves on and on. Without language the human being has no reason, and without reason no language."[36]

Herder does not want to get out of this circle. He only wants "to stop" the spinning top, look at it properly and more than ever give it credence. Those who maintain the superhuman character of the human and its language as well as those who maintain the subhuman character of the human and its language stop the spinning top in an illegitimate way. Both miss the obvious point.

> One can see that if one once misses the exact point of genesis, then the field for error on both sides is immeasurably large! — then language becomes now so superhuman that God has to invent it, now so inhuman that any animal could invent it if it gave itself the trouble. The goal of truth is only one point! But, set down on it, we see on all sides: why no animal can invent language, why no God must invent language, and why the human being as a human being can and must invent language.[37]

Herder moves in the circle that he noted throughout and made a theme by emphasizing that one can never "give reason and humanity to someone through instruction when he does not already have them."[38] Reason and instruction thus merely give the human being what it already has. And the human could neither hear nor answer if it did not understand from the outset what was given to it to hear and think. This is the difference between human learning and that of the "parrot" or dog, about whose conditioning he writes: "The dog has learned to under-

---

35. Herder, "Treatise," 91 (translation altered). On *ratio et oratio* cf. below chapter 10, "Natural Right and Social Life," note 50.

36. Herder, "Treatise," 91.

37. Herder, "Treatise," 96.

38. Herder, "Treatise," 94.

stand many words and commands; however not as words but as signs associated with gestures, with actions; if it were ever to understand a single word in the human sense, then it no longer serves, then it creates for itself art and republic and language."[39]

To understand a "single word in the human sense" means *always from the outset* to understand it. According to Herder this applies even in view of the human's being addressed by God. If God anticipates the human in the word, the human must understand this prevenience, must be able to understand it. If in the last century Rudolf Bultmann insisted on the intelligibility of the *kerygma* and saw in the existential interpretation the condition for the possibility of being able to understand it, it is the same argument as that of Herder: "In order to be capable of the first syllable in the divine instruction, he of course had to be a human being, that is, to be able to think distinctly, and with the first distinct thought language was already present in his soul; hence it was invented from his own means and not through divine instruction."[40]

Remembering and Inventing

"I know of course what people usually have in mind with this divine instruction, namely, parents' instruction of their children in language. But let it be recalled that this is not the case here at all. Parents never teach their children language without the children constantly themselves inventing it as well; . . . parents . . . facilitate and promote for them the use of reason by means of language,"[41] which they already have.

"To be able to receive the first word as a word, that is, as a characteristic sign of reason, even from God's mouth, reason was necessary; and the human had to apply the same taking-awareness in order to understand this word as a word as if he had originally thought it up."[42] *In this proposition of Herder, the entire problem of the conflict between modern consciousness and Christian faith is concentrated.* For this reason it is paradigmatic. First, it shows that the thesis of modernity as a falling away from God does not hold. The human's modern autonomy

39. Herder, "Treatise," 96.
40. Herder, "Treatise," 92.
41. Herder, "Treatise," 92.
42. Herder, "Treatise," 92.

may not be understood as if the human were master of itself in a radical way, as if it established itself. It does not establish itself but makes sure of itself and of God, its origin. The freedom it claims is indeed "not emancipation from the divine cause," but indeed a "self-originating reflection upon it."[43] It is not a self-empowering constitution in every respect, but indeed a self-empowering anamnesis. If the anamnetic element identified here is united to the operative concept of truth, according to which "truth" is what one can make, then it in fact posits a consciousness to which the Christian faith cannot adapt or accommodate, but can only relate critically, but not in a sweeping dissent such as the thesis of the fall from God will have it.

If for Herder the reception of the word from the mouth of God is both sheer recollection[44] and sheer invention, then it is precisely this thesis that Hamann opposes: "Learning in the true understanding is neither invention nor sheer recollection."[45] In the thesis just cited lies the apex of Hamann's criticism of Herder's understanding of language and thus of Herder's entire anthropology, the significance of which for current anthropology was already addressed with the reference to Gehlen. The thesis cited forms the core of the *Philological Ideas and Doubts about an Academic Prize Essay,* those ideas and doubts that Hamann, the philologist of the cross, puts forward against Herder's treatise. This writing, in comparison with Hamann's other flying leaves, consisting of "little jars," as he puts it, almost amphora-like in size, and with *To the Solomon of Prussia* forming a twin, is the basis for the following presentation.

Hamann's "Philological Ideas"

In its first section, this piece offers Hamann's own anthropology, that is, his "ideas" on the theme of "language" and on anthropology as such. In the second section, "Doubts," he deals with Herder's prize essay in an

---

43. W. Beierwaltes, "Subjektivität, Schöpfertum, Freiheit. Die Philosophie der Renaissance zwischen Tradition und neuzeitlichem Bewusstsein," in *Der Übergang zur Neuzeit und die Wirkung von Traditionen* (Göttingen: Vandenhoeck & Ruprecht, 1978), (15-31), 30.

44. Though Herder argues sensualistically, the structure of the argument in the midst of the sensualistic-behavioristic material is Platonic, as Hamann correctly notes and parodies Herder with critical intent. For details cf. E. Büchsel, HH IV, 251-53.

45. "Philological Ideas and Doubts," in Haynes, 119 (N III, 41, 11) (translation altered). Cf. below note 55.

expressly metacritical way, in a metaschematism, and offers a spirited analysis of Herder's proof, a grand parody[46] in which what was earlier dealt with positively is now reflected on negatively. In forms peculiar to his authorship he produces a "proof." By it he demonstrates that he is master at adducing evidence. But at the same time he parodies Herder's adducing of evidence and reduces it *ad absurdum*. This second section is thus a negative demonstration in "metaschematism" form.

Hamann derives this concept from the Greek text of 1 Corinthians 4:6: "I [Paul] have applied *(metaschematisa)* all this to me for your benefit." In Hamann, this verb becomes a peculiar figure that he then plays out. He sees himself in the mirror of others[47] and others in the mirror of his own experiences. He puts himself in their place; he sees, as it were, the world with their eyes. In such an exchange of roles, places, and words he takes up in parody and other forms specific figures of argument from the Pauline epistles ("to make oneself a fool," "to boast in human fashion," and so on).

The third section situates the argument in time. It is the biographical, contemporary historical section. Herder, who earlier was so vehemently criticized, is now publicly rehabilitated, recognized as victor, and celebrated by Hamann as friend, though in ironic distance. Hamann excuses Herder by conceding that he had no other way of getting a hearing and recognition within the "wicked, adulterous generation"[48] of his time than through anthropologizing the theological, which Hamann, however, clearly contradicts. Herder is excused; his treatise is *"un Discours aussi méchant que le Siècle"* (a discourse as wicked as the century).[49] Nevertheless, after what was said in the first and second section of the *Philological Ideas* this excuse will retract nothing of the criticism.

Divine and Human Simultaneously

Hamann criticizes Herder's anthropologizing of the theological in which the image of God in the human is taken so one-sidedly that God's *humanitas* (Titus 3:4),[50] his love for humankind, is reversed and becomes

46. For this see the impressive commentary by E. Büchsel, HH IV, (232-56), 244.
47. Cf. ZH III, 246, 34-36 (to Nicolai; 1776).
48. "Philological Ideas and Doubts," in Haynes, 134 (N III, 51, 21f.).
49. "To the Solomon of Prussia," in Haynes, 139 (N III, 57, 5).
50. "Aesthetica in nuce," in Haynes, 79 (N II, 207, 2-5).

the divinity of the human. In conjunction with this, the divinity Herder claims for the human is defined primarily by the distinction between the human and the beast in "formation," or in "work," called by Karl Marx the "self-engendering act of the human."[51]

It is Hamann's great service to the history of theology as well as to systematics to have immediately recognized and incisively criticized the anthropological *incurvatio in se ipsum* (a curving in upon oneself) beginning in Herder, the perversion of the human relationship to God in a pure self-referentiality,[52] long before Ludwig Feuerbach tried to prove anthropology as the true essence of religion.

Recalling Feuerbach's criticism of religion supported by the Christological doctrine of the two natures, by the proposition that "God is human," indicates how sensitive the point is on which the controversy between Hamann and Herder turns.[53] In his *Willensmeinung über den göttlichen und menschlichen Ursprung der Sprache (Intention of the Will in the Divine and Human Origin of Language)* Hamann insists upon the simultaneity of the divine and human, and he draws from it consequences other than Feuerbach's.

Hamann sets the major thesis of his positively developed anthropology at the end of the first section, of the "Ideas." Though composed sequentially, Hamann's writings are often to be read from the end. "The end is what matters."[54] This corresponds to an anthropologically intelligible way of reading and hearing, of orienting oneself, a procedure set down in rhetorical rules and often observed by Hamann, not merely in the *Philological Ideas*.

Learning Is Neither Mere Invention nor Mere Remembrance

Hamann's most important "idea" in his debate with Herder is contained in the idea that language is learned, that we can know of no other "origin" (if this word is to be used) than this origin in learning. "Man learns

51. Karl Marx, cf. chapter 4, note 30.

52. Compare above at note 38.

53. E. Büchsel speaks of the two poles of "actualizing and secularizing" Christian faith: "We would have to look for Hamann's authorship at the first and Herder's authorial work at the second pole" (HH IV, 74).

54. ZH I, 358, 36–361, 2 (to his brother; 1759); H VII, 161, 25-27; 162, 26-30 (to Jacobi; 1787).

to use and to govern all his limbs and senses, and therefore also the ear and tongue, because he can learn, must learn, and equally wants to learn. Consequently the origin of language is as natural and human as the origin of all our deeds, skills, and crafts. But notwithstanding the fact that every apprentice contributes to his instruction to learn in keeping with his inclination, talent, and opportunities, learning in the true understanding is neither [sheer] *invention* nor sheer *recollection*."[55]

Hamann arrives at a specific concept of "learning." It is constituted by a twofold negation as well as by a positive element. The negation reads that "learning in the true understanding is neither [sheer] *invention* nor sheer *recollection*." Hamann explains this concept in a positive way in the already oft-cited formula of the "critical and archontic dignity" of the human as "political animal," or in the formula of "critique and politics."

Hamann's chief idea has wide-ranging significance. Until modern pedagogy and educational theory the Socratic-Platonic understanding of learning as "remembrance," as anamnesis, has been authoritative, represented primarily but not only in the Platonic dialogue *Meno*.[56] Instruction is understood as anamnesis, as an aid to self-discovery, as a *maieutic* art, the art of midwifery. What is already there in the pupil is drawn out. Accordingly, to think means to achieve, to remember what one already has. In this sense Herder asks: "And then what would it mean to give reason and humanity to someone through instruction when he does not already have them?"[57] The difference from Hamann is obvious.

With respect to the Platonic concept of learning through remembrance, Herder has an ally against Hamann in Kant, who writes to Johann Plücker: "That I was so to speak only the midwife of your thoughts and everything, as you said, long ago, lay in you, though not arranged, means precisely to arrive at the proper and only way of basic and illuminating knowledge. For only what we can make ourselves, do we understand in a basic way; what we are to learn from others in dealing with intellectual matters, we can never be certain, whether we correctly understand, and those who rely on interpreters even less."[58] Everyone must think for oneself.

---

55. "Philological Ideas and Doubts," in Haynes, 119 (N III, 41, 4-12) (translation altered).

56. Plato, *Meno*, 80a5-86c3.

57. Herder, "Treatise," 94.

58. Kant, *Briefwechsel*, Akademieausgabe, vol. XII, 57, 7-14 (= Kant, *Briefe*, ed. and introduced by J. Zehbe, 1970, 244).

One can only interpret what one has "made," construed, and constituted by oneself. Only in such self-construing can one be certain of truth, be really aware of it and have it in one's own possession. Only what we ourselves make, as expressed in the *Critique of Pure Reason*, is "completely a priori in our power."[59] What is true is what we ourselves are able to do. But now since only the purely rational and not the empirical is completely in our power,[60] that "what we can make ourselves," must always be *in* us. By virtue of what is always in us, what is empirical must be constituted in its objectivity and find its identification and evaluation. Thus, at the depth of the Kantian concept of reason a considerable Platonic element is at work, the element of anamnesis.

Hamann's Understanding of Learning

What is learning if it cannot be identified with the extremes of sheer recollection and sheer invention, or with a combination of both as would correspond to Kant's concept of reason? According to Herder as well, the two condition each other. The human must "invent what is natural to him."[61] This is the thesis that gives Hamann offense: "I called this supernatural proof of the human origin of language 'Platonic' because it starts with the neologic coinage of awareness *('Besonnenheit')*, as an 'individual point and shining spark of the perfect system' and in the end returns to a Greek synonymy, and because the Platonists chewed over and over . . . the inner and the outer word."[62]

Speaking of the inner ("a characteristic word for me")[63] and the outer word ("a communication word for others")[64] Herder was once more talking in a circle in which the one always assumes the other. There is thus never a real hearing, but only a hearing of what is already in me. No real communication occurs other than the communication of what is always shared with the other and the other can understand from the out-

59. Kant, *Critique of Pure Reason*, A 843, p. 660.

60. Kant, *Critique of Pure Reason*, A 842f., p. 659.

61. "Philological Ideas and Doubts," in Haynes, 125 (N III, 45, 24f.); cf. Herder, "Treatise," 79.

62. "Philological Ideas and Doubts," in Haynes, 127 (N III, 47, 7-15); cf. Herder, "Treatise," 101, 82, 77-79.

63. Herder, "Treatise," 82.

64. Herder, "Treatise," 82.

set. Hamann does not see Herder's circular argument as proof. Such "proof" consists of "arbitrarily assumed postulates" and "false axioms about the nature of language."[65] In the same context Hamann refers to Herder's "legislation,"[66] his determinations and divisions. Hamann regards the thesis of the human's immanent self-constitution in terms of its becoming what it already is as far from possibility as the supernatural counterthesis of Süssmilch — that God as it were gave humans speech from above and they receive it as a finished product.

To oppose both theses, Hamann insists on both the divine and the human origin of language *simultaneously.* Since God himself speaks in a human way, the human is able to understand God, without already finding in itself beforehand the ability to understand. Thus anthropomorphism, which according to Herder is unworthy of God,[67] is the ineradicable characteristic of the speech of God; Hamann is able to cite the entire Bible as witness. Since God speaks in a human way, the human can understand him. One need not have in oneself the ability to understand, since God encounters one in a human way and speaks as human to the human. This is how immanentism with all its forms of circular self-understanding is burst open.

Entirely at the margin of his treatise Herder speaks of the "Creator." What does this mean? Does he intend to exclude theological speech on merely methodological grounds, but by retaining vestiges of theology suggest he would prefer not to surrender his theological background? But theological anthropology can never exclude what is theological because God's address to the human makes the human and without this address the human would be trapped in itself, would not be free at all, could not be thought of as completely human, but would be shattered into a multitude of roles and be without identity.

Freedom Given in Advance

For Hamann's concept of learning two elements are constitutive, the element of prior gift and the element of freedom received with it. Both are important. The sequence is likewise important. As a learner the human

65. "Philological Ideas and Doubts," in Haynes, 128 (N III, 47, 21-23).
66. "Philological Ideas and Doubts," in Haynes, 128 (N III, 47, 26).
67. Herder, "Treatise," 163.

is a hearer. In Hebrew, learning is hearing and ultimately has its basis in the hearing of the first commandment: "Hear, O Israel: The Lord is our God, the Lord alone" (Deut. 6:4f.), wherefore fearing and loving God are the beginning and end of knowledge. "The fear of the Lord is the beginning of wisdom, his evangelical love the goal and *punctum* of wisdom."[68] The fear and love of God coming from the word intend to be learned by the ear, just as the entire world can be perceived through hearing. "Morning by morning he wakens — wakens my ear to listen as those who are taught," as disciples (Isa. 50:4). All my senses are opened with the ear.[69]

The learner is the hearer. One can only hear, learn, and perceive with all the senses what is given beforehand, what comes to me, what I did not invent myself but is prepared for me. Whatever can be perceived in this way is something concretely sensuous. It cannot be identified by mere anamnesis or construction however much perception always includes the anamnetic and constructive. But it lives from what is given to the senses beforehand. It is the first element of learning. The second is free appropriation.

Hamann's concept of free learning is the counterconcept to Herder's concept of awareness. If Herder can only speak in a circular way of awareness and thus of the relation between reason and language, and in this way arrive at the immanence of a self-entanglement, for Hamann the circle is burst in at least one respect because the element of *address* comes into effect; freedom is *awarded* to the human. The human "is a feudal tenant,"[70] given dignity through promise, owned neither by one's own reason nor strength. As Hamann states in citing Luther's *Small Catechism,* it is given and promised "without merit or worthiness." The meaning of the "judicial and administrative dignity of a political animal," in which, according to Hamann, "the true character of our nature" consists, is that "now this dignity like all honorific positions assumes neither an inner worth nor merit in our nature; rather it is, as the latter itself is, direct gift of grace from the great All-Giver."[71]

---

68. H V, 333, 16-18 (to Jacobi; 1785); compare "Biblische Betrachtungen," in N I, 152, 22f. And above chapter 2, "Style and Form," note 79.

69. N III, 32, 21-31.

70. "The Last Will and Testament of the Knight of the Rose-Cross," in Haynes, 108 (N III, 32, 9) (translation altered).

71. "Philological Ideas and Doubts," in Haynes, 114 (N III, 37, 24–38, 3) (translation altered).

The fact that along with this dignity freedom to learn is given "from divine and fatherly goodness," "without merit or worthiness,"[72] applies as well to sin's misuse of the freedom given. "Every hero or poet, whether he is a type of the Messiah or a prophet of the Antichrist, has periods in life when he has full cause to confess with David: 'I am a worm, and no man' [Ps. 22:6]."[73]

This complaint cited repeatedly[74] by Hamann is in contrast to the majesty of the feudal tenant who is promised the judicial and administrative dignity of a political animal. Not only the luster but also the misery of the human comes into focus.

72. Martin Luther, "The Small Catechism," in *The Book of Concord*, ed. Robert Kolb and Timothy J. Wengert (Minneapolis: Fortress, 2000), 354. (Interpretation of the First Article of the Creed.)

73. "Philological Ideas and Doubts," in Haynes, 115 (N III, 38, 4-7).

74. "Philological Ideas and Doubts," in Haynes, 115 (N III, 38, 7); "Golgatha and Scheblimini," in Haynes, 192 (N III, 311, 30f.); "Königsbergische Zeitungen," in N IV 282, 22f.; "Le Kermès du Nord, ou la Cochenille de Pologne," in N II, 317, 5 (Motto).

Chapter 6

Criticism and Politics

(Hamann–Herder–Frederick the Great)

Hamann's concept of "politics" is included in the founding of an anthropology together with its chief concept, freedom. In metacritical reference to Herder's *Treatise on the Origin of Language* which, as the reference to Gehlen made clear, has become the Magna Charta of modern anthropology, the philologist Hamann not only airs his doubts respecting Herder's immanent and circular theory, but also his own ideas on the theme. His vote of no confidence is constructive. If Herder's thought experiment is concerned with setting the human "in the condition of awareness which is one's very own"[1] — the human is to be what he is — if the human must still discover "what is natural to him,"[2] and "is himself the purpose and goal of his endeavor," then Hamann sees such circular relation to self burst apart by the fact that the human is addressed, and in such fashion that the address that creates him is mediated in worldly, in human fashion. As creature the human is addressed by the Creator through the creature, initially through one's parents, through whose care speaking becomes as easy "as a child's game." The word draws near to the human. In the word of address which is God, "with this word in his mouth and in his heart the origin of language was as natural, as close and easy, as a child's game," so reads the end of *The Last Will and Testament of the Knight of the Rose-Cross.*[3]

1. Cf. above chapter 5, "Freedom as a Fundamental Concept of Anthropology," note 32.
2. "Philological Ideas and Doubts," in Haynes, 124 (N III, 45, 23-25).
3. "The Last Will and Testament of the Knight of the Rose-Cross," in Haynes, 109

To attain to language, the human need neither sink anamnetically into the depths nor through invention grasp at the heaven of pure construction.[4] In a specific way language is obvious, "natural"[5] — if only sin, this deception of language, this lie, did not exist.[6] The question as to whether language is of divine or human origin rends asunder what inseparably belongs together.[7] It follows "a despotic-dictatorial use of language,"[8] an imperious rule that Hamann deals with in citing but to which he does not submit, no more than to the term "origin," better to be avoided if it denotes the distance of a beginning only to be remembered with effort and the distance of a goal first to be discovered, constructed. Otherwise everything boils down to "word-play and scholastic prattle."[9] The absolute beginning and goal are given here and now, at a center, in the midst, in which divinity and humanity unite and the Creator comes so close to us that a more fervent "union, fellowship, and communion,"[10] a more intimate *communicatio* of God and the human, God and world, cannot be conceived. "This *communication* of divine and human *idiomatum* is a fundamental law and the master-key of all our knowledge."[11] Hamann widens the Christological use and expands it to the sphere of the first and third article of the creed.

The human "voice" of God, heard by humans, discloses to them their "political destiny: to people the earth and to rule by the word of

---

(N III, 32, 26-28); cf. John 1 and Deuteronomy 30:11-14 and Romans 10. In addition: "Biblische Betrachtungen," in N I, 291-97.

4. "Prolegomena über die neueste Auslegung," in N III, 132, 10-19; compare ZH III, 86, 23ff. (to Kant; 1774). Additionally: "Philological Ideas and Doubts," in Haynes, 119 (N III, 41, 4-12); "Selbstgespräch eines Autors," in N III, 75, 14-20.

5. "Selbstgespräch eines Autors," in N III, 75, 20 and "Philological Ideas and Doubts," in Haynes, 119 (N III, 41, 7; cf. "The Last Will and Testament of the Knight of the Rose-Cross," in Haynes, 109 (N III, 32).

6. "The Last Will and Testament of the Knight of the Rose-Cross," in Haynes, 108 (N III, 32, 15-21).

7. Cf. all of "The Last Will and Testament of the Knight of the Rose-Cross," but especially Haynes, 117 (N III, 40, 2ff.) ("bill of divorcement": line 4; "marriage": line 10).

8. "Selbstgespräch eines Autors," in N III, 75, 19.

9. "The Last Will and Testament of the Knight of the Rose-Cross," in Haynes, 99 (N III, 27, 8)

10. "The Last Will and Testament of the Knight of the Rose-Cross," in Haynes, 108 (N III, 32, 23f.).

11. "The Last Will and Testament of the Knight of the Rose-Cross," in Haynes, 99 (N III, 27, 12-14).

their mouth."[12] Freedom is given to name the beasts (Gen. 2:19f.), thus to move in ordered association with fellow creatures. Thus, on one hand, the world according to the Creator's will is incomplete insofar as he brings the human's fellow creatures to him "to see what he would call them; and whatever the man called every living creature, that was its name" (Gen. 2:19). On the other, the world is not merely the material of the human's duty, as though the human had first to establish the world as the not-I! Rather, the human is in a world already prepared and ordered, with the rhythm of night and day, summer and winter, youth and old age, in a world its Creator *has already spoken*, in "the world set in order by word of his mouth."[13] The human is already "set in order" in and with language and reason, "set" — instituted — in its political destiny.[14] The human is in such a "setting," such an institution beforehand. It need not first "invent" language or justify it by reverting to an origin, as the prize question of the Royal Academy of Sciences in Berlin suggested. One is and remains set in it.

However, to quote Büchner *(Dantons Tod),* a fissure goes through creation "from top to bottom."

The Fissure of Sin

The human, who "by the word of [its] mouth,"[15] in "analogy" to the Creator and the "word of his mouth,"[16] as "a feudal tenant"[17] of the Creator, is to endow "all creatures with their substance and their stamp, on which depends fidelity and faith in all nature,"[18] has become unfaith-

---

12. "The Last Will and Testament of the Knight of the Rose-Cross," in Haynes, 107 (N III, 31, 30-33 and 39f.).

13. "The Last Will and Testament of the Knight of the Rose-Cross," in Haynes, 108 (N III, 32, 10 — the parallel, Haynes, 107 [31, 32f.]).

14. "The Last Will and Testament of the Knight of the Rose-Cross," in Haynes, 108 (N III, 32, 2).

15. "The Last Will and Testament of the Knight of the Rose-Cross," in Haynes, 107 (N III, 31, 33).

16. "The Last Will and Testament of the Knight of the Rose-Cross," in Haynes, 108 (N III, 32, 10).

17. "The Last Will and Testament of the Knight of the Rose-Cross," in Haynes, 108 (N III, 32, 9).

18. "Aesthetica in nuce," in Haynes, 78-79 (N II, 206, 32–207, 2); cf. "Golgatha and Scheblimini," in Haynes, 176-77 (N III, 301, 18ff.).

ful to its political destiny, has betrayed it. The human distorts language into a lie and involves all fellow creatures against their will in such a perversion of the word and thus in the ruination of "fidelity and faith."[19]

Hamann sets the scene for this fissure of sin extending through creation from top to bottom in his "translation"[20] of the Old and New Testament narrative of creation[21] by directly including Romans 8:18-25 merely between dashes: "The creature was not yet made subject, unwillingly, to the vanity and bondage of the corruptible system under which they now yawn, sigh, and are dumb. . . ."[22]

Unlike Herder, subservient to the age in his *Treatise on the Origin of Language* and viewing the human neither in the strict sense as creature nor as sinner, Hamann can only speak of the human in just this way, that is, with equal emphasis on the human as God's creature and as sinner. The effect is that the philologist is now also a theologian, though he wished to have nothing in common with the theologians of his century.[23]

In fact, no anthropology other than Hamann's has placed such stress on biblical concerns, an anthropology that can be cast and performed only in those biblical figures and images:

> "For he spake, and it was done" [Ps. 33:9] "and whatever the man called every creature, that was the name thereof." According to this model and image of definiteness, every word of a man ["one man, one word"!] ought to be and to remain the thing itself. It is on this likeness of stamp and motto to the perfect type of our race [Gen. 1:26] and to the guide of our youth [Jer. 3:4] — it is on this law of nature to make use of the word as the primary, noblest, and most powerful means of revealing and communicating our inward declaration of will — that the validity of all contracts is based, and this mighty fortress [Ps. 31:3] of truth in the inward parts is superior to all frenchified practices, machinations, pedantries, and monger-

---

19. Cf. "Aesthetica in nuce," in Haynes, 78 (N II, 207, 1) with "Essay of a Sybille on Marriage," in Dickson, 507 (N III, 199, 34) and "Golgatha and Scheblimini," in Haynes, 175 (N III, 300, 22ff.).

20. "The Last Will and Testament of the Knight of the Rose-Cross," in Haynes, 96 (N III, 25 [Title Page]): "Hastily translated from an original cartoon hieroglyphic. . . ."

21. At issue is a skillful interweaving of references in the Old and New Testaments.

22. "The Last Will and Testament of the Knight of the Rose-Cross," in Haynes, 108 (N III, 32, 15-18).

23. "Kreuzzüge des Philologen," in N II, 115, 8-11.

ing. The misuse of language and of its natural testimony is there-fore the grossest perjury; it turns the transgressor of the first law of reason and its justice into the worst misanthrope, the traitor and opponent of German uprighteousness and honesty, on which our dignity and felicity are based.[24]

If God's creative word is a clear unambiguous Yes or No, then in anal-ogy to it our human word in its proper, free usage should likewise be a clear unambiguous Yes and No, as Jesus in the Sermon on the Mount de-finitively interpreted the Creator's will (Matt. 5:37). Hamann takes up the word of Jesus, well known but scarcely ever recognized in its creation-theological and fundamental anthropological gravity: The "great Archi-tect and cornerstone of a system that will outlast heaven and earth, and of a patriotism that overcomes the world, has said: let your speech be yes, yes, no, no; everything else is of the devil — and herein lies the whole spirit of the law ['*L'esprit des lois*"] and social settlement [of the contract, the social contract], whatever names they may wish to have —."[25]

Not only sociality but the coherence of the world as such rests on such a clear, distinct, and reliable word, even in the human's relationship to the nonhuman fellow creature. For Hamann a "contract" of the hu-man with nature was an obvious idea derived from the Old Testament. It radically questions the current dominance of instrumental reason.

Judicial and Administrative Dignity

In freedom for the word, in which the human's political destiny lies, though it has perverted this freedom and committed the "serpent's de-ception of language,"[26] the human is always a creature. Even as a fallen creature the human does not escape its "judicial and administrative dig-nity"[27] or responsibility. It must give account of every "useless," ineffec-tive word, every word irrelevant to life it has spoken (Matt. 12:36). It must give account of what it has done and not done.[28]

---

24. "Golgatha and Scheblimini," in Haynes, 176-77 (N III, 301, 18-33).

25. "Zwo Recensionen," in N III, 24, 7-13.

26. "Golgatha and Scheblimini," in Haynes, 172 (N III, 298, 3) and "Zwo Recen-sionen," in N III, 22, 15-21.

27. "Philological Ideas and Doubts," in Haynes, 114 (N III, 37, 25).

28. Cf. H V, 88, 17 (to J. M. Hamann; 1783). On the meaning of the word "tongue," cf. James 3:6 and Hamann's citation of James 3:6: "Zwo Recensionen," in N III 19, 34f.

Hamann's ingenious anthropological formula secured in his debate with Herder, namely, that the true character of our nature consists in its judicial and administrative, critical and archontic dignity of a political animal,[29] interprets the summons in the primeval biblical history to subdue the earth (Gen. 1:28) and harks back to Aristotle. Hamann corrects and deepens Aristotle's definition of the full citizen as participant in judgment, in *"krisis,"* as well as in governing and ruling, in *"archē,"* by assigning it along with the biblical primeval history to *every* human. Aristotle had assigned it only to the full citizen but denied it to the *banausos* (artisan) and above all to the slave as a mere "human-footed animal." With Hamann, therefore, Aristotle's politological definition becomes a fundamental anthropological definition, on the basis of its politological definition in the narrower sense.

Mimicking the "scholarly argot" of his *siècle philosophique,* Hamann takes hold of the critical and archontic in two definitions, but not without tongue in cheek, aware that definitions "are laws and belong to the monopoly of the monarch":[30]

> *Criticism* is a partly natural, partly acquired skill in recognizing and appropriating what is true and false, good and bad, beautiful and ugly, either through perceptive knowledge and revelation or through acclamation and tradition, according to the relation between our areas of activity. By contrast, *politics* is a partly inherited, partly acquired capacity through wonders and signs to make into a plus or minus the true and false, the good and bad, the beautiful and ugly according to the standard of our critical taste.[31]

Humans live out their freedom and use their reason in criticism and politics. The perversion of their use of reason does not indicate the need for flight from it, but for its liberation and renewal. But even renewed reason situates the human at a distance from the environment and always includes behavior that makes of nature an object. In view of the ecological crisis it would be foolish to concede to the natural-Romantic inclination to regard every kind of objectification as contrary to creation — an inclination now more and more on the increase, even in theology

---

29. "Philological Ideas and Doubts," in Haynes, 114 (N III, 37, 24-26).
30. "Selbstgespräch eines Autors," in N III, 72, 4-8; cf. ZH III, 104, 23-29.
31. "Selbstgespräch eines Autors," in N III, 72, 9-17.

and church. That would miss a chief element of the freedom given to humans. The *homo faber*, the worker, who intervenes in nature and reshapes it, must retain this critical and archontic dignity, and thus be aware of limits and refrain from gesturing in the absolute while at work.

Hamann symbolizes these limits since, as already indicated, he brings sharply into focus the human's misery along with its dignity and splendor.[32] Alongside praise for the majesty of the "feudal tenant" (Ps. 8:7) reads the complaint of the one in misery: "I am a worm, and no human!" (Ps. 22:7).

Dependence and Autonomy

Since in complaint and confession of sin the human bends God's ear or praises him, and since the human answers because the human was addressed by him and hears him, the human is a human. The human is defined wholly by relationship to God, which in sin it has perverted into a disproportion.[33] On the basis of this understanding Hamann criticizes Herder, who however resists Hamann's criticism and explains the point of dispute to Friedrich Nicolai as due to another way of speaking. According to Hamann, "in everything the human has heard the word of God, has seen God, et cetera. We, as prosaic people, are saying that the human has formed a language after the standard of nature, of the beasts."[34]

Yet Herder is deceived. The way of speaking is not arbitrary. Hamann does not have the same thing in mind as Herder. He speaks of the human in a categorically different way. Where Herder speaks of the human's awareness lodged in a relation to self, Hamann speaks of human freedom, not of a primarily reflexive freedom, but a freedom promised and for whose use or misuse the human is responsible toward the One who gave it as "a direct gift of grace."[35] It "assumes neither an inner worthiness nor merit in our nature. . . ."[36] As he frequently does,

32. "Philological Ideas and Doubts," in Haynes, 115 (N III, 38, 4-7); cf. above chapter 5, "Freedom as a Fundamental Concept of Anthropology," note 74.

33. "Golgatha and Scheblimini," in Haynes, 195 (N III, 312–13, 25).

34. Herder, *Briefe, Gesamtausgabe* (1763-1803), vol. 2, ed. W. Dobbek and G. Arnold (Weimar: Böhlau, 1977), 188 (#88 to Fr. Nicolai; 1772) (own translation).

35. "Philological Ideas and Doubts," in Haynes, 114 (N III, 38, 2f.) (translation altered).

36. "Philological Ideas and Doubts," in Haynes, 114 (N III, 37, 28–38, 2) (translation altered). Cf. H VI, 68, 29ff. (to Scheffner; 1785); 492, 1ff. (to Wizenmann; 1786).

Hamann cites Luther's *Small Catechism* at this point in his explanation, namely the first article, the article of creation: "All this is done out of pure fatherly, and divine goodness and mercy without any merit or worthiness of mine at all!"

The gift of grace for which the human is responsible is "freedom." Hamann's anthropology is summarized in this one concept: "Without the freedom to be evil there is no merit, and without the freedom to be good no responsibility for one's own guilt, and indeed no knowledge of good and evil. Freedom is the maximum and minimum of all our natural powers, as well as both the fundamental drive and the final goal of their entire orientation, evolution, and return."[37]

"Hence neither instinct nor the *sensus communis* determines man. . . . Everyone is his own legislator but also the first-born and neighbor of his subjects."[38] "Every man, by virtue of the autonomy of pure reason or its good will, is his nearest law giver and natural judge." From these propositions, belonging to the most remarkable set forth by Hamann, it is clear in what way Hamann deals with the Enlightenment and here especially with Kant, as a contemporary, but as a contemporary in dissent. For Hamann, dependence and autonomy do not exclude but include each other. By virtue of the granted freedom the human moves beyond mere receptivity and mere spontaneity. The human is neither a mere listener nor a mere speaker, neither merely one who obeys nor one who commands, but always and in every case both, though according to the situation, with a different accent. The human's freedom is a game together with others between gift and appropriation, reception and transmission. The human does not have in hand the beginning and end of this game, but remains a learner.

This game together with others does not occur in a social space that is free from domination and does not exist in anticipation of it. It is defined by the fact that others have power over me and I over them, as both lord and servant, "the two natures of lord and servant in one person,"[39] a free lord over all and subject to none and a dutiful servant of all and subject to everyone.

Remarkably, Hamann conceives his fundamental-theological con-

---

37. "Philological Ideas and Doubts," in Haynes, 115 (N III, 38, 8-13).

38. "Philological Ideas and Doubts," in Haynes, 115 (N III, 38, 14-17). Oetinger for example is of another opinion. On the subject, cf. R. Piepmeier, *Aporien des Lebensbegriffs seit Oetinger* (Freiburg im Breisgau; München: Alber, 1978), especially 112ff. The following quotation: "Ein fliegender Brief," in N III, 361, 23-25.

39. ZH III, 48, 2 (to Nicolai; 1773).

cept of communicative freedom that issues neither from instinct nor the *sensus communis,* as personal but entirely nonpersonalistic. It occurs through his observing[40] the human's physiological-sensualistic dimension of free learning, "for man by nature is the greatest pantomime among all the animals."[41] "Everything that is in our understanding has previously been in our senses, just as everything that is in our entire body has once passed through our own stomach or our parents'. The *stamina* and *menstrua* of our person are thus in the truest understanding revelations and traditions which we accept as our property, transform into our fluids and powers, and by this means we become equal to our destiny, both to reveal the critical and archontic dignity of a political animal,"[42] but not without passing it on within the context of generations, institutions, and within a comprehensive perception of the world.

As regards the observation of the human physiological dimension, its special biological condition, Hamann is not inferior to Herder and Gehlen, even though he places the accent elsewhere and in a remarkable way sees "experiences" and "traditions," nature and society in an interplay.[43]

Beyond Materialism and Idealism

It is characteristic of Hamann that he is as opposed to monistic models of explanation as he is to dualistic models and instead tries to think of them in greater number, at least in threes. "In order to arrive at a comprehensive concept of the fullness within the unity of our human essence, several distinguishing earthly marks must be recognized."[44] In connection with this postulate Hamann tries to imagine an anthropological "Third," but in such a way that the figurative language and graphic character of the biblical primal history do not fade. "Man therefore is not only a living field but also the son of the field, and not only field and seed (in the system of materialists and idealists) but also the king of the

40. "Philological Ideas and Doubts," in Haynes, 115 (N III, 38, 21).

41. In the "Philological Ideas" he presents it in a detail uncommon in his writings; cf. Haynes, 115 (N III, 38-40).

42. "Philological Ideas and Doubts," in Haynes, 116 (N III, 39, 10-19). On "stamina" compare below chapter 2, "Style and Form," note 8.

43. "Philological Ideas and Doubts," in Haynes, 117 (N III, 39, 25ff.); cf. 39, 15 ("revelations and traditions"). Cf. below chapter 9, "Reason Is Language," note 73. With "stamina" and "menstrua" Hamann views the biological as well as the historical origin of our reason.

44. "Philological Ideas and Doubts," in Haynes, 118 (N III, 40, 12-15).

field, who is to grow good seed amid hostile tares; for what is a field without seeds and a prince without land and income? These Three in us are therefore One, namely *theou georgion* ['field of God'], just as the three profiles on the wall are the natural shadow of a single body illuminated by a double light behind it."[45]

Hamann illustrates his anthropological Third by a comparison with an optical event. Two sources of light are directed toward a screen. Between them is a solid body. The projection causes three shadows or "masks" to emerge — two half shadows, and in the center a full shadow.

With this threefold scheme Hamann overcomes the alternative between materialism and idealism dominating discussion since Hegel and Marx. The right to speak of the *materia* is held to as strictly as the right to speak of the *forma*. Both, however, are not left to an immanent process. Rather, the human as "king of the field" installed by God has the task of preserving the balance of both in the use of the given critical and archontic dignity, thus in the use of freedom.[46] Criticism and politics bring the element of *materia* and of *forma* into a proper relation, into a balance, without the one dominating the other. They do not, for example, add a third to the human's Being-in the world or to its free formation, but rather the two in a proper relationship. Criticism and politics hold both *forma* and *materia* in balance.

Though it sometimes gives the appearance, Hamann does not represent any sort of sensualism or materialism, just as he does not represent any sort of dualism. He acknowledges *forma* as well as *materia*. Neither of these two elements may presume to usurp power over the other. The balance is so to be maintained that neither triumphs over the other, so that neither the idealistic suppresses the sensuous-material element, nor conversely, does the materialistic element govern in its obscurity. This is the human being's task, an office. In this the human is "king of the field." In this lies the human's critical and archontic dignity.

To Frederick the Great

Hamann's dual piece from 1772 offers an impressive anthropology, centered in the freedom given the human "without merit or worthiness." This freedom is characterized by the fact that from the very first it ap-

45. "Philological Ideas and Doubts," in Haynes, 118 (N III, 40, 16-24).
46. Cf. above chapter 5.

pears as political, as political freedom in a comprehensive sense. The freedom promised to every human is a royal freedom, the freedom of the "king of the field."

What only recently has been generally recognized in the exegesis of Genesis 1:26-27 was obvious to Hamann, the interpreter of scripture. This text of the creation narrative refers to the human's likeness to God and the task of dominion, in analogy to the king whose presence and power is represented by a statue, a plastic image. In his image of the divine, the human is the "king of the field."

Hamann perceives this royal freedom promised to each, itself existing critically and politically, by critiquing the royal ideology in eighteenth-century Prussia, that is, its enlightened absolutism. The critique is contained in his French writing *To the Solomon of Prussia*, which together with the *Philological Thoughts and Doubts* comprises a dual piece. Hamann appeals to the king who as stated later in a letter to Bucholtz stops "his ears against all the cries of his subjects and tax collectors."[47] He addresses the first servant of his state as such, as the "lowest servant," thus making use of Frederick's own self-designation, his own claim, and urges him to become what he as lowest servant, by virtue of the humiliation and exaltation of Jesus Christ, already is.[48]

> But Sire! You thought it not robbery the form of a Supreme being which is able to destroy souls and bodies all the way to the fires of Hell, and You have made yourself of no reputation, even making Yourself in the likeness of this King of the Jews, who is the King of Kings, and who nonetheless was numbered among the transgressors, the bandits, the rogues. You humbled Yourself and being found in fashion as an unhappy Prussian, You will at last succeed in becoming our FATHER, who will know well how to give good things, like our Father who is in Heaven.[49]

In this way the king is addressed with the Christ-predicate Voltaire assigned him at his coronation in 1740. Voltaire's ode *Au'roi de Prusse*

47. H V, 208, 34f. (to Bucholtz; 1784).

48. By this means Hamann gives currency to a decisive thought in Luther's interpretation of the "Magnificat" (WA 7, 544-604; 1521), which he might have read during the course of his study of Luther (cf. for example ZH I, 297, 5-7: to Lindner; 1759).

49. "To the Solomon of Prussia," in Haynes, 141-42 (N III, 58, 17-26). Cf. above chapter 1, "Life and Work," note 69.

sur son avènement au trône celebrates Frederick the Great as the true "image of God" (Col. 1:15):

> Quelle est du Dieu vivant la véritable image?
> Vous, des talents, des arts et des vertus l'appui,
> Vous, Salomon du Nord, plus savant et plus sage,
> Et moins faible que lui.[50]

As absolute lord the king represents the political embodiment of the philosophical concept of a supreme rational being, just as the metaphysics of the Enlightenment used it as a title for God. Thus Hamann speaks of the monarch abstracting himself from his "unhappy Prussia" as the "Supreme Being of the Prussia."[51] As such an *ens supremum* the monarch in his enlightened absolutism is the political incarnation of the metaphysical concept of God as the "Being of the Being of reason," likewise abstracted from the sensuous-particular, and of which the *Letzte Blatt* speaks. To this "supreme rational being" Hamann opposes the humanity of the incarnate God. His strategy in *To Solomon of Prussia* consists in a critique of ideology by staging this correspondence of metaphysics and politics as he sees it in a direct address to the king.

At the same time, with an uncommon freedom Hamann sets before the king the question of conscience, as to what represents the real power in enlightened Prussia, the majesty of the king or of the biblical God, the Lord, who as Lord is servant and as servant is Lord. In imitation of the well-known "Carmen Christi" (Phil. 2:5-11) the king's claim to be the first servant of his state is accepted as fulfilled, and thus in sharp contrast to it the actual reality is all the more garishly illumined: "Your century, Sire!, is a day only of trouble and of rebuke and blasphemy."[52]

In his prophetic vision Hamann speaks of another Prussia ruled by a "Paradigm of Kings, the Prince of Virtues," "the true Father of Your

50. "What is the true image of the living God? You, the support of talents, arts, and virtues. You, Solomon of the North, more learned and more wise, And less feeble than he," *Exchange of Letters between Frederick the Great and Voltaire*, ed. R. Koser and H. Droysen, 2nd part (1740-1753). Publications from the *Königlich-Preussischen Staatsarchiven*, vol. 82 (Leipzig: Hirzel, 1909), 2f.

51. Compare Bayer and Christian Knudsen, *Kreuz und Kritik. Johann Georg Hamanns Letztes Blatt. Text und Interpretation* (Tübingen: Mohr, 1983), notes 284 and 341.

52. "To the Solomon of Prussia," in Haynes, 140 (N III, 57, 34f.); translation (cf. above note 49), 174.

Prussian Peoples."[53] He summons his king to become this "Solomon of Prussia."

> Be ye therefore, Sire, perfect, even as YOUR Father which is in heaven is perfect, and Your Name will be hallowed above every name. The honor, brightness, and glory of Your Kingdom will be established and added unto, for the Eternal has highly exalted You in giving you a Royal Majesty such as no King before YOU has had, and YOU will be seated on the Throne of the Eternal to be the King of Kings. All Prussia will obey YOU and YOUR will will be done in earth as it is in Heaven.[54]

The irony in this piece, which together with the passage just cited edges toward the blasphemous, is just as effective in its acuity today. It is no wonder Hamann found no publisher for it.

For Hamann irony and kerygma, jesting and seriousness intersect. A year later, Hamann applies the same sharp contrast that could only pass for bitter irony, and in a piece written in French, aimed at the Fredericum, in particular at the tax system: *Lettre perdue d'un sauvage du nord à un financier de Pe-kim* (1773):

> Whoever rules subjects must compel them or delude them. Justice is never done in this dual task other than in hate and contempt for a people, with all the evil of a tyrant and a sophist, but behind the mask of a hypocritical morality and humanity. The lord, who loves his subjects, will always be betrayed by them, just as the great God, or will be their sacrifice, just as his dearly beloved Son. Whoever will quickly become rich [at issue is Prussia's tax system] must therefore turn his back on the great God and his dearly beloved Son.[55]

---

53. "To the Solomon of Prussia," in Haynes, 142 (N III, 59, 4f.); translation (cf. above note 49), 175.

54. "To the Solomon of Prussia," in Haynes, 142 (N III, 58, 32–59, 3); translation (cf. above note 49), 175.

55. "Lettre Perdue d'un Sauvage du Nord à un Financier de Pe-Kim" (N II, 302, 16-23); translation. Cf. *Johann Georg Hamann und Frankreich. Acta des dritten Internationalen Hamann-Colloquiums im Herder-Institut zu Marburg/Lahn* 1982, ed. B. Gajek (Marburg: Elwert, 1987), especially 181.

Chapter 7

What Is Enlightenment?

(Kant–Hamann)

The same understanding of freedom articulated in Hamann's writings on Herder and in the *Lettre perdue* strikingly reappears more than ten years later in Hamann's approach to Kant's famous, much cited, but seldom analyzed "Answer to the Question: What Is Enlightenment?" (1784),[1] which till now enjoys almost uninterrupted agreement. In particular the introductory sentences, functioning as sacrosanct canons not least among theologians, are no longer thought through or tested. This, to be sure, contradicts their real intention, though according to Kant "enlightenment" consists precisely in "always thinking for oneself."[2]

Immediately after the publication of Kant's article, Hamann, his friend and critic, undertook such a test, evidence enough of his critical power of thought, though not drawn from the power of his thought but from elemental concern. It appears in his letter of December 18, 1784, to Christian Jacob Kraus,[3] Königsberg professor of practical philosophy

1. Kant, "An Answer to the Question: What Is Enlightenment?" in *Perpetual Peace and Other Essays*, trans. Ted Humphrey (Indianapolis: Hackett, 1983), 41-48.

2. Kant, *Was heißt: Sich im Denken orientieren? Akademieausgabe* (1968), vol. 8 (131-47), 146 note.

3. H V, 289-92 (to Kraus; 1784); printed in its totality together with a precise analysis and commentary on the text in Oswald Bayer, *Vernunft ist Sprache: Hamanns Metakritik Kants* (Stuttgart: Frommann-Holzboog, 2002), chapter 6 (427-68). The quotations from the preceding chapter that are not indicated all derive from H V, 289-92, and are cited individually in *Vernunft ist Sprache*.

and political science, student and friend of both Kant and Hamann. On December 20, 1784, Hamann writes to Lavater: "What our Kant has published in the December edition of the *Berlinische Monatsschrift* about self-inflicted immaturity rather than guardianship cuts me to the quick."[4]

In its acuity and critical power the response to Kant's article by Hamann, "cut to the quick," has not been surpassed. In view of the status of Kant's propositions still held even today, it is particularly relevant to call to mind Hamann's controversy with Kant, to a great extent lost to the general consciousness, so that Kant's defining propositions are not read undialectically but "metacritically," by testing.

Pursuit of this controversy yields rich insight. Two texts precisely dated have significance far beyond the situation of that time. Scarcely a comparable controversy, documented as it is within a specific textual context, would have exemplary character to such high degree or would inquire in such a terse and multilayered way after true, radical enlightenment.

Philosophical Claim and Reality

Hamann's rejoinder is critical of ideology. He tests Kant's propositions and their philosophical claim against sensuous-practical reality; he confronts and contrasts claim and reality. He illumines the claim implicit in the term "enlightenment," uncovers the blindness paradoxically hidden beneath this title, and combines thought and sensuous-practical existence, which on his view were torn asunder in Kant.

Hamann shows himself to be not only a passionately sensuous and politically existent person, but also one who thinks passionately, who detects inaccuracies in Kant — for example that Kant does not perceive the character of simile or analogy in "maturity." He illumines what Kant, more likely unaware than aware, leaves in the dark, that is, the correlate of the immature, namely, the guardian who is Kant himself. He uncovers the partisanship in Kant's *Laudatio* of Frederick the Great and identifies him as an observer, which strongly contrasts with Kant's claim to think with practical intent. Hamann, personally affected by the political and economic situation of Frederician Prussia, on the basis of this el-

---

4. H V, 294, 32-35 (to Lavater; 1784).

emental concern and by virtue of faith as the "fear of the Lord," the beginning of wisdom,[5] becomes both "courageous toward guardians" as well as "merciful toward our immature fellows" and in the process suresighted and keen, in contrast to those "blind" philosophers "of our enlightened century," "who do not know the evil that they do."[6]

Hamann's controversy with Kant belongs to those lessons of history in which a special form of language results in the interpenetration of political and existential, philosophical and theological dimensions in such a paradigmatic way that they dare not be forgotten, are able to penetrate the present and alter attitudes in feeling, thinking, and acting.

Through the "fear of the Lord" Hamann is emboldened to a *parrhesia*, to a freedom that allows him to be critical in signal fashion. His letter to Kraus states with desirable clarity what Christian freedom is.

In this freedom Hamann shows he is clearly related to his time but contradicts the performance of the philosophers insofar as their thinking is nothing but their "own time comprehended in thoughts."[7] He opposes the prevailing ideas and the ideas of those who govern on behalf of his "immature fellows." He will not be guilty of an immature guardianship, but hold to it "with an immature innocence."

However, the political dialectic of immaturity and guardianship in which all are involved, to the point that others have power over them and they over others, must also be considered in all severity. But to consider it cannot mean to abstract from what is thought, thus to arrive at a sphere of "pure" reason. Rather, thinking itself must participate in the sensuous-practical. Accordingly, in dispute with perverted thinking one cannot take to its abstract plane. Such dispute can be carried on only in order that the contradiction succeeds logically and intellectually, but also, and essentially, that it occurs in the sensuousness of a linguistic form suited to facilitate awareness of the contradiction in the elementary dimension of existence and the political.

In his letter to Kraus Hamann moves in all these dimensions just cited, the logical, the linguistic, and the political. This coheres with the fundamental significance of the linguistic dimension that, together with the point of the entire text, it first of all creates its own theme.

---

5. Cf. above chapter 5, "Freedom as a Fundamental Concept of Anthropology," note 68.

6. H V, 299, 5-9 (to Reichardt; 1784).

7. G. F. W. Hegel, *Elements of the Philosophy of Right*, trans. Allan W. Wood and Hugh Barr Nesbit (Cambridge: Cambridge University Press, 1991), 21.

"My transfiguration of the Kantian statement has as its goal that true Enlightenment consists in the immature person's exit from the most extreme self-inflicted guardianship." By transfiguration he does not mean a surmounting but a metamorphosis, a transformation, even a reversal of the Kantian statement. Quoting Kant himself, Hamann wants to show that Kant's position is perverse, that it rests on a self-deception, actually, on a falsehood that defines the entire epoch. In this conversion of a perverse to a true enlightenment lies the point of Hamann's letter.

Converting what is perverted will serve the truth and secure its validity. In what medium? A specific linguistic shape, more precisely, a specific linguistic action; the action of an author befits the matter of conversion. Though Hamann's conversion has an odd effect, it is understandable precisely because it takes up what is known, Kant's text. Hamann engages Kant so totally that he not only relates to him, but also makes continuous use of him. This is done with a "macaroni quill," that is, in the style of a language mix that according to its customary use[8] aims at a satirical-comic effect, but with Hamann aims at bringing out the truth. Hamann does not take what Kant says at face value but alienates and shifts it to another level.

What marks this second, new level is reflected in Hamann's remark that he is thanking Kraus for the loan of Kant's article "in cant-style," that is, in language that reduces Kant's language to a "diminuendo,"[9] brings it to a "lower"[10] level. Below the *niveau* of Kant, at the lower level of language the issue is not "pure" thought, not the transcendental I in its universality, loosed from place and time, gender and profession. The issue is rather this Immanuel Kant or his pupil in their concrete existence and status over against their fellow humans, a matter Kant unconsciously hides but Hamann brings to light, consequently "enlightens," and by asking: "Who is the indeterminate other, who twice appears anonymously?"[11]

Despite the logic functioning in this question about the "*correlatum* of the immature*" implied in Kant, Hamann does not move solely on the level of Aristotle and Kant, thus will argue neither in terms of traditional

---

8. Cf. G. von Wilpert, *Sachwörterbuch der Literatur* (Stuttgart: Kröner, 1969), 467.

9. Cf. M. Seils, *Theologische Aspekte zur gegenwärtigen Hamann-Deutung* (Göttingen: Vandenhoeck & Ruprecht, 1957), 38-56.

10. Cf. C. F. Flögel, *Geschichte der komischen Literatur* (Liegnitz: Siegert, 1784), vol. 1, 174: "Humble speech (at times called cant-style in England). . . ."

11. Cf. Kant, "What Is Enlightenment?" 35, 36.

nor of transcendental logic alone. He rather combines his question about the logic of the Kantian view with the use of a specific composition technique. He engages Kant with a "macaroni quill," in a language mix. Kant's tidy analyses are disrupted by sharp illumination of what retreated to the background and became obscure, that is, the guardian implied but not named in Kant's exposition, or only mockingly observed at a distance and with which Kant identifies himself.[12] The guardian, Kant himself, is now inserted into the Kant-text, by which it, however, becomes another text.

Such a language mix upsets the unidimensionality of the reflections of the "professor of logic and pure reason," as well as his "rules of explanation." It puts the question of the guardian squarely in a way painful for Kant; it upsets the purity of his style of reason and calls him critically to account for it. What as "macaroni style" may be mere play from a literary perspective Hamann uses as a means to bring the truth to light.

In this way the logical and linguistic dimensions interpenetrate, and in its sensuousness the linguistic extends to the dimension of the human-practical. When Hamann rewrites the text of Kant in "cant-style," using Kant's concepts and phrases to reduce Kant's speech to the level of a lower language, he intends to bring those who look down on and judge the immature to the level at which Kant in his manifest wisdom looked down from the higher lookout of a historical view (as an "animated gawker," one who stands aside as onlooker).

Self-Inflicted Guardianship

Dealing with Kant, Hamann deals above all with his concept of "immaturity." If Kant supposed he had to speak of a self-inflicted immaturity, then Hamann convicts him of self-inflicted guardianship. The harshness of the judgment by which Kant judged the immature is now meted out to him as guardian. Unexpectedly but quite understandably, everything suddenly turns on the "self-inflicted guardianship, not immaturity."[13]

More precisely at issue is not an abstraction, guardianship, but in fact the guardian, indeed, as the letter pointedly makes clear, the guardian whose name is Kant, who has it "in mind but has not the heart to ad-

---

12. Kant, "What Is Enlightenment?" 35, 9–36, 35, especially 35, 12.20f.
13. H V, 290, 12 (cf. above note 3).

mit" his own guilt as guardian, since "he himself belongs to the class of guardians." Hamann will not be culpable of the abstraction of the philosophers (the "metaphysicians"), of whom he states that they "are loath . . . to call their persons by their right names and like cats pussyfoot around." On the other hand, he names the one who is actually guilty by name and identifies him: "This is the man of death!"

This quotation (2 Sam. 12:5), so important in the context of Hamann's letter that he repeats it, allows its process and intent to become clear. In his "authorial action" he intends nothing other than what Nathan did. He wants to convict concretely. The one addressed cannot escape the word, because this word is his own which he cannot deny. His own word flung back to him by Hamann turns against its author supposing himself to be sublime and innocent. So "the transfiguration of the Kantian statement," that is, its critical conversion, does not remain in the purely conceptual. It occurs less in *raisonnement* than in the sensuous-practical sphere, arrived at by means of the linguistic form of the parable. Nathan's task is repeated in a new situation. 2 Samuel 12 is so concretely preached that the judge, the critic Kant, is struck by his own judgment. The result is a surprise: "The guilt of the falsely accused immature" consists "in the blindness of the guardian who masquerades as one who sees [as an enlightener!] and for this very fact must be held accountable for all guilt." The guilty party is addressed, even if not formally in the second person ("You are the man!"), but in the indirect statement of a clause. Accordingly the verdict not only applies to the one directly affected (Kraus/Kant) but also lays claim to political reach.

Thus, in only a formal sense is Hamann's letter a written piece. Even as a letter, there is something "oral" about it, so that it represents an intervention in a situation, is related to something concrete and intends a radical alteration of the situation and not merely of the discussion of the question, "What is enlightenment?" Hamann's letter is a negotiation discourse.

We understand in what sense Hamann does not want to be at the level of the "professor of logic and critic of pure reason," perhaps in order "to remind him of the rules of explanation." He is not concerned with argument in the same area, at the same level, with the obvious acceptance of universal assumptions. On the contrary, he is calling attention to the limit of reason, but in a criticism that differs materially from that of Kant. He does this by reflecting on this limit not only in the medium of thought, but would have it become existentially experiential, through the figure of the parable pushing his addressee in sensuous-concrete fashion to the limit of his rational plea for reason and enlightenment.

It is worth making clear what gain in knowledge and what change in the addressee's situation are achieved by the communication Hamann uses. His refusal from the outset to take his place at Kant's level and acknowledge his presuppositions does not denote a rupture but actually an intensification of communication. The Enlightenment is extended, radicalized. Hamann voices concrete dissent in a specific negation, and in such a dialectic avoids rendering his conversion of the Kantian position irrational. We will not be able to reproach Hamann for not understanding Kant or for negating him in the abstract, or even of having opposed him with what is irrational.

Hamann's controversy with Kant indicates how a contemporary seeks understanding in a targeted dissent. Hamann has not spoken past Kant, has not mistaken him. He has rather struck him a blow with his "macaroni quill."

Hamann wants to convict his addressee, change him, bring him to *metanoia,* to conversion, by using the means to render what the addressee knows, his own word, so alien that it critically strikes back at its author, unable to avoid his own word.

Public and Private Reason

The postscript,[14] in which Hamann specifically formulates the intention of his transfiguration, his conversion of Kant, requires special attention.

The blame does not lie beneath, among the minors, the immature, but above, among the guardians with all their "highest self-inflicted guardianship," as Hamann formulates it in ironic allusion to court language. In this context the person referred to as "immature" is the guardian. His immaturity is either that of the philosophical guardian who is politically patronized and needs the army as protector and guarantee of his thought, or that of the one who makes use of his private reason and over whom the philosopher sets himself as guardian.

The "fear of the Lord"[15] is acknowledged as source of true enlightenment, thus the faith that we should "fear, love, and trust in God above

14. H V, 291, 21–292, 11 (cf. above note 3).
15. Cf. Job 28:28; Psalm 111:10; Proverbs 1:7; 9:10.

all things." For Hamann, who never has "anything up his sleeve but an evangelical Lutheranism,"[16] to validate, to hear, and to recognize the first commandment even in thought, in the sphere of wisdom, goes without saying — here with Luther's explanation of the first commandment in the *Small Catechism*.

As Hamann pointedly puts it in critical reference to Kant, faith in God makes us "cowardly about lying and lazy about inventing — all the more bold toward guardians, who at most can kill the body and suck the purse dry — all the more merciful toward our immature fellows and more fruitful in good works of immortality."[17]

What Hamann represents is the Pauline-Reformation freedom, in which the Christian by faith "is a free lord . . . subject to none" and thus in love is "a dutiful servant . . . subject to all."[18] Faith, the "fear of the Lord," creates freedom and boldness "toward guardians" in merciful advocacy for "our immature fellows."

Hamann's bold behavior corresponds exactly to the bold word of his letter. For years he tried to improve the economic situation of his "poor colleagues,"[19] the Königsberg *"commilitones in telonio."*[20] In particular, he protested against the illegal withdrawal of the "fooey amounts" due the "tax collectors,"[21] which comprised an essential part of their income, but had now to be siphoned off to the state till.[22] The letter of December 26, 1784, cited above, written to his friend the Kapellmeister Johann Friedrich Reichardt living in Berlin, indicates the direct link of this protest to the "authorial action" of the letter to Kraus. Hamann wants to gather "all the printed and written acts" of the events into a memorial ("for memoirs and confessions") in order to document that it is "not the innocent immature, but the all highest self-inflicted guardianship" that is the real scandal "of our enlightened century."[23]

16. H VI, 466, 23f. (to Schenk; 1786).

17. E. Büchsel attempts to indicate the reminiscences of biblical passages in this section in "Aufklärung und christliche Freiheit . . . ," in *Neue Zeitschrift für Systematische Theologie und Religionsphilosophie* 4 (1962): (153-57) 154.

18. Martin Luther, "On the Freedom of a Christian," in LW 31:344.

19. H V, 294, 27 (to Lavater; 1784).

20. H V, 298, 32 (to Reichardt; 1784).

21. H V, 294, 22 (cf. above note 19).

22. H IV, 447, 29–449, 6 (to Jacobi; 1785) and others.

23. H V, 299, 2-10 in relation to 298, 32-34 (cf. above note 20) and 294, 21-31 (cf. above note 19).

This reaches the decisive point of the entire argument. From this point Hamann explicitly unhinges (a continuous occurrence but only by implication) what is crucial to Kant, his way of knowing, the shape of his argument, which even breeds pupils today. He unhinges "the distinction between the public and private service of reason," and scorns it as "comical."[24] It is that distinction which according to the famous Halle professor of theology, Semler, allows the theologian to speak differently in the pulpit than the academic.

From here on up to its "Amen!" the postscript is nothing but a contesting of the right to this distinction. Kant errs because his distinction is not what it intends to be. It is really not a distinction but a separation that, by pretending to be meaningful, propagates a false reconciliation.

Immaturity and Guardianship

First of all, drawing a direct parallel between the public and private use of reason, the guardian and the immature, serves to prove the legitimacy of this critical thesis. In this way the threads of Kant's thoughts are tangled. Kant saw the "private use" of reason limited by obedience, thus by immaturity, but in its public use took no notice of guardianship, not to mention self-inflicted behavior. He thus separated immaturity and guardianship instead of distinguishing and holding them together in a *unio personalis*, though "the task is to unite[25] the two natures of an immature person and a guardian," the one who hears and the one who speaks, the one who obeys and the one who commands, not with long-winded philosophical speculations on history but with direct and concrete advocacy on behalf of "our immature fellows."

If one separates the two "natures" one turns them into "two self-contradictory hypocrites," fancies them as isolated from each other and assigns them two unconnected roles within a single existence or even to different existences. In this way both become "hypocrites," untrue. Their untruth consists in their "contradicting themselves." Since what is in fact separated or perversely united in the political-existential sphere

---

24. Cf. H V, 258, 15f. (to Scheffner; 1784).

25. This takes up the Christological conceptuality of Chalcedon. Cf. above chapter 5, "Freedom as a Fundamental Concept of Anthropology," note 53, and chapter 6, "Criticism and Politics," note 39.

seeks to justify itself theoretically as something to be sensibly distinguished, the distinction becomes hypocritical, it conceals the perverted union of the two natures of the guardian and the immature.

Now this perverse union is a fact, not a mystery *("Arcanum")* first uncovered by philosophical wisdom, something one would have to publish, which "must first be preached." On the contrary, it has long been obvious; it is a public scandal, as a matter of fact, the chief political problem. "Precisely here is the knot of the entire political task." The cosmopolitical-public use of reason in the presence of the learned reading public does not enter into the oppressive relations of Prussian daily life but remains solemnly at the sidelines. "Of what help to me is the festive garment of freedom, if I am at home in the smock of a slave?"

The meaning of the following passage is summed up in these sentences: "Thus the public use of reason and freedom is nothing but a dessert. . . . The private use is the daily bread that we should do without for the sake of the public use."

Other than Kant, Hamann is concerned with the use of reason *in concreto.* In the ordinary relations and tasks of life lies true publicity. In them, when resistance is offered, one may not allow the use of reason to be limited without protest, may not blindly obey and merely nurse the inner reservation of that speculative "cosmopolitical-Platonic chiliasm," according to which the course of history, "when considered in its totality,"[26] is rational, in any case justified as such on the basis of its rational purpose.

According to Hamann, the truly public place is for Kant "at home."[27] Where this place is concerned, Hamann sees Kant engaged in a guardianship in which guardians at the lectern, stage, and pulpit perform compulsory service "to the state in their own self-inflicted immaturity." Here, "at home," the guardians could and would have to use their reason, even if by it they put their office and their own lives at risk. If they bow to the power of the state in this concrete place, then they behave, as Kant says, like "the fair sex." Hence the question, "Does Plato [= Kant] also belong to the fair sex [= to the immature]?" but of course "Plato" is silent where he should speak. With this question, Kant's accusation of the immature

---

26. Kant, "What Is Enlightenment?" 41, 28f.
27. Kant, "What Is Enlightenment?" 38, 23 . . . taken up by Hamann with the adverb "at home." The following quotations of Hamann refer entirely to Kant, 38, 21-26, and then Kant, 35, 18ff.; likewise to 1 Corinthians 14:35.

strikes back at him, at the guardian who in his guardianship is nevertheless guilty of immaturity, in contrast to the immature who are innocent.

Hamann regards the judgment "self-inflicted immaturity" as insulting to those concerned and in their name forbids it. In such advocacy he exercises that guardianship he proudly and self-consciously affirms: *"Anch'io sono tutore!"* (I too am a guardian).[28] In such guardianship one does not grovel before the investor and ruler, to flatter him and at the same time harshly and scornfully distance oneself from the immature. Rather, the two natures of the immature and the guardian are united by the one who lives in "fear of the lord." Thus the two relations between fellow humans are so effectively held together that one is upright before superiors and hunched toward inferiors, whereas Hamann sees Kant hunched toward superiors and upright toward inferiors. The political dialectic between immaturity and guardianship in which all are implicated by the fact that others have power over them and they over others can only be perceived by Christians in the freedom promised and given them, so that they are "merciful in relation to their immature fellows" and thus "bold toward guardians." Hamann concludes, "I am not a lip server nor hired hand of an overseer, but I am on the side of immature innocence," thus to right-side Kant's upended answer to the question "What is enlightenment?" into a true enlightenment and concretely to perceive the freedom of a Christian as "mature childlikeness."[29]

---

28. By this means, Hamann changes the *"Anch' io sono pittore"* ("I too am a painter"), which Correggio is supposed to have called out in front of a painting of Raphael's.

29. Hamann, *Entkleidung und Verklärung,* quoted according to R. Wild, *"Metacriticus bonae spei . . ." Johann Georg Hamanns "Fliegender Brief"* (Bern: Lang, 1975), 343 (= appendix to the text 58, 32). Hamann is referring to Romans 8:19-23.

Chapter 8

History and Reason

(Reimarus–Lessing–Mendelssohn–Hamann)

The collective noun "history" appears between 1750 and 1770,[1] apparently not without the midwifery of Bengel and Hamann. Earlier one spoke in the plural of "histories." With the emergence of the singular "history" and interest in its "unity" can be identified the beginning of an earlier nonexistent philosophical approach to "history." Since Aristotle, "history" had not been an object of philosophy but a matter of rhetoric — more precisely, of the *genus demonstrativum*. Now for the first time philosophy makes history a theme.

With this is likewise first connected a particular interest in the future. The view is directed towards what is ahead, toward a period in which what is so far universally human is not repeated, so that one could speak of what history "teaches" and what one can learn from it. What is awaited as absolutely new and is to be put to work cannot be historical knowledge through experience which, as the pragmatic historiography of Thucydides views it, one would eternally possess as a directive for action. Rather, the chief expectation was that everything changes. The new is at hand. If for the fifteenth- and sixteenth-century humanists the "old" was criterion of truth, to the pure source of which one was to return, then since the eighteenth century at the latest the

---

1. R. Koselleck, "Geschichte V. Die Herausbildung des modernen Geschichtsbegriffs," in *Geschichtliche Grundbegriffe. Historisches Lexikon zur politisch-sozialen Sprache in Deutschland*, ed. O. Brunner, W. Conze, R. Koselleck (Stuttgart: Klett, 1975), vol. 3, 647-91.

"new" to be produced is opposed to the old as the criterion of truth and verification.

Their totally new orientation is briefly and pregnantly represented in the self-designation of the epoch, in the German word for "modernity," namely *"Neuzeit,"* literally translated, "new time." By this very name summarizing its self-understanding, "modernity" is connected with a salvific claim to bring about the completely, unsurpassably new as the good. Modernity seeks to set in motion the incomparably new, but it must overtake what currently exists in order to promote salvation in a permanent revolution. But in its wake it has also brought the horror, the terror not only of conscience, but of that razor applied wherever a historically random angle obstructs the level highway. Not only cities and French gardens were planned and built *more geometrico* (according to geometric custom), but the entire face of the earth was altered, judged by Karl Marx to be the humanizing of nature, and spiritedly celebrated in the *Communist Manifesto* (1848).

In the concern to articulate a modern self-understanding one cannot overlook its theological aspects, above all its "hope for better times," its chiliasm (Revelation 20), which in secularized form, along with belief in universal progress, had particular effect. Hence historians of philosophy are agreed that the modern philosophy of history in all its forms can only be appropriately understood as an answer — one that varied according to time — to the Old and New Testament concept of history and time.

However, this understanding of history and time, as indicated for example in Galatians 4:1-7, underwent specific reshaping. The answers were given with philosophical means. This took the sting from the cross of Jesus Christ as well as from the contingency and finitude of the human, its sin and the judgment.

The Age of Criticism

Chladenius, carefully observed by Hamann, made the first attempts to cope philosophically with the problem of history.[2] As a student of Wolff he wanted to apply Wolff's method of demonstration to the sphere of

---

2. ZH I, 334-36 (to Lindner; 1759). Cf. V. Hoffmann, *Johann Georg Hamanns Philologie. Hamanns Philologie zwischen enzyklopädischer Mikrologie und Hermeneutik* (Stuttgart: Kohlhammer, 1972), 154-61.

history and here also to arrive at an "immutable coherence and essential connection of ideas, according to which they either presuppose or exclude one another" — as Hamann polemically remarks with a quotation from Mendelssohn, likewise a pupil of Wolff.[3]

We will return to Hamann's critique of the Leibniz-Wolffian philosophy, above all to his criticism of its impact on the understanding of history, after we have gained a sense for the importance of the overall formulation of the question. Not only for church and theology, or for academic and philosophical awareness, but for the public consciousness beyond all of this its importance can scarcely be overestimated. At issue is the dissolution of the old *heilsgeschichtlich*, apocalyptic concept of history and its understanding of sin, versus the modern optimistic notion of progress for the sake of a radical transformation — not only in thinking of history but in experiencing it, and thus of history itself. To the degree one promises oneself something new from the shaping of the future, one breaks off from the old, from a tradition become contingent, and which if to be preserved must first be justified before the forum of reason.

In a survey of modern history Friedrich Engels's *Anti-Dürung* reads: "Religion, natural science, society, the state, all were subjected to the most unsparing criticism, and everything was compelled to justify its existence before the judgment seat of reason or perish."[4]

What has historically become is, as such, not rational. Reason occurs in history first and through testing, through the validation of a criterion. In any case, reason adheres in history only to the extent that it is always first to be critically demonstrated. Everything that exists is under the pressure of having to justify itself, of always having to prove its right to exist. "Our age," Kant defines, "is in especial degree, the age of criticism, and to criticism everything must submit. Religion through its sanctity, and law-giving through its majesty, may seek to exempt themselves from it. But they then awaken just suspicion, and cannot claim the sincere respect which reason accords only to that which has been able to sustain the test of free and open examination."[5]

---

3. "Golgatha and Scheblimini," in Haynes, 180 (N III, 303, 15f.) (translation altered). Cf. Moses Mendelssohn, *Jerusalem or On Religious Power and Judaism*, trans. Allan Arkush, Introduction and Commentary by Alexander Altmann (Hanover and London: University Press of New England, 1983), 33-139, p. 91.

4. Friedrich Engels, "Landmarks of Scientific Socialism," in *Anti-Dühring*, trans. Austin Lewis (Chicago: Charles Kerr, 1907), 36.

5. Kant, *Critique of Pure Reason*, A xii, p. 9.

In their critical reason humans are aware they are the creatures who can stand the things of the world on their head, can arrange them in freedom according to rational reflection. The world must be directed according to their notion, according to my head. Humans are not subject to their drives and passions, their inclinations, or to positive laws, custom, and convention. They can think of everything that exists in a different way. At any rate, in thought they can venture the experiment of an *annihilatio mundi,* an annihilation of the world. In this experiment they can call the existence of everything back to nothing and from this nothing think everything anew. In this way humans can allow things to succeed each other in a way different from nature and produce what is new after their own sketch. If Descartes had claimed such freedom from the world,[6] but limited it to the sphere of the natural sciences as the only sphere of "truth" (everything else being the sphere of probability) then Hobbes applied the method to the area of the social, an application Descartes had not considered, and tested it in the purely conceptual construction of a social contract. Even Kant situated himself in the tradition of this "revolution in the manner to think,"[7] according to which "reason has insight only into that which it produces after a plan of its own."[8]

What characterizes modern thought in contrast to past epochs is that push and pull to justify everything in principle and establish the new from absolute zero and, in any case according to the claim, to construct without bias. What cannot be comprehended rationally cannot be "explained," thus justified by reconstruction within the context of the unity of self-consciousness, and has lost its right to exist.

The demand and execution of such an explanation bent on vindication are an excellent means of emancipation, of getting rid of historical, traditional demands and claims. What is near needs shaking off, or in any case, keeping at a distance in which it is no longer a threat, no longer claims or invites, no longer demands and obliges.

We cannot keep clearly enough in mind that from the outset the interest of the Enlightenment in historical research does not serve communication with what is researched or even agreement with it, but rather distantiation from it as the method dictates. It intends no estrangement

---

6. Cf. Oswald Bayer, "Descartes und die Freiheit," in *Leibliches Wort: Reformation und Neuzeit in Konflikt* (Tübingen: J. C. B. Mohr [Paul Siebeck], 1992), 176-204; cf. above chapter 7, "What Is Enlightenment?," note 3.

7. Kant, *Critique of Pure Reason,* B xii, p. 20 (translation altered).

8. Kant, *Critique of Pure Reason,* B xiii, p. 20.

that would allow what had become strange to be newly seen and heard. Rather, it dispenses with it, whether in the form of a sharp and solemn elimination not only of the *ancien régime*, but also of the old God of the Christians and their chronology, or in the French Revolution, or in the seemingly much less ominous sublation advocated and undertaken by the philosopher Hegel. Hegel's concept of sublation made history's resistance and thus the encounter with it disappear, set it aside.[9] The historicizing of reason, dominant in the nineteenth century, coheres with the rationalizing of it already attempted a century earlier, beginning with Chladenius.

When, in the attempt to test it critically for its rationality, such a philosophical treatment of history applies to the proclamation of Jesus of Nazareth as the Christ, then this proclamation is struck at a nerve. For the life, suffering, and death of Jesus Christ is bound to a specific place, a specific time. It is contingent. It can no more be justified in principle and derived from a previously devised universality than the history of the Jewish people. It too is contingent. Its precise locality, individuality, and personality cannot be sublated. Rather, they have abiding, eternal weight.

This is in tension with that pressure that before all others has made unavoidable the still unanswered question of the relation between reason and history, between the "truths of reason" and the "truths of history." The distressing and painful history of religious and civil wars fought on confessional grounds, particularly in France and England, required seeking beyond or this side of a positive and in fact always particular confession for a pure essence of Christianity, as Friedrich von Logau stated it in his motto: "Lutheran, Papist, and Calvinist; these faiths exist, all three. But there is doubt as to where Christianity would be."[10] Furthermore, it would necessitate inquiring after a universal, natural religion that united all, in any case after a natural and human right which according to Hugo Grotius applies "even if we were to assume . . . there is no God *(etiamsi daremus . . . non esse Deum)*."[11]

---

9. D. Jähnig, "Die Beseitigung der Geschichte durch 'Bildung und Erinnerung' (zu Hegel)," in *Welt-Geschichte: Kunst-Geschichte. Zum Verhältnis von Vergangenheiterkenntnis und Veränderung* (Köln: Dumont Schauberg, 1975), 29-37.

10. F. von Logau, *Sämtliche Sinngedichte*, ed. G. Eitner (Tübingen: Fues, 1872), Bibliothek des literarischen Vereins in Stuttgart, CXIII, 246 (under the heading "Faith," in second thousand, in first hundred, Number 100).

11. Hugo Grotius, *De Jure Belli ac Pacis libri tres* (Parisiis: apud Nocelaum Buon, 1625, 1712), VIII.

The Fragments Dispute

Within the context of this essential regression to the universally human with its claim to settle the demands made by positive claims for recognition and therein to be rational, we must now observe that event which as no other in eighteenth-century theological history was epochal, and even today represents a great challenge and demands an answer. The event is the "Fragments Dispute," conducted from 1777 to 1780 between Lessing and his opponents of various theological and philosophical origins.

Bit by bit Lessing published *Fragmente eines Ungenannten*, not in order to do justice to the author he did not name, the Hamburg Orientalist, Hermann Samuel Reimarus (1694-1768), but to set in motion the discussion of the problem, the significance of which Lessing clearly recognized. Lessing did not at all share the deistic reduction of Reimarus to the purely historical on the one hand and the purely moral on the other, but he was also not content with Lutheran orthodoxy, in any case in the shape in which it encountered him. He nevertheless expected something from the investigation and public treatment of the problem.

Reimarus had written an *Apologie oder Schutzschrift für die vernünftigen Verehrer Gottes (Apology or Defense for the Rational Worshipers of God)*, but understandably, in order not to jeopardize his bourgeois existence, did not publish the book. After his death Lessing acquired a manuscript of the *Apology*. As G. Gawlick puts it,

> [h]e recognized the significance of the work and resolved to make it accessible to the public. In order not to endanger the family, he published it only in fragments and pretended they originated in a manuscript of the Wolfenbüttel library (which he managed since 1774), thus the title *Wolfenbüttel Fragments*. In 1774 a section of the first book appeared with the title *Von Duldung der Deisten (On the Toleration of Deists)*, which remained unnoticed. The plan to have the entire manuscript printed in Berlin miscarried due to difficulties from the censor. In 1777 Lessing published five further sections in the *Beiträge zur Geschichte und Literatur aus der Herzoglichen Bibliothek zu Wolfenbüttel (Contributions to History and Literature from the Ducal Library in Wolfenbüttel*; this journal was not subject to censorship). In 1778 the final fragment *Von dem Zwecke Jesu und seiner Jünger (On the Purpose of Jesus and His*

Disciples) followed. At that time Lessing was required to turn over the manuscript.[12]

Natural and Positive Religion

Since it is not Lessing but Reimarus who is Hamann's precise antipode, we need at least briefly to get an idea of the "natural religion" that the deist Reimarus represents. "Natural religion" is separated from every positive religion or even confession. According to his writing of 1754, titled *Die vornehmsten Wahrheiten der natürlichen Religion (The Most Distinguished Truths of Natural Religion)*, these truths are the "existence of God, the dependence of the world on God, the manifestation of the attributes of God in nature; the dualism of body and soul, and the destiny of the human as the highest perfection possible for a rational creature, the special providence of God for humanity and its defense in a theodicy; immortality as the medium which allows the virtuous to ascend to a higher blessedness than can be attained in this world."[13] "Sin, guilt, grace, and redemption do not even appear, since they belong to positive religion." The "usual reference to the transition from natural to positive religion" is "totally" lacking in Reimarus.[14]

According to Reimarus's basic conviction, "all claims to supernatural revelation are unfounded; a positive" religion bound to a specific history and tradition, "in which all could be saved, is an absurdity."[15] "The human is not made for a religion grounded on *facta*, indeed on such supposed to have happened in a tiny corner of the earth."[16] In their individuality, such contingent facts are not universally binding, lack capacity for consensus, and lack universalizability. How should what happened at a point in history, at a specific place and time, say, *sub Pontio Pilato*, have universal significance? If a single, contingent event could have any

---

12. G. Gawlick, "Hermann Samuel Reimarus," in *Die Aufklärung*, Gestalten der Kirchengeschichte, ed. M. Greschat (Stuttgart: Kohlhammer, 1983), vol. 8, (299-311) 309.

13. Gawlick, "Hermann Samuel Reimarus," 300. Cf. Hamann's reference to Reimarus, who "explained and rescued the noblest truths of our naturalized religion in an understandable way . . .": "Konxompax," in N III, 225, 31f.

14. Gawlick, "Hermann Samuel Reimarus," 302.

15. Gawlick, "Hermann Samuel Reimarus," 308.

16. H. S. Reimarus, *Apologie oder Schutzschrift für die vernünftigen Verehrer Gottes*, ed. G. Alexander (Frankfurt am Main: Insel Verlag, 1972), vol. 1, 171.

universal significance, it would have to have it from the outset, and only then would universal significance appear or be seen in it.

Reimarus solves the problem posed by the confession that the historical Jesus is identical to the eternal Son of God by sharply separating the temporal from the eternal, the historical from the existentially relevant and obligatory, in brief, the "positive" from the "natural." The "natural" is in essence defined by the fact that it was not "posed," did not become, was not generated. While the "positive" is bound to a specific place, time, and person, the "natural" always applies everywhere and for everyone.

Since Reimarus separates "positive" from "natural" religion, he is a "separation artist," to use the then customary word for chemists, a term also used by Kant, who thinks no differently than Reimarus at the decisive point. At the end of the *Kritik der Praktischen Vernunft (Critique of Practical Reason)*, Kant expressly states that he recommends and follows a method "almost like a chemist," specifically that of separating "the moral (pure) determining ground from the empirical,"[17] further, the a priori from the a posteriori, the contingent truths of history from the necessary truths of reason, the human Jesus from the Christ as the eternal type, the humanity of the Bible from its divinity. Quite in terms of the disjunction sharply marked and with ideally typical clarity in Reimarus, the section dealing with "The Conflict between the Philosophical and Theological Faculties" in Kant's *The Conflict of the Faculties (Der Streit der Fakultäten,* 1789) reads: "Tenets of faith which are also to be conceived as divine commands are either merely statutory doctrines, which are contingent for us and [must be] revealed . . . or moral doctrines, which involve consciousness of their necessity and can be recognized a priori — that is, rational doctrines."[18] Either — or! Revelation and reason fall asunder like chance and necessity. A rational faith is opposed to faith in revelation, the necessary is opposed to the contingent, the historical and temporal to the a priori knowable eternal.

Reimarus is not only like Kant a "chemist" by virtue of his separating chance and necessity, revelation and reason, "positive" and "natural" religion. Unlike Kant who lacked the philological tools, as a philol-

17. Kant, *Critique of Practical Reason,* trans. Mary Gregor (Cambridge: Cambridge University Press, 1997), 78.

18. Kant, *The Conflict of the Faculties,* trans. Mary J. Gregor (Lincoln: University of Nebraska, 1979), 87.

ogist and historian Reimarus plies his art of separation as an exegete of the Old and, particularly important, of the New Testament. His treatment of the New Testament shows that the method of separation is particularly successful (Hamann rigorously dubs this artistic tearing asunder a "divorcing, adulterating"[19] procedure, in which is separated what inseparably belongs together). Spinoza's critical Bible exegesis had spared the New Testament. Now, for the first time Reimarus applies Spinoza's separation of the historical and metaphysical, the positive and natural to the New Testament with unrelenting and most impressive results. For the first time in the history of New Testament research, with total rigor and radicality the New Testament is separated from the Old, Jesus' teaching from that of the Apostles, and along with it the historical Jesus from the kerygmatic Christ.[20] In the fragment *Von dem Zwecke Jesu und seiner Jünger (The Goal of Jesus and His Disciples)* published by Lessing in 1778, Reimarus writes, "I find ample cause, however, to separate completely that which the apostles set forth in their own writing from that which Jesus himself really spoke and taught in the course of his own life."[21] Since then the problem of the historical Jesus has existed, and Jesus has been played off against Paul.

For two hundred years Reimarus's formulation of the question, his art of separation, has had a powerful effect in theology and church. The Christology of Rudolf Bultmann, for example, and with it all of his theology, cannot be understood apart from Reimarus. Whatever position one takes toward Reimarus, the enormity of his work is not to be denied. According to Albert Schweitzer's *Geschichte der Leben-Jesu-Forschung (Quest for the Historical Jesus)* the fragment *On the Purpose of Jesus and His Disciples* is

> not only one of the greatest events in the history of criticism, it is also a masterpiece of world literature. The language is as a rule

19. Bayer, Oswald, "Vernunftautorität und Bibelkritik in der Kontroverse zwischen Johann Georg Hamann und Immanuel Kant," in *Autorität und Kritik. Zu Hermeneutik und Wissenschaftstheorie* (Tübingen: Mohr Siebeck, 1991), 59-82, especially 59-61.

20. Cf. Gawlick, "Hermann Samuel Reimarus," 306.

21. Hermann Samuel Reimarus, *The Goal of Jesus and His Disciples*, trans. George Wesley Buchanan (Leiden: E. J. Brill, 1970), 37. The text was edited by G. E. Lessing, and printed in Braunschweig in 1778. This sentence is cited in: G. E. Lessing, *Sämtliche Schriften*, ed. K. Lachmann, 3rd edition, furnished by F. Muncker, 1897 (reprinted in Berlin: De Gruyter, 1968), vol. 13 (215-327), 223. Cf. *Apologie* (cf. above note 16), vol. 2, 20.

crisp and terse, pointed and epigrammatic, the language of a man who isn't engaged in literary composition but is wholly concerned with the facts. At times it rises to heights of passionate feeling and then it is as though the fires of a volcano were painting lurid pictures on dark clouds. Seldom has there been a hate so eloquent, a score so lofty; but then it is seldom that a work has been written in the just consciousness of so absolute a superiority to contemporary opinion. And throughout there is dignity and serious purpose.[22]

According to Schweitzer "this was the first time that a really historical mind, thoroughly conversant with the sources, had undertaken the criticism of the tradition."[23] It is necessary to make clear, however, that "criticism," the term for the underlying force of the person gifted with critical and archontic status, is used in a quite specific sense, that is, in the sense of the art of separation cited, that "adulterous" procedure in which what only lives together is torn apart, divorced. Despite, indeed, *in* his decisive opposition to Reimarus's art of separation Hamann did not surrender the term "criticism." In this respect he differs from many theologians today who do not dare to rescue this term. Hamann battled for its proper use and thus also for the proper use of the human gift and capacity for analysis.

Schweitzer rightly calls Reimarus a "historian."[24] But the truth that Reimarus as historian serves is not historical truth but as already emphasized, the "natural," the rational, the timeless. Historical research is pursued here in order to keep the truth of history at a distance and silence it. This paradox is characteristic of the entire history of the Life of Jesus Research. Its direct intention is not toward the historical but the metaphysical. For this reason the weighty systematic problem we are touching cannot merely be formulated as a question of the relation between reason and history but must, at the same time, also be put as a question regarding the truth. What is truth? What kind of truth is involved in defining the relation between reason and history?

In his interpretation of truth by way of veracity *(Wahrhaftigkeit)* Schweitzer, who stands entirely in the tradition beginning with Reimarus

22. Schweitzer, *The Quest for the Historical Jesus*, trans. John Bowden (Minneapolis: Fortress, 2001), 15.

23. Schweitzer, *The Quest for the Historical Jesus*, 15.

24. Schweitzer, *The Quest for the Historical Jesus*, 15, 22 ("a historical performance of no mean order"); 25 ("historian by the grace of God").

and himself plies the art of separation, of separating the historical and the rationally ethical, sees in the Life of Jesus Research "an act of veracity on the part of Protestant Christianity."[25] He is concerned with nothing less than the essence of Christianity, its core. The "imperturbable veracity" shown in Reimarus, as in all of Life of Jesus Research, belongs "to the essence of genuine religiosity."[26] He concludes the foreword to the sixth edition of his *Geschichte der Leben-Jesu-Forschung (History of the Life of Jesus Research)*, written in 1950 in Lambarene, with the following sentence: "We may take for our comfort, whenever historical knowledge raises difficulties for faith, Paul's words: 'we can do nothing against the truth, but only for the truth' (2 Cor. 13:8)."[27]

It should have become clear that no point in the history of modern theology would be more sensitive. All the other problems are implicit in it. Only those who consider the depth of the problem and note its explosive force will be able to evaluate Hamann's treatment of it in its significance. For this reason it was necessary to take the path we took. Before we take note of Hamann's position against Reimarus, we need to hear Lessing of whom Hamann writes that he "himself thought, and was serious about paving a new way."[28]

Lessing's *Proof of the Spirit and of Power*

It was Lessing who ignited the Fragment Dispute, but as was already made clear, not to agree with Reimarus. He absolutely did not, as a still prevailing misunderstanding will have it, repeat the disjunction of history and reason represented by Reimarus. His famous maxim that "the contingent truths of history can never be proof of necessary truths of reason," to which Hamann also relates, though critically, intends something strikingly different than would be expected of Reimarus, without being identical to what Hamann positively opposes to the separation of history and reason.

Lessing writes his celebrated maxim during the Fragment Dispute in his dual writing *On the Proof of the Spirit and of Power (Über den*

25. Schweitzer, *Geschichte der Leben-Jesu-Forschung,* sixth edition (Tübingen: J. C. B. Mohr, 1951), xviii.

26. Schweitzer, *Geschichte der Leben-Jesu-Forschung,* xviii.

27. Schweitzer, *Geschichte der Leben-Jesu-Forschung,* xix.

28. H V, 403, 13f. in relation to 10-17 (to Herder; 1785).

Beweis des Geistes und der Kraft) and *The Testament of John (Das Testament Johannis)*.[29] By it he answers the attempt of Hannover School Superintendent Schumann to secure the truth of the Christian religion against the attacks of the anonymous one, that is, of Reimarus. Schumann's apologetic serves Lessing "as a negative example of a theological method that betrays its object, a method that is so spirit-less that it argues 'About the evidence of the proofs for the truth of the Christian religion' without allowing the Spirit and the power of the matter dealt with to be shared."[30] "In the conversation between Schumann and Lessing . . . the possibility and legitimacy of securing the truth of Christian faith by way of argument" is disputed; thus Lessing's dual writing is not "to be interpreted as a dogmatic tract but as a teaching guide on the method of theological reflection."[31] In this sense the sentence immediately preceding the famous maxim must be heard: "If no historical truth can be demonstrated, then nothing can be demonstrated through historical truths." Everything depends on the verb. At issue is the range of the method of "demonstrating," of proving. What can be demonstrated? What cannot? Not everything can be demonstrated. According to the assumption of Wolff's philosophy, determinative for Schumann as well as Reimarus, according to the assumption the method of "explanation" and "demonstration" dominant since Descartes, no historical truth can be perceived. More precisely, if historical research follows the Cartesian method only general characteristics can appear, that is, only those of which the method of demonstration and explanation are aware at the outset as being clearly and distinctly perceptible. Hamann recognized this state of affairs,[32] as did Lessing.

Bitter, ironic, with all the literary means at his disposal, Lessing attempts to make clear to his theological contemporaries that in view of Reimarus's radical attack they are ineffectively conducting their apology for Christian truth when as Schumann they want to secure "evidence of proof for the truth of the Christian religion." They do not see that the proof of the truth at issue here is not at all a matter of demonstration, in

---

29. *Lessing's Theological Writings*, trans. Henry Chadwick (London: Adam & Charles Black, 1956), 53.

30. J. Von Lüpke, *Wege der Weisheit. Studien zu Lessings Theologiekritik* (Göttingen: Vandenhoeck & Ruprecht, 1989), 76. The title of Schumann's writing is *Über die Evidenz der Beweise für die Wahrheit der Christlichen Religion* (Hannover, 1778).

31. Von Lüpke, *Wege der Weisheit*, 77.

32. "Biblical Reflections," in Smith, 123 (N I, 11, 31ff.)

any event not the demonstration of modern reason, which from the outset has faded out what is decisive in order to meet its "objective" observations. The vitality and totality of the "object" must first be silenced; the object must first be killed so that it becomes recognizable and available in the way envisaged and desired. To call this to attention, to "demonstrate" this in his own way, with a "theater logic"[33] that summons up figures and quotations and involves one in the action of conversation, Lessing allows the apostle Paul to present his own theological-critical viewpoint and takes 1 Corinthians 2:4 as the title for the first part of his dual writing, *Über den Beweis des Geistes und der Kraft.*

According to Lessing the truth of religion is demonstrated in the Spirit and power of love: "Little children, love one another!" This apocryphally transmitted apophthegm of John, his "testament," effectively staged by Lessing in the second section of his dual writing, not least by continual repetition, is his own positive answer to the question of the truth of Christianity dealt with in the Fragments Dispute. The proof is the proof of deed (cf. John 7:17). In *Nathan,* with which he intends to preach in his own pulpit, the theater,[34] Lessing gave the same answer, and in the drama condensed it in the "Ring Parable."

In his answer Lessing did not exclude the necessity for faith and its historical, "positive" mediation. Rather, he expressly reflected on and included it.[35] However, such mediation and thus the history merely concerns the path needed for instruction. Lessing would never be able as Hamann to speak of the "eternal truths" as "incessantly temporal." For Hamann, on the other hand, truth is "the daughter of time"[36] in the ultimate, eschatological sense.

---

33. With his term "theater logic" Goeze criticizes the connection between the imagistic and the reasoned in Lessing's theological-critical writings (cf. G. E. Lessing, *Werke,* ed. G. Göpfert (München: C. Hanser, 1979), vol. 8, 171. Lessing defends his method and style in *Anti-Goeze* II (*Werke,* vol. 8, 193-96).

34. Lessing to Elise Reimarus on September 6, 1778, in *Werke* (Berlin: De Gruyter, 1971), vol. 2, 719. Cf. von Lüpke, *Wege der Weisheit,* 129-32, 190-94. On the "ring parable" cf. *Wege der Weisheit,* 150-57.

35. *Nathan the Wise,* trans. Walter Frank Charles Ade (New York: Barron's Educational Series, Inc., 1972). Cf. von Lüpke, *Wege der Weisheit,* 111f., 154f.

36. L. Schreiner, HH VII, 105. Cf. H VI, 162, 26 (to Jacobi; 1785). Cited is: Francis Bacon, *Novum organum,* Pars Secunda, Aphorismi de Interpretatione Naturae et Regno Hominis LXXXIV (*The Works of Francis Bacon,* Facsimile reprint of the edition of Spedding, Ellis, and Heath, London 1857-1874 in 14 vols. (Stuttgart–Bad Cannstatt, 1963), vol. 1, 191.

Truth as "Daughter of Time"

With his confession to know "of no eternal truths save as incessantly temporal,"[37] Hamann contradicts not only Reimarus, Mendelssohn, Kant, and many others of his time such as Michaelis and Semler, but Lessing as well, with whom he usually battles as against "shallow" philosophy[38] and theology.

Lessing's maxim that "the contingent truths of history can never be proof of the necessary truths of reason" is polemically taken up by Hamann in his *Konxompax*, which appeared in 1779 in midst of the Fragments Dispute. The subtitle, *Fragmente einer apokryphischen Sibylle über apokalyptische Mysterien (Fragments of an apocryphal Sybil concerning apocalyptic Mysteries)*,[39] already betrays Hamann's conscious engagement. The fragments offered by the anonymous editor are fragments of an anonymous someone, an "apocryphal" Sybil who remains hidden and speaks of apocalyptic mysteries, of the "mystery of the kingdom of heaven from its genesis to the apocalypse."[40] Two books furnish the occasion for the writing: Christoph Meiner's *Über die Mysterien der Alten (On the Mystery of the Ancients)* (Leipzig, 1776), but chiefly Johann August Starck's *Apologie des Ordens der Frey-Mäurer (Defense of the Order of Freemasons)* (Berlin, 1778).

Starck, the Königsberg Freemason, theology professor, and court preacher, Hamann's own father confessor, represented the purist strain of modern willing and thinking evidenced in the forms of the mastery of nature and humans but also in the methods of abstraction and reduction on the part of representatives of a natural religion, to which Deists such as Reimarus belonged.

Reference was already made to the historical distress caused by the religious and civil wars that opened the way to Deism and its natural religion. Yet, Hamann more sharply than any other recognized that re-

---

37. "Golgatha and Scheblimini," in Haynes, 180 (N III, 303, 36f.) (translation altered). Hamann combines *Jerusalem* 39 (JubA8, 108) with 89 (156).

38. Cf. "Biblical Reflections," in Smith, 120 (N I, 9, 15f.)

39. "Konxompax," in N III, 215-28. Cf. in addition I. Manegold: *Johann Georg Hamanns Schrift 'Konxompax'* (Heidelberg: C. Winter, 1963), and the commentary by E. J. Schoonhoven (HH V, 165-262). Lessing is cited in N III, 218, 26-29.

40. "Konxompax," in N III, 226, 21f. On New Testament apocalyptic expectation compare especially N III, 218, 32–219, 17. Cf. the parallel in "Golgatha and Scheblimini," in Haynes, 182 (N III, 305, 17-19).

course to the universally human, nearing its zenith at the end of the eighteenth century in Kant's transcendental philosophy, and calling for settling the demands made by positive claims for recognition and therein to be rational, is monstrously abstract, "thin, as a hungry dog."[41]

Here, Hamann's criticism focuses on a premise that by itself is highly plausible. Its gist is that the more universal the idea, the more abstract and empty. It brushes against the nothing. So, as early as in his 1764 review of the second volume of Robinet's *De la Nature (On Nature)*, Hamann points out that "worldly wisdom" begins "to degenerate from universal knowledge of the possible to universal ignorance of the real."[42] "The modesty of the author . . . to allow nothing to be said of the God of the Christians belongs to the high taste of the enlightened century where denial of the Christian name is a condition without which one may venture no claims to the title of a philosopher. So it is . . . always easier for authors to charm the public with an idle nothing, without their detestableness being recognized."[43]

Again, even in Starck Hamann sees such a process of abstraction and reduction as is characteristic of the representatives of natural religion. In the *Hierophantic Letters (Hierophantischen Briefen*, 1775) he makes the following claim against Starck: "If with pharisaic criticism one wished to sunder all Jewish and heathen components from Christianity, then there would remain as much as would remain of our body by a similar metaphysical art of separation, that is, a substantive Nothing or a spiritual Something, which at bottom . . . would amount to the same thing."[44]

Hamann is referring to Starck's Königsberg dissertation, which attached to the evidence of traditions reaching Christianity from Judaism and Hellenism the requirement that everything be separated from Christianity that is not purely Christian in order by such chemistry to arrive at the true essence of Christianity, identical to the essence of "natural" religion.

The Something of natural religion identical to a Nothing and just as senseless as a "natural language"[45] can only be avoided by one who

---

41. "Zweifel und Einfälle" [1776], in N III, 192, 2 (*"hundemager"*).
42. "Königsbergsche Zeitungen," in N IV, 271, 30-32.
43. "Königsbergsche Zeitungen," in N IV, 271, 48–272, 6.
44. "Hierophantische Briefe," in N III, 142, 4-9.
45. H IV, 195, 13f. (to Herder; 1780).

is not intent on separating the rational and empirical, reason and history, the contingent and the necessary, the a priori and the a posteriori, in order willy-nilly but in fact only later to relate the two dead halves[46] to each other again. The "idle nothing"[47] of a natural religion arrived at by artificial abstraction and reduction can only be avoided by one who in the given situation perceives both as vital elements in their interplay and does not adulterously divorce them. In this interplay I always find myself, which does not mean I would have to resign myself to rigid, ironclad rules. The interplay is not rigid but living. It lives in the freedom of receiving and transmitting, hearing and speaking, perceiving and answering. Otherwise, reason would stand still, would be dead.

Historical Truths of Future Times

On essentially the same front as against Starck Hamann battles Mendelssohn in the second section of that writing in which he published what was most accessible and significant on the problem of the relation between the "contingent truths of history" and the "necessary truths of reason," namely, in *Golgatha and Scheblimini* (1784).[48] In its very title the writing reveals where Hamann sees the solution to the problem,[49] that is, in the one history of Jesus Christ, in which humiliation and exaltation, cross ("Golgatha") and resurrection (*"Scheblimini"* = "Sit at my right hand," Ps. 110:1), indissolubly belong together.

In his *Jerusalem oder über religiöse Macht und Judentum (Jerusalem or on religious power and Judaism)*, appearing in 1783, Mendelssohn had plied Reimarus's art of divorce and correspondingly separated the historical-positive from rational-natural religion. The "eternal truths about God and his government and providence, without which man cannot be enlightened and happy," are not "made known through *word* and *script,* which are intelligible only *here* and *now,*" but are "revealed . . . to all rational creatures through *things* and *concepts,* and inscribed

46. Cf. "Golgatha and Scheblimini," in Haynes, 179 (N III, 303, 7).

47. "Königsbergsche Zeitungen," in N IV, 272, 5.

48. "Golgatha and Scheblimini," in Haynes, 180-98 (N III, 303, 33–315, 8). This is the second part of Hamann's piece to which L. Schreiner in his commentary gives the appropriate heading: "Faith and History" (HH VII, 100).

49. Cf. even "Zweifel und Einfälle," in N III, 192, 5-35.

in the soul with a script that is legible and comprehensible at all times and in all places."[50]

By contrast, Hamann insists on the vital connection of what in Mendelssohn and his entire *siècle philosophique* is separated. He maintains it by taking up the wording of Mendelssohn's text and altering it. For example, where Mendelssohn speaks of "propositions" representing ideas, he places "facts."[51] The "temporal truths of history" negatively apostrophized by Mendelssohn and separated from "eternal truths" are set forth positively with emphasis as "temporal truths of history, which occurred once and never came again — of facts which have become true at one point in time and place through a coherence of causes and effects, and which, therefore, can only be conceived as true in respect to that point in time and space, and must be confirmed by authority."[52]

For Mendelssohn the link of the truth of history to "authority" in the wake of the modern criticism of prejudice and its demand for direct, timeless evidence is the salient argument against the eternal weight and rational universality of "truths of history." Strictly speaking for this reason, no truth but only probability attaches to them.[53] "Without authority the truth of history vanishes along with the event itself."[54] By contrast, concerned with the vital, fruitful relationship between authority and criticism, history and reason, Hamann turns this proposition intended critically by Mendelssohn into the positive: If the eternal truth is temporal and thus history, and if it intends to be perceived at all and will not escape from me, then it can be accepted only on "authority," thus "not . . . in any other manner than on faith."[55] It is not captive to an internal view allegedly free of presuppositions and prejudice, but to the

---

50. Mendelssohn, *Jerusalem*, 126; cf. 93, 127; taking up Psalms 19 and 50, cited by Hamann, "Golgatha and Scheblimini," in Haynes, 180-81 (N III, 304, 2-6).

51. "Lettre perdue d'un sauvage du nord à un financier de Pe-kim" ("a lost letter by a savage of the north to a financier of Pe-kim"), in N II, 304, 33. On the appearance of the word "fact" *(Tatsache)* in the middle of the eighteenth century: cf. R. Staats, "Der theologiegeschichtlich Hintergrund des Begriffes 'Tatsache,'" in *Zeitschrift für Theologie und Kirche* 70 (1973): (316-45), 326.

52. "Golgatha and Scheblimini," in Haynes, 182 (N III, 304, 32-37); the quotation is from *Jerusalem*, 91, 93, and 126-27. Here and in what follows Hamann's citations of Mendelssohn are indicated by quotation marks.

53. In distinction from Descartes' *Principia Philosophiae* (Londini, 1664), I, 3.

54. "Golgatha and Scheblimini," in Haynes, 182 (N III, 304, 39f.; *Jerusalem*, 93, is cited).

55. "Golgatha and Scheblimini," in Haynes, 182 (N III, 305, 5f.; *Jerusalem*, 126-27, is cited); compare further (ll. 6f.): "Jewish authority alone gives them the required evidence."

hearing of a word that must be uttered and "proclaimed in advance"[56] and thus is its author and source. It is "the sure prophetic word [2 Peter 1:19] within the most ancient documents of the human race and within the holy scriptures of genuine Judaism."[57]

> Hence the revealed religion of Christianity is called, rightfully and with reason, faith, trust, confidence, firm and childlike reliance on divine pledges and promises and on the majestic progress of its life unfolding itself in representations from glory to glory until the full uncovering and apocalypse of the mystery which was hidden and believed from the beginning in the fullness of beholding face to face.[58]

This proposition reveals Hamann's understanding of history with particular clarity. What was merely hinted at in the first, indirect statement respecting the object of the Fragments Dispute, that is, in the *Fragmente . . . über apokalyptische Mysterien,* is here powerfully developed in the second section of *Golgatha and Scheblimini,* in hand-to-hand battle with Mendelssohn.

As usually happens in research, one may term Hamann's understanding of history *"heilsgeschichtlich"* provided it is not connected with the idea of chronological constructions and arithmetic as practiced, for example, by Johann Albrecht Bengel. Hamann was averse to them, not in spite of but precisely in appeal to his apocalyptic hope. Hamann writes to Häfeli in 1781, "If his advent will be like a thief in the night: then neither political arithmetics nor prophetic chronologies can turn it into day."[59] This contradicts contemporaries who suppose they can escape the present twilight between creation and eschaton into the would-be clarity of a hope for better times attaching to a this-worldly history.

This chronological-critical word must be called to mind lest that bivalent definition of the truths of history be misunderstood that gives special shape to Hamann's understanding of history and stands out, not least in *Golgatha and Scheblimini* as well as in the *Fliegender Brief:*

56. "Golgatha and Scheblimini," in Haynes, 182 (N III, 305, 3f.).

57. "Golgatha and Scheblimini," in Haynes, 185 (N III, 306, 28-31).

58. "Golgatha and Scheblimini," in Haynes, 182-83 (N III, 305, 13-19) (cf. 2 Cor. 3:18 and 1 Cor. 13:12); *Jerusalem,* 100, is cited.

59. H IV, 315, 3-5 (to Haefeli; 1781).

Hamann speaks of "historical truths not only of past times but also of times to come."[60]

This concerns in the first place the enlightened Judaism of Mendelssohn, who "severs"[61] from "eternal truths and doctrines" and from "ceremonial and moral law" the "temporal truths of history"[62] and with this Wolffian conception of the law, of the Pentateuch, "likewise did not know, overlooked, and did not want to know about the Psalms and Prophets."[63] Whoever historicizes history rejects it as a collection of contingent and particular events that took place then and there, and in its place reveres allegedly universal, necessary, and eternal truths of reason; and along with what has happened, but has not passed away, loses the future, denies the prophetic, the "spirit of prophecy," which in Mendelssohn as with all the Wolffians is inseparably linked to the absolutized "spirit of observation." In the *Fliegender Brief* Hamann inquires, "What would the most exact, most meticulous knowledge of the present time be without a divine renewal of the past, without an intimation of the future . . . ? What kind of Labyrinth would the present time be for the spirit of observation without the spirit of prophecy and its guides from the past and future?"[64]

In a figure from the area of the sexual Hamann speaks of the "inseparable bond between the spirit of observation and prophecy,"[65] between the present on the one hand and the past and future on the other; Ecclesiastes 4:11 is explicitly cited: "If two lie together, they keep warm; but how can one keep warm alone?"[66] For Hamann, such figures are more than mere figures.[67] Life, everything living, communal, even the vital, experienced connection of time and space,[68] knowledge of them as all

60. "Golgatha and Scheblimini," in Haynes, 182 (N III, 305, 2) (translation altered).
61. "Golgatha and Scheblimini," in Haynes, 179 (N III, 304, 30-32); cf. *Jerusalem*, 126-27.
62. "Golgatha and Scheblimini," in Haynes, 182 (N III, 302, 35f.).
63. "Fliegender Brief," in N III, 385, 9f.
64. "Fliegender Brief," in N III, 398, 10-16.
65. "Fliegender Brief," line 5f.
66. Cf. "Fliegender Brief," line 10.
67. Cf. below chapter 11, "Essay of a Sybil on Marriage," note 13f.
68. Mendelssohn, "the Jewish worldly wise," was "not in position to make clear to himself the extraordinary fates of Jerusalem revealed in these documents or the temporal, historical truths of the holy city according to all seven dimensions of the past, present, future, length, breadth, height, and depth in all their coherence" ("Ein Fliegender Brief," N III, 385, 8.14-19). The entity "Jerusalem" can only be conceived as seven-dimensional, as a

knowledge roots in the sexual.[69] With this Hamann is probably going beyond the Bible he intends to interpret; yet the uncommon intensity in which he reflected on the difference between the sexes and their union is remarkable since at this point most Bible interpreters lag behind.

The Old Testament as the Historical A Priori of Knowledge

No doubt, Hamann gained his understanding of history and time chiefly and decisively in relationship with the Bible, an understanding that largely through Herder's mediation and reshaping helped produce the historical consciousness of the nineteenth and twentieth centuries. What is striking about this and was harshly offensive to his contemporaries is his high esteem for the Old Testament. Not least at this point Hamann was a contemporary in dissent. In his passionate objection to the art of separation plied by the Jewish and worldly-wise Moses Mendelssohn, which "severs . . . the temporal from the eternal"[70] and thus separates a living totality "into two dead halves,"[71] Hamann arrives at an impressive defense of the Old Testament as a book of history, not only of any sort of history book but of the book of history absolutely, of the historical, linguistic-sensuous a priori of all history. Instead of constructing a pure a priori of all knowledge, Hamann allows this historical a priori of all knowledge, of an all-encompassing perception of the world to be predetermined with the Old Testament. He allows it to be permanently predetermined, as he pithily expresses it in the following section of *Golgatha and Scheblimini* against Lessing's understanding of the Old Testament as an outdatable and outdated "primer." Once more the section is woven from shreds of Mendelssohn's *Jerusalem* into a sharp rejection of Mendelssohn: "However, if all human knowledge can be reduced to a few, fundamental concepts, and if the same sounds often occur in the spoken language as do the same images in different hieroglyphic tablets, though always in different combinations, by means of which they multiply their meaning; if this were true, then this observa-

---

spatial-temporal unity in which space and time are understood as *creatura verbi*, as creatures of the sure prophetic word.

69. "Schürze von Feigenblättern," in N III, 213, 7-13. According to Hamann's use of Ezekiel 1:27, God himself, the Creator, is concentrated in the sexual: N III, 207, 11f.

70. "Golgatha and Scheblimini," in Haynes, 179 (N III, 302, 35f.) (reversed).

71. Haynes, 179 (N 303, 7), in relationship to Haynes, 179-80 (N 302, 32–303, 31).

tion would also apply to history, and the entire range of human events and the whole course of their vicissitudes would be encompassed and divided into subsections just as the starry firmament is divided into figures, without knowing the stars' number — Hence the entire history of the Jewish people, by the allegory of their ceremonial law, appears to be a living, mind- and heart-rousing *primer of all historical literature in heaven, on and under the earth,* — an adamantine hint forward to the Jubilee year and a state-plan for divine rule over all creation from its beginning to its close. The prophetic riddle of a theocracy is reflected in the fragments of this smashed vessel. . . ."[72]

This unsurpassable and inexhaustible history of the promise of God to Israel and of the wreckage of the Jewish people is concentrated and totally fulfilled in the history of Jesus Christ, "in the ambiguous form of his person; his message of peace and joy, his travails and sorrow; his obedience unto death, even the death of the cross!; his being raised from the mortal dust of a worm to the throne of immovable majesty — toward the kingdom of heaven, which this David, Solomon, and Son of Man would plant and complete as a city which has foundations, whose builder and maker is God, as a Jerusalem above, which is free and mother of us all, as a new heaven and a new earth, without sea and without temple therein."[73]

In this Bible cento[74] that marks Hamann's language his understanding of history arrives at its zenith. If we tried to abstract from it a theory of history capable of being universalized, thus from the outset subject to the possible consensus of all, it would burst apart. The Jewish and Christian particularity that constitute this understanding of history remains an offense to this very day.[75] Whoever wants to transform it, as Hegel transforms the historical into the speculative Good Friday, annihilates it.

Hamann summarizes and indicates how *he* understands history in the collective singular, that is, solely as the present, past, and future his-

---

72. "Golgatha and Scheblimini," in Haynes, 191-92 (N III, 310, 36–311, 12); italics added (according to the original). Cf. *Lessing's Theological Writings,* 91 ("primer"; "hint"); the reference is to *Jerusalem,* 101, 109, 102; on Theocracy cf. 128f.

73. "Golgatha and Scheblimini," in Haynes, 193 (N III, 311, 27-36) (translation altered).

74. The references are to Isaiah 53:2; Isaiah 52:7; Isaiah 53:4; Philippians 2:8; Genesis 2:7; Psalm 22:7; Jeremiah 4:21 (17:12); Hebrews 11:10; Galatians 4:26; Revelation 21, 1:22.

75. Cf. "Golgatha and Scheblimini," in Haynes, 189 (N III, 309, 12: "the Jew nevertheless is still the authentic first nobleman of the entire human race."

tory of Jesus Christ, from which no one and nothing is excluded: "These historical truths, temporal and eternal, of the king of the Jews, the angel (messenger) of their covenant, the firstborn and head of his church, are the A and Ω, the foundation and the summit of our wings of faith. . . ."[76]

As much as Hamann makes precise and metacritical reference to Mendelssohn in *Golgatha and Scheblimini,* and from it this writing achieves its unmistakable character, we can no more overlook the fact that in it once more, as in all Hamann's other writings, the original motif of the journalist and writer appears as we learned to know it from the source, from the *Biblical Meditations,* the *Thoughts about My Life-Story,* and the other texts directly belonging to them from the life-changing event in London in 1758. What makes the uniqueness of the original motif of his life and work is that Hamann allows the themes of the metaphysical triple stars — God, world, and self — to be worked out and decided beforehand by way of a book, the "Book of God,"[77] the one book of the Old and New Testaments, in order to move freely in the exposition and application of Holy Scripture, once he has experienced it as a liberating authority empowering him for criticism.

This also gives us a look into the origin of Hamann's understanding of history. A signal passage in *Thoughts about My Life-Story* reads:

> I found the unity of the divine will in the redemption of Jesus Christ, so that all history, all miracles, all commands and works of God flowed towards this center, to stir the soul of man from the slavery, bondage, blindness, folly and death of sins to the greatest happiness, the highest blessedness and an acceptance of goods whose greatness, when revealed to us, must terrify us more than our own unworthiness or the possibility of making ourselves worthy of them. I recognized my own crimes in the history of the Jewish people, I read the course of my own life and thanked God for his longsuffering with this his people, since nothing but such an example could justify me in a like hope.[78]

---

76. "Golgatha and Scheblimini," in Haynes, 193 (N III, 309, 37-40) (translation altered); the references are to John 19:19; Malachi 3:1; Romans 8:29; Ephesians 1:22; Revelation 1:8; 1 Corinthians 3:11. Cf. "Zweifel und Einfälle," in N III, 192, 19-26; "Konxompax," in N III, 226, 20-25.

77. "Thoughts about My life," in Smith, 152 (N II, 40, 15).

78. "Thoughts about My life," in Smith, 152-53 (N II, 40, 18-29).

Hamann reads the Old Testament as a book of remembrance that becomes hope by the power of the Holy Spirit. It reminds of hope. Since from it are to be heard "historical truths, not only those of past times but also of times to come,"[79] the Bible is the primer by which one simply learns to spell "history." Therefore "the entire history of the Jewish people . . . is a living, mind- and heart-rousing *primer of all historical literature in heaven, on and under the earth,*"[80] thus of historical writing at all.

For history that does not directly occur in the Bible, or for nature that does not directly occur in it, this means that they are not excluded but first disclosed by the Bible. According to a graphic word in the *Socratic Memorabilia,* "the whole of history . . . like nature" is "a sealed book, a concealed witness, a riddle that cannot be solved, without plowing with another heifer than our reason."[81]

If the sphere of reason is perceived solely in terms of the "spirit of observation," separated from the "spirit of prophecy" and thus "one-eyed,"[82] if it is perceived as the circle of "the sciences, where hypotheses — systems — and observations are the first and last thing,"[83] then one understands Hamann's appeal to "another heifer." Here again Hamann shows himself to be a thoroughgoing, radical enlightener. He does not allow the other of reason, that is, sensuousness and feeling,[84] to be severed, but holds them together in the appropriate word, in language. Whoever shatters this marriage and merely with the heifer of analytic

79. "Golgatha and Scheblimini," in Haynes, 182 (N III, 305, 2f.) (cf. above note 60).

80. "Golgatha and Scheblimini," in Haynes, 192 (N III, 311, 4-8) (cf. above note 72). On "Primer" cf. K. Gründer, *Figur und Geschichte. Johann Georg Hamanns "Biblische Betrachtungen" als Ansatz einer Geschichtsphilosophie* (Freiburg: Alber, 1958), 160, note 3.

81. "Socratic Memorabilia," in Dickson, 383 (N II, 64, 10-13). Cf. "Biblische Betrachtungen," in N I, 148, 19f. ("nature" as a "sealed book"). Hamann takes his figure ("to plough with another heifer") from Judges 14:18. Cf. H. Veldhuis, *Ein versiegeltes Buch. Der Naturbegriff in der Theologie J. G. Hamanns (1730-1788)* (Berlin/New York: De Gruyter, 1994) (Theologische Bibliothek Toepelmann 65).

82. "Cloverleaf of Hellenistic Letters, Third Letter," in Haynes, 58 (N II, 183, 3) in relationship to (182, 16–183, 4). Cf. "Selbstgespräch eines Autors," in N III, 69, 20; 71, 15 (by contrast: 71, 21).

83. "Cloverleaf of Hellenistic Letters, Second Letter," in Haynes, 43 (N II, 175, 6-8). Cf. above Introduction, note 13.

84. Since the beginning of his authorship Hamann is concerned with communication between sensuousness and understanding, with a living whole, the "meeting" between ideas and perceptions ("Socratic Memorabilia," in Dickson, 379 [N II, 61, 28f.]; cf. "Socratic Memorabilia," in Dickson, 391 [N II, 73, 10-12]).

reason[85] wants to plow the field of history seeks "the art of living and ruling"[86] in a "historical skeleton,"[87] an "anatomical skeleton."[88] "The field of history," Hamann writes in the *Second Hellenistic Letter*, "seemed to me like that open field that was full of bones — and, lo, they were very dry. No one but a prophet can prophesy of these bones that sinews and flesh will be brought up upon them and skin will cover them. — Nor is any breath in them — until the prophet prophesies unto the wind and says the word of the Lord to the wind — ."[89]

We can only surmise from afar the explosive power of such Bible interpretation, such free converse with the given word for methodological, scientific-theoretical, and hermeneutical reflection, for that earnest quest of the relation between truth and method.[90] Hamann's understanding of history, his historical understanding of reason is castrated by historicism and is not even revived by dialectical theology, in any event, not by Bultmann's existential interpretation that repeats the chemistry of Reimarus and Mendelssohn. Otherwise, Bultmann would have had to write his *History and Eschatology* (1958) differently.

Impure Word and Pure Spirit

In conclusion, special emphasis should be given the chief element in Hamann's understanding of history and reason, his understanding of God the Holy Spirit, the *spiritus creator*. This element is indissolubly connected with a particular understanding of word and scripture, of sounds and letters, thus of a particular aesthetic and understanding of space and time, poetry and art, rhythm and the succession of figures, and can be set off in bold relief against Lessing's understanding.

The leading insight concerning word and Spirit in Lessing's *On the*

---

85. Cf. "Cloverleaf of Hellenistic Letters, Second Letter," in Haynes, 46 (N II, 176, 2), and "Ein fliegender Brief," in N III, 385, 33ff.

86. "Cloverleaf of Hellenistic Letters, Second Letter," in Haynes, 46 (N II, 176, 9f.).

87. "Cloverleaf of Hellenistic Letters, Second Letter," in Haynes, 46.

88. "Socratic Memorabilia," in Dickson, 391 (N II, 73, 12).

89. "Cloverleaf of Hellenistic Letters, Second Letter," in Haynes, 46 (N II, 176, 9f.) (translation altered).

90. Cf. my attempt to take up this passage of the Second Hellenistic Letter in Bayer, *Umstrittene Freiheit: Theologisch-philosophische Kontroversen* (UTB 1092) (Tübingen: J. C. B. Mohr [Paul Siebeck], 1981), 152-61 (form of communicative judgment), 159f.

Proof of Spirit and Power (Über den Beweis des Geistes und der Kraft)[91] is marked by the assumption of an immediacy that according to Hamann cannot even be conceived except as an illusion. According to Lessing this immediacy is seen in contrast to "mediation," to a "medium," which as such is given with "reports," but from what is reported of them, as Lessing states, "all force is removed."[92] For Lessing, the report of miracles, their narration, is precisely "*nothing* but reports of miracles,"[93] thus not the miracles themselves. Hamann avows the opposite: "That this word of God performs just as great miracles in the soul of a pious Christian, be he simple or learned, as the miracles that are recorded in it; that therefore the understanding of this book and its contents is to be attained only through the very same Spirit who impelled its authors. . . ."[94]

With Lessing and Hamann the understanding of *Spirit* is in dispute, and this always means the relation between word and Spirit. Hamann congenially repeats the insight and struggle of Luther against the fanatics, the spiritualists. Luther emphasized that when the Spirit comes in the freedom of God, he comes in no other way than through the bodily, oral, public, and external word, not unmediated. On the other hand, the Enlightenment was entirely possessed by the idea of the immediacy, unconditionality, and purity of the spirit of reason, a secularization of the old idea of the *verbum internum*, the internal word.

Far more acutely than Lessing, whom the problem of mediation and thus the history of reason occupied throughout, Immanuel Kant insisted on immediacy, on the unconditionality and purity of reason. What is not purely rational, but empirical and historical, is not worthy to be a criterion of truth, can never settle claims to validity. Kant's thesis awakens Hamann's passionate dissent: "*Pure reason* and *good will* are still words for me whose concept I am not in a position to arrive at with my senses, and for philosophy I have no *fidem implicitam*" (implicit faith).[95] "Still" means that the four years that have passed since the appearance of the *Critique of Pure Reason* and the two years since Kant's *Prolegomena* (1783) have not rendered the *fides implicita* super-

---

91. Cf. above note 29.

92. "On the Proof of Spirit and Power," in *Lessing's Theological Writings*, 4.

93. "On the Proof of Spirit and Power," 6.

94. "Thoughts about My Life," in Smith, 156 (N II, 43, 19-24).

95. H V, 434, 24-26 (to Scheffner; 1785), "implicit" faith: not one's own faith, but blind assent to authorities.

fluous, an attitude he does not at all intend to levy against philosophy. He wants to think altogether on his own, just to do in his own way what Kant required.

Hamann thought and judged on his own, not "purely" but "impurely," with explicit reference to the friend and opponent whom he "by chance" saw opposite him, Immanuel Kant. The contingency of this encounter was not merely ephemeral, but lifelong. Its high point is Hamann's metacriticism, his reexamination of Kant's *Critique of Pure Reason*.

The method in all Hamann's writings, in his speaking and thinking generally, is "metacritical" insofar as he judges only in a precise, reflected, and responsible relation to what is earlier said and thought, not in an allegedly pure relation to self that imagines it is without prejudice, independent of tradition, or in any case is so stylized as can be observed in classical form in Descartes. Thus, although Hamann's procedure, his "method," can generally be called "metacriticism" (in a wider sense) it is nonetheless instructive that Hamann first arrives at the term in the course of his dispute with Kant's *Critique of Pure Reason*. The term "metacriticism" occurs in Hamann, and thus for the first time in history, in a letter to Herder dated July 7, 1782.[96] The word is Hamann's own invention and ever since belongs to current philosophical vocabulary. In the total context of Hamann's letters and works its formation is not surprising, though he usually speaks of "re-reading," "re-mocking," and "re-enacting,"[97] always emphasizing the given text to which, however, he relates "critically," freely appropriating or reshaping it and thus always preserving the "critical dignity" of the *zoon politikon* (political creature).

Thus, a brief philological view of the origin and formation of the word "metacriticism" shows that in the narrower and narrowest sense Hamann's metacriticism, his reexamination of Kant's *Critique of Pure Reason*, is not an erratic fault line on the terrain of his life and thought.

Still, Hamann's metacriticism represents something new that would be incomprehensible without the radical challenge which the appearance of the *Critique of Pure Reason* signified. It can be compared to the challenge Erasmus presented to Luther. Just as Luther's answer in the *Bond-*

96. H IV, 400, 18 (to Herder; 1782).
97. H IV, 340, 35 (to Herder; 1781); "Ein fliegender Brief," in N III, 401, 27; "Wolken," in N II, 83.

age of the Will, his most important writing, would not have come about without Erasmus's *Discourse on Free Will*, so Hamann would not have written his *Metakritik* without Kant's *Critique of Pure Reason*. Kant's *Critique of Pure Reason* is not just any material at all for demonstrating what Hamann already knew and said.

With his *Metakritik* Hamann delves most intimately into Kant's thought; he does not simply judge from the outside. In one particular respect the *Metakritik* is thoroughly indebted to Kant. In its precise relation to Kant's formulations of the question it is a novum. But the leading viewpoint in the reference, briefly describable by the catchword *"communicatio idiomatum"*[98] (communication of properties), is not new. Its "application," however, does not at all occur without friction and further ado. As he complains to Herder, it gave Hamann many headaches: "My poor head is a broken pot against Kant's — clay against iron."[99]

For the *Critique of Pure Reason*, on behalf of which he served as mediator with the publisher Hartknoch in Riga, and which he had read already piecemeal in the galleys, Hamann sketched a review as early as July 1, 1781, and which even then, as all his reviews and writings, represents a metacriticism.[100] Hamann labors on, waits for Kant's proposed appearance of the *Prolegomena*, a writing intended to make the great work more intelligible. He will let Kant first "talk himself out,"[101] "before I come out with my Metacritique."[102] What he finally manages to produce, and at Herder's urging gives him in a copy dated September 15, 1784,[103] the *Metacriticism on the Purism of Reason (Metakritik über den Purismum der Vernunft)*, he himself thought had misfired.[104] It was only in 1800 that the text was published posthumously, and in a collective work titled *Several Things on the History of Metacritical Invasion (Mancherlei zur Geschichte der metakritischen Invasion)*, edited by Rink, a Kantian. This title, which according to Hamann Herder also used against Kant, shows how the term invented by Hamann has become common.

---

98. Cf. above chapter 1, "Life and Work," notes 48-49.

99. H V, 108, 4f. (to Herder; 1783).

100. "Kritik der reinen Vernunft," in N III, 275-80.

101. Cf. for example H IV, 333, 17 (to Hartknoch; 1781); 336, 34 (to Herder; 1781); 350, 29 (to Hartknoch; 1781).

102. H IV, 400, 18 (to Herder; 1782).

103. H V, 210, 17–216, 31 (to Herder; 1784).

104. H V, 217.

In the following chapter an attempt will be made to give a comprehensive description of the significance of this text, which together with *Golgatha and Scheblimini* Hegel described as Hamann's chief work.[105] It is concentrated in the following terse sentence, which in the context of his dispute with Kant's *Critique of Pure Reason* Hamann wrote to Herder on August 8, 1784: "Reason is language."[106]

105. *Hegel on Hamann*, 33-40.

106. HV, 177, 18. Cf. Oswald Bayer, *Vernunft ist Sprache: Hamanns Metakritik Kants* (Stuttgart: Frommann-Holzboog, 2002).

Chapter 9

Reason Is Language

(Hamann–Kant)

S ince Heraclitus and Plato, Western philosophy has been inquiring after the relationship between reason and language. For the most part,
it insists on the unity of reason and perceives the plurality of languages
as an unproductive vexation that must be overcome as soon as possible.
This dominant characteristic of philosophy in which the chief element in
its identification of its awareness of the problem is to be seen throughout the history of its changes, takes on a particular shape in the thinking
of modernity. It is characterized by a desire for purism. It intends to be
purified of all prejudices and thus from the contingency of traditional
language and history, so that language may not lead thought astray.
Reason's dominant desire for unity takes offense at the multiplicity of
languages and seeks to subvert their conflicts, perhaps by assuming the
meanings of words as established a priori, or by assuming a capacity for
language on the part of all humans as rational creatures as rigidly fixed
a priori. In fact, it is at work even in the assumption of a communicative
a priori, whose representatives fancy themselves hermeneutically enlightened, but with their transcendental-hermeneutical concept of language defer to reason's dominant desire for unity and are thus forced to
give an ultimate foundation.

Hamann offers an alternative to the usual handling of the problem.
His life's work lies in having worked through the problem of the relation
between reason and language, not only in its importance, but in its precise dissent toward the prevailing philosophical intent. But, he does not
claim he can solve it. At the end of his life he writes to Herder: "I am

gnawing on this marrowbone and will gnaw myself to death. For me it keeps getting darker and darker over the deep" [Gen. 1:2]. I am waiting for an apocalyptic angel with a key to this abyss [Rev. 20:1]."[1]

This is not an allegorical paraphrase of a conundrum that can be solved, but the attempt to speak of what can scarcely be conceived, that is, the primeval and apocalyptic dimension of the "eternal dispute over boundaries"[2] between reason and language. According to Hamann this dispute cannot be settled within history. It "will remain so long till languages cease with prophecy and knowledge."[3] Then "I will know fully, even as I have been fully known" (1 Cor. 13:12). Only then will "our knowledge" no longer be "in part," (1 Cor. 13:9f.), a fragment.

No philosophical orientation can renounce the eschatological or protological equation. For this reason Habermas allows his anticipation of the eschaton a social space that is free from domination to correspond to the a priori of reason he believes resides in language. And with Popper the openness that method demands with the affirmation of the falsification principle coheres with the quasi-religious anterior decision on behalf of critical rationality, an openness that can promise the relatively best outcome of human histories. The unavoidability of the question concerning the protological and eschatological and their correspondence does not, however, demand a specific answer. What is decisive about that answer is whether and how the desire for unity, metaphysical in substance and subject, has the upper hand in it.

In his critique of such a desire for unity Hamann includes even Rousseau's criticism of metaphysics. In the conjuring up of pure nature and the original, infallible sentience of the heart, in Lessing, for example, following Rousseau, the criterion of truth and portrayed in the figure of Recha in *Nathan*, he sees the failure to acknowledge sin, and in the *Biblical Meditations* engages such conjuring with irony: The story of the Tower of Babel (Gen. 11:1-9) tells of "an unprecedented unity among people, a unity which got its strength from the foolishness and evil thoughts of their hearts. For only in this are people by nature perfectly *equal* and *one*."[4]

If humans' natural perfectibility, their equality and unity, consists

---

1. H V, 177, 18-21 (to Herder; 1784).
2. Cf. below note 60.
3. Cf. below note 60. The reference is to 1 Corinthians 13:8f.
4. "Biblische Betrachtungen," in N I, 29, 36-39. Cf. the text cited in note 82.

in the "evil thoughts of their hearts,"[5] then the "preservation and governing of the world," directed toward its consummation through judgment and thus "toward a unity of humankind . . . toward a single language, toward the single true knowledge," can only be "a continuous miracle."[6]

Hamann can never marvel enough at it. For him it is a miracle to be called into life along with all creation, which even in sin can hear and answer on its own. To be united with everything through hearing and speaking means to be defined through the word. "Without word, no reason — no world. Here is the source of creation and government."[7]

Even if at present the unity of reason, as the unity of humans with their fellow creatures, not in a lie but in truth, can no more and not yet be perceived, it is nonetheless promised. However, contrasted with the promised unity of the hearing world,[8] the present world shut off from the word is all the more painfully felt; it "sighs [Rom. 8:22] and becomes silent."[9]

So it is clear: Hamann's celebrated axiom, "reason is language," affirms no timeless state of affairs that would be self-evident once expressed. It is a creation-theological and simultaneously eschatological axiom. The writer feels that he and his world are in contradiction and tension, the solution for which he waits. "Reason is language, Logos, on this marrowbone I am gnawing. . . ."[10]

Conflict of Languages

The one reason as the one language is a matter of faith in creation and expectation of the consummation of the world through judgment of the world. Hence, whoever would flee from the present conflict of the many reasons and languages and by reflection enter into or return to a univer-

---

5. "Biblische Betrachtungen," in N I, 29, 36-39.

6. "Biblische Betrachtungen," in N I, 31, 4-13.

7. H V, 95, 21f. (1783). Cf. "Biblische Betrachtungen," in N I, 322, 8f. (1785).

8. There is an uncommonly graphic and attractive reference to the hearing world, to reason truly aware as language in "The Last Will and Testament of the Knight of the Rose-Cross" (1772): Haynes, 107 (N III, 31, 27-32, 31), especially Haynes, 108 (32, 31-28). Cf. above chapter 6, "Criticism and Politics," notes 3-14.

9. Haynes, 107 (N III, 32, 18).

10. H V, 177, 18ff. (cf. above note 1).

sal language would be prey to an illusion. The scandal of the plurality and rivalry of languages and reasons cannot be avoided. Hamann faces up to it.

Since for us at present "nothing but Turbatverse" — scraps of original unity — remain,[11] no one can from the outset assume to be in agreement with the other. No one can speak with the other in anticipation of an ultimately successful understanding. Rather, there is only the hard work of translation. It is the *signum* of language after the Fall.

So Hamann's perception of the fallen world and its language is contained in the laconic sentence, "To speak is to translate."[12] The various languages and reasons are not systems that would harmoniously interplay, be variously joined or happily subordinated to each other. Hearing and understanding, speaking and being understood occur in the intersecting of various perspectives, in the rivalry of various prejudices, in the conflict of various languages.

In a letter to Jacobi, Hamann gives an impressive description of the task of translating given with the conflict of languages and inherent in hearing and reading. "No one can forbid your knowing that what others call reason is illusion. Just as no one can forbid your calling the disputed thing faith. In another philosophy, in another religion, another language is unavoidable, as are other ideas, other names for the same objects, which everyone describes from the viewpoint of his necessity or freedom. Since each works on the analysis of the other and on the synthesis of his own concepts, no constancy is possible from either side, but an interminable turning and unavoidable change."[13]

When assumed and dealt with, this conflict can have a productive effect and yield a gain for language. Hamann, however, refuses to expropriate this experience for the productivity of modern subjectivity and thus wring surreptitiously from necessity a virtue "of the dear I."[14] Hearing and reading as continual converse in translation with the natural and social world cannot simply be reshaped into the function of an individuality that opens itself to the other and strangers only in order to expand and enrich itself, thus in the understanding of the other always returns to the self and uses the variety of languages or reasons only to

11. "Aesthetica in nuce," in Haynes, 45 (N II, 198, 34f.).

12. "Aesthetica in Nuce," in Haynes, 66 (N II, 199, 4).

13. H VII, 175, 4-12 (to Jacobi; 1787).

14. "Zweifel und Einfälle," in N III, 179, 6; compare 180, 30-35 (". . . I, deified by abstraction as a universal reason . . .").

enjoy itself. Romanticism and Schleiermacher along with it misunderstood Hamann's hermeneutic.[15] The same is true of Hegel, for whom the contemplative Spirit is enriched by emptying into the other but in this emptying merely comes to itself, becomes aware of itself, "through sinking, being sunk in the other,"[16] and gains nothing but *itself*.

Hamann does not pursue total communication that functions noiselessly and smoothly in thought, but as if anticipating Levinas,[17] respects the unsurpassable strangeness of the other and his or her story. History's factor of resistance is not broken and resolved.[18] Rather, for the communication Hamann advocated, "the indissolubility of the distance and the contingency of participation is constitutive."[19] Thus what is decisive for him is "the most precise locality, individuality, and personality."[20] These cannot be tallied up in some mutual communication and exchange but only translated. The risk of such translating is not to be hedged against and mastered, for example, by the calculating assumption of a universal communicability as Kant had in mind.[21] Like Leibniz (in his program of a *mathesis universalis*) and his disciples to the time of the Vienna Circle, one may dream of a "universal character of philosophical language as already invented."[22] In such a dream one flees from the language characteristic of our present *condition humaine*.

This language exists only in a plurality of languages in competition with each other, so that arriving at understanding is not an obvious rule but always a miracle. In conflict the language existing only in plurality is

---

15. Stephan for example is of another opinion. He sees in Schleiermacher the perfecter of Hamann: H. Stephan, "Hamanns Christentum und Theologie. Eine Studie zur neueren Kirchengeschichte," in *Zeitschrift für Theologie und Kirche* 12, 1902, 345-427.

16. Hegel, *Die Absolute Religion*, ed. G. Lasson (Hamburg: Meiner, 1929, 1966), 81 (PhB 63).

17. Cf. especially E. Levinas, *Die Spur des Anderen. Untersuchungen zur Phänomenologie und Sozialphilosophie*, trans. and ed. W. N. Krewani (Freiburg: Verlag Karl Alber, 1983); Levinas, *Die Zeit und der Andere*, trans. L. Wenzler (Hamburg: Meiner, 1984).

18. Cf. above chapter 8, "History and Reason," note 9.

19. K. Gründer, "Erfahrung der Geschichte," in *Reflexion der Kontinuitäten. Zum Geschichtsdenken der letzten Jahrzehnte* (Göttingen: Vandenhoeck & Ruprecht, 1982), (118-36) 136.

20. "Ein fliegender Brief," in N III, 352, 25f.

21. Kant, *The Critique of Judgment*, trans. J. H. Bernard (New York: Hafner, 1951), § 39, 133-35. See below note 65.

22. H V, 216, 18f. (= Haynes, 217, "Metacritique of the Purism of Reason" [1784], in N III, 289, 9f.)

always a "tyrant" and a "sophist."[23] As sophist it deals in seductions and temptations. As tyrant it forces specific distinctions and divisions. By means of the prevailing language rules it is also violent. Thus Hamann's understanding of language and his definition of the relation between language and reason is without illusions.

What frees Hamann's understanding of language from illusion is the cross of Jesus Christ. It is for him the source of his critical contact with the conflict of languages and rationalities. The tyrant and sophist can be "disarmed by nothing than *mathemata pathemata,* suffering erudition, aesthetic obedience to the cross."[24]

This axiom contains an understanding of learning and experience whose significance cannot be overestimated.[25] It bursts the alternative which since Hegel's controversy with Kant (we are thinking particularly of Hegel's preface to his *Philosophy of Right,* 1821) not only characterizes the discussion between philosophy and theology, but to a great extent determines the historical and political climate, that is, the alternative of conceiving what is and realizing what is to be.

According to Hamann's axiom, neither by conceiving nor by protesting and postulating may we avoid the force and rigor of contentious reality in the conflict of the various languages and rationalities. The established philosophical, political, and theological language rules are not to be negated in the abstract. Nor can they be transcended nostalgically or by addiction to the future. But dealing with them in no way spells seamless appropriation or painless reproduction. It means avoiding flight from "the irksome cross of indication by experience,"[26] the painful acceptance and assimilation of the most everyday and resistant experiences. This brings a "learning" that is "just as little [mere] *invention* as mere *recollection,*" neither pure anamnesis nor pure construction.[27] This learning occurs in listening to the truth disclosed in a linguistic-historical way

---

23. "Zwei Scherflein," in N III, 234, 20f.; cf. note 24. On language as "seducer of our understanding": H VII, 173, 3-7 (to Jacobi; 1787).

24. "Zwei Scherflein," in N III, 234, 21-23.

25. For an explanation: Bayer, *Umstrittene Freiheit. Theologisch-philosophische Kontroversen* (UTB 1092) (Tübingen: J. C. B. Mohr [Paul Siebeck], 1981), 152-61 (communicative judgment), 154.

26. J. G. Hamann, Draft B to *Metakritik* (see above note 22), 1782 in Bayer, *Vernunft is Sprache,* 179, line 22.

27. "Philological Ideas and Doubt," in Haynes 118 (N III, 41, 10-12). Cf. above chapter 5, "Freedom as a Fundamental Concept of Anthropology," note 55ff.

in which one engages the history of nature and humanity and in doing so suffers. Thus "in experience" the explosive point is "the dear cross."[28]

In his *Letzten Blatt* Hamann relates knowing and doing, metaphysics and morals to suffering as their criterion.[29] This makes it possible to question the right and extent of the current distinction between knowing and doing as well as to revise the usual opposition between *passio* and *actio*. This revision and with it the indissoluble connection between suffering and acting, receiving and passing on, hearing and speaking, is to be kept in mind as we proceed to lift out the concepts of "action" and "author" so decisive for Hamann's understanding of reason and language.

Translation as Action

"For me, what Demosthenes says of *actio* is language, not as a work of memory but as a mathematic, as a true art of thinking and acting or of communicating, understanding and interpreting others."[30] Hamann writes this axiom succinctly, indicating his understanding of *"mathesis universalis"* in a context involving pedagogical association with children and thus a paradigmatic situation of hearing and speaking as the arduous labor of translation. *Fünf Hirtenbriefe das Schuldrama betreffend (The Five Pastoral Letters Concerning School Drama)* (1763)[31] relate to this situation: "Answering children is in fact a rigorous examination; and to sound out and to sharpen their minds by questioning is a masterstroke."[32] For this, one must "either have the help of actions or know how to invent questions."[33] In any case the translation of one's own language into that of children consists in "descending to their weakness; becoming their servant when one wants to be their master; following them

---

28. "Leser und Kunstrichter," in N II, 347, 28.

29. Cf. Bayer and Christian Knudsen, *Kreuz und Kritik, Johann Georg Hamanns Letztes Blatt. Text und Interpretation* (Tübingen: J. C. B. Mohr, 1983), 110f. In the context of the entire section (100-114: "Offenbarung und Passion"), of the interpretation of the third section of *Letztes Blatt*, and further: H VI, 534, 10-22 (to Jacobi; 1786). Cf. H VII, 158, 16f. (to Jacobi: 1787).

30. H V, 25, 17-19 (to Lindner; 1783). Cf. "Fünf Hirtenbriefe," in N II, 358, 26 (dead memory work) in the context of N II, 358f.

31. "Fünf Hirtenbriefe," in N II, 351-74.

32. "Fünf Hirtenbriefe," in N II, 358, 36–359, 2.

33. "Fünf Hirtenbriefe," in N II, 358, 35f. Here "or" does not denote an alternative. The questions are actions and answered by actions. Cf. ZH I, 330, 5 10 (to Lindner; 1759).

when one wants to rule them; learning their language and soul, when we want to induce them to imitate ours."[34] In doing so we show ourselves "a match for the God of love who never ceases to be a child, though his small arm does great wonders."[35]

In dramaturgy Hamann sees not only a key to didactic,[36] but construes "all human life expressions including learning and teaching as in essence actions."[37] He thus takes up the experience of the rhetor Demosthenes, whom an actor told what actual importance in speaking belongs to the "presentation" *(hypokrisis), and* the *"actio,"* the "action."[38] This experience already prefigures the mixture of genres that marked Hamann's understanding of language, as well as of reason![39] He was supported in this understanding by Johann Jakob Engel's *Über Handlung, Gespräch und Erzählung (On Activity, Conversation, and Narration)* (1774).[40] "Action," at home in drama first of all, is also "the soul of eloquence" as well as of the "manner of writing."[41] At any rate it is the moving force of the author Hamann, "who loves action"[42] and eagerly spoke of his "actions as an author."[43]

---

34. "Fünf Hirtenbriefe," in N II, 373, 12-16. Cf. 363, 10-14 and 364, 7-11 (to Lindner; 1759).

35. "Fünf Hirtenbriefe," in N II, 362, 33-35 (God is man. This is an eternal definition, the everlasting temporal definition of the eternal). Compare "Gedanken über meinen Lebenslauf," in N II, 14, 15-28 and below note 88.

36. Cf. G. Hausmann, *Didaktik als Dramaturgie des Unterrichts* (Anthropologie und Erziehung), ed. O. F. Bollnow and others (Heidelberg: Quelle u. Meyer, 1959), vol. 2.

37. Hausmann, *Didaktik als Dramaturgie des Unterrichts,* 70.

38. Cf. F. Blass, *Die attische Beredsamkeit* (II, 1: Demosthenes) (Leipzig: B. G. Teubner, 1877), 21f. Further: A. Schaefer, *Demosthenes und seine Zeit,* vol. 1, 1856, 297f.

39. Cf. already the foreword to the "Kreuzzüge des Philologen" (1762): below note 41 and 42.

40. The first version (1774) appeared in the *Neue Bibliothek der schönen Wissenschaften und der freien Künste.* In 1964 E. T. Voss published a facsimile edition in the Metzler collection and furnished it with an epilog.

41. "Kreuzzüge des Philologen," in N II, 116, 17f. The Greek equivalent of "action" is expressly noted on line 36.

42. "Kreuzzüge des Philologen," in N II, 116, 18f.

43. Cf. the text of "Fliegender Brief," indicated in note 70 below. The correspondence aside, in this (incomplete) writing Hamann speaks most often of his "authorship" (references: N VI, 41, cf. the term "Autorschaft"). On "author" and "action" R. Unger offers rich material in *Hamann und die Auflärung. Studien zur Vorgeschichte des romantischen Geistes im 18. Jahrhundert* (cf. above Introduction, note 18) (Tübingen: Max Niemeyer Verlag, 1968), 537-41.

An "author filled with action"[44] shows in a particularly plastic way what constitutes every person in relation to the world and self, in fact, in relation to God, if as Martin Luther holds that God "deals" with the person in the word, and the person "deals" with God in faith.[45] Hamann's concept of "action," neighbor to the understanding of "action"[46] developed by Max Weber, in substance validated by and in its essential features given material validity by Arnold Gehlen,[47] contains a fundamental anthropological understanding of reality as an ambivalent process of communication. It can be briefly explained as Hamann does by merely drawing out the meanings of a single Greek word, the verb *hypokrinesthai.* With the gift of freedom the person responds to a question containing a challenge by judging and interpreting the address that is heard. This responsive *actio* of the person as speaker is at the same time a mimic representation, the action of an actor, a thespian who plays a role, with which the person must not be identical but can be distanced and for this reason "feigns" it. The concept of *hypokrisis* allows Hamann to offer the basic fundamental anthropological description reported above and by assuming it, to perceive poetry and rhetoric, aesthetics and logic, natural science and politics in their context.

Thinking is also defined from the perspective of language as action. Accordingly, in opposition to Idealism Hamann emphasizes in an exaggeration that our "powers of thinking . . . taken altogether make up the most contingent and abstract modes of our existence."[48] Hamann thus arrives at the insight "that all our philosophy consists more of language than of reason."[49] "For me the question is not so much, what is reason?

44. "Hamburgische Nachricht [1763]," in N II, 255, (17-25) 20. Livy is meant as the "author filled with action [*handlungsvoller Schriftsteller*]": *Historiarum ab urbe condita libri* . . . , I, 54. Compare below note 71.

45. LW 36, 42 (WA 6, 516, 30-32).

46. For Weber it is the task "of sociology (and the sciences of action as such): clearly to interpret actions directed at meaning" (M. Weber, *Soziologische Grundbegriffe* [special edition by M. Weber, *Wirtschaft u. Gesellschaft,* 5th revised addition, furnished by J. Winkelmann, Tübingen: Mohr, 1976, 1-30], UTB 541, 1978, [9-33: § 1: "Begriff der Soziologie und des 'Sinns' sozialen Handelns"] 13f.). The difference between the idea of "action" in Weber and Hamann can be shown from the category of "meaning."

47. Gehlen, *Man: His Nature and Place in the World* (see above chapter 5, "Freedom as the Fundamental Concept of Anthropology," note 11).

48. "Zweifel und Einfälle," in N III, 191, 32-34. Cf. H VI, 27, 30 (to Auerswald; 1785): "the heart beats earlier than our head thinks").

49. H V, 272, 5f. In the context of 3-18 (to Jacobi; 1784).

but rather what is language? And here I am assuming the basis of all paralogisms and antinomies with which one burdens it."[50] The question that Kant relegates to the margin, "How is the faculty of thought itself possible?"[51] Hamann makes the chief question[52] and seeks its answer in language; "the entire faculty of thought rests on language."[53] As though in a somersault he alters Kant's transcendental question concerning what is possible and lets it return to what is linguistically actual, not least in the demonstration of Kant's actual dependence on language. "Without language we would have no reason, without reason no religion, and without these three essential components of our nature neither intelligence nor social bond."[54]

Kant fails to recognize this. He thinks of pure reason as timeless and eternal, as some see the laws discovered by Galileo and Newton "transfigured into eternal laws of nature," rather than taking them as "the impromptus" of human language, as improvisations, ideas, as human actions of inventive response.[55] Kant fails to recognize that he himself is an author and acts. Hamann's *Metakritik* of the transcendental critique of reason as oblivious to language states, in "mimic style,"[56] that Kant's relation to Leibniz and Locke, Plato and Hume is a historical action. The *Critique of Pure Reason* is not pure at all; it has a "pedigree,"[57] which though unwilling betrays it. "This much is certain that without Berkeley there would have been no Hume, just as without Hume no Kant. Yet finally everything comes down to tradition just as all abstraction comes down to sensuous impressions."[58] Hamann could see Kant only as a historical author dependent on tradition, experience, and language, who

---

50. H V, 264, 34-36 (cf. the continuation to Jacobi; 1784). Cf. H V, 213, 24-28 (= "Metacritique of the Purism of Reason," in Haynes, 211 [N II, 286, 9-13]: "but language is also the center point of reason's misunderstanding with itself. . . ." Hamann is citing *The Critique of Pure Reason* A XII metacritically.

51. Kant, *Critique of Pure Reason*, A XVII, p. 12.

52. Note the striking shift in the comparison between HV, 213, 18-20 and the *Critique of Pure Reason*, A xvii, p. 12.

53. H V, 213, (18-28) 22f. (= Metacritique of the Purism of Reason in Haynes, 211 [N III, 286, [1-13] 6f.)

54. "Zwei Scherflein," in N III, 231, 10-12.

55. "Zwei Scherflein," in N III, 240, 1-3. Cf. above chapter 4, "The Modern Concept of Nature in Crisis," note 5.

56. ZH I, 378, 24 (to Kant; 1759).

57. "New Apology of the Letter h," in Haynes, 163 (N III, 107, 6).

58. H IV, 376, 16-19 (to Herder; 1782).

writes what he has read and thereby shows how he, Kant himself, not, say, reason absolutely, has read, heard, and judged. Kant's own thought as free response is *one* of the histories of reason. But the historical actions of reason are the critique of its purity.[59]

Language is not only the *"organon"* but also the *"kriterion* of reason."* Thus, for a critique of reason as critique of language there is nothing left but to wash dirty glasses with a filthy towel in dirty water. "What Demosthenes calls *action*, Engel calls mimic, and Batteux calls imitation of beautiful nature is *language* for me — the *organon* and *kriterion* of reason, as Young says. Here lies *pure reason* and at the same time its *critique* — and the eternal boundary disputes will endure till languages together with prophesies and knowledge cease."[60]

In the present conflict of languages and rationalities there is no frictionless arrangement marking the traffic in money and wares. Interested very early in economic questions,[61] Hamann is thinking of the communication established by the word, not least in its relation to the circulation of money.[62] The "exchange of words" on which the "wealth of all human knowledge rests,"[63] is however in certain respects comparable to the exchange of money,[64] not, however, in its limitless communicability or capacity for transfer without noise and further ado. Rather, in the arduous labor of translating I encounter resistances and cannot simply raise myself above them so that in the illusion of unhindered, universal communicability I can, as it were, painlessly think in place of another[65] and form a concept of reason that the other must always be able to share and be able to agree.[66] The impossibility of a universal and perfect communication and mediation applies particularly to the exchange of words between the justi-

---

59. Cf. Oswald Bayer, *Vernunft ist Sprache: Hamanns Metakritik Kants* (Stuttgart: Frommann-Holzboog, 2002), 21-62: "The Histories of Reason Are the Critique of Its Purity."

60. H V, 359, 37-360, 4 (to Scheffner; 1785).

61. Cf. the "Beilage zu Dangeuil's Anmerkungen . . . ," in N IV, 225-42; 1756.

62. Cf. "Das Triumvirat," in N IV, 460, 39–461, 4 ("not in great sacks of current small change").

63. "Word Order in the French Language," in Haynes, 22 (N II, 129, 5f.). Cf. "Aesthetica in nuce," in Haynes, 63 (N II, 197, 14) ("exchange of words").

64. "Word Order in the French Language," in Haynes, 22 (N II, 129, 5f.).

65. Cf. Kant, *Kritik der Urteilskraft* (Hamburg: F. Meiner, 1963), §40 ("to think in place of everyone else"), and above note 21.

66. On the debate with Habermas cf. my description of the "form of communicative judgment" in Bayer, *Umstrittene Freiheit*, 153f.

fying God and the sinful human, for the communication of faith. It is "not communicable like a ware but the kingdom of heaven and hell in us."[67]

If theories of communication and mediation current in the modern era do not connect with Hamann's understanding of language and reason, and if communication does not occur in that soundless and unresisting medium as is suggested by the metaphor of the mirror dominant since antiquity, then we must all the more take note of Hamann's specific understanding of language as action. This understanding distinguishes him from behaviorism[68] as well as dialogue-ism.[69] "Every action apart from its original, natural, material, and mechanical description is still capable of all kinds of figurative, formal, tropic, and typical meanings which can no more be peeped at and tasted than the intentions and dispositions of the actor, but like all intellectual and moral impressions without sensuous expression are amenable to neither mediation nor reproduction. Consequently an author's intentions and dispositions must typify his actions as author, must be revealed through the clothing and expression of his ideas or at least betray them."[70]

In a few instances, though altered, Hamann's concept of "action" has entered Kierkegaard's "indirect communication."[71] If according to

67. H VII, 176, 7f. (to Jacobi; 1787).

68. In the following quotation we should especially note that the "intentions and dispositions" of the one who acts cannot "be peeped at and tasted." At the same time the element of truth in the "sensuous expression," absolutized in behaviorism and constitutive for action, is effective.

69. Rightly, Buber does not begin his sketch "Zur Geschichte des dialogischen Prinzips" with Hamann but with Jacobi. Cf. *Das dialogische Prinzip* (Heidelberg: L. Schneider, 1979). On the other hand, Ferdinand Ebner appeals to Hamann (*Das Wort und die geistigen Realitäten. Pneumatologische Fragmente* [1921] (Vienna: Herder Verlag, 1980), 16, 18, 20, 27-29, 31, 56f., 60, 78f., 84f.) — incorrectly as the following sentence indicates: "Man must turn his eyes away from the world, then it will no longer block his sight of God" (ibid., 213 in the context of 213f.). Kierkegaard represents this idea, but not Hamann. Kierkegaard practices Christianity by repelling the sensuous, Hamann on the other hand by retrieving it and allowing it to be disclosed by the language of the Bible, especially by that of the Old Testament.

70. "Fünf Hirtenbriefe. Fünfter Brief," in N III, 366, 5-14. Cf. "Biblische Betrachtungen," in N I, 128, 18-29.

71. Hamann's heritage is clearly shown for example in the motto Kierkegaard chooses for *Fear and Trembling*: "What Tarquinius Superbus spoke in his garden with the poppies was understood by his son, but not by the messenger." Cf. ZH II, 195, 11-13 (to Nicolai; 1763); what is characteristic is that Hamann replaces "deed" with "speech": ll. 12f. and ZH II, 202, 31f. (to Lindner; 1763). The story handed on by Livy (cf. above note 44) might also be in "Socratic Memorabilia," in Dickson, 379 (N II, 61, 5-9).

Kierkegaard the indirect communication of existence is within a context in which "suffering . . . will hinder you from sneaking out into the world again,"[72] and if this means communication is in essence negatively defined by the world, that is, by its negation, by "de-secularization." Then according to Hamann's understanding, "action" perceives the world in an altogether positive way, nevertheless in learning through suffering. Indeed, action is itself worldly, that is, historical and sensuous in the indissoluble connection of "traditions" and "experiences."[73]

In terms of such language as action and of action as language[74] and of our life as "a series of symbolic actions,"[75] that exchange of words[76] does not denote a dialogue apart from the world and history on the part of an I and Thou free of the It of nature and culture. On the contrary, it is worldly. It discloses and shapes the world. One's own life history is not only reflected in it but is first and foremost in it, is formed in it, and experiences its unity in it. This unity is not that of an individual rational substance or of a rational subject that would accidentally have a history. There is no I beneath my life's history which I myself would be. The fact that the human does not dissolve into continually changing shapes and relations, that in the changes continuity rules without one's having the power to integrate one's changes on one's own, results from the fact that God is the author of my life history as well as of all world history.[77]

God, the Poet

Titling God as "author," as "poet,"[78] himself "the best interpreter of his own words,"[79] his actions, and their ultimate critic ("arbiter"),[80] Ha-

72. S. Kierkegaard, *Erbauliche Reden in Verschiedenem Geist,* trans. Hayo Gerdes (Düsseldorf/Köln: Eugen Diederichs Verlag, 1951), 273.

73. Cf. especially "Philological Ideas and Doubt," in Haynes 117 (N III, 39, 25-40, 15). Cf. above chapter 6, "Criticism and Politics," note 43.

74. On the subject matter, cf. also O. Bayer, *Living by Faith: Justification and Sanctification,* trans. Geoffrey Bromiley (Grand Rapids: Eerdmans, 2003), 45-47 ("deed as word" — "word as deed").

75. "The Wise Men from the East," in Smith, 191 (N II, 139, 25-29).

76. Cf. above note 63.

77. Cf. above chapter 3, "Original Motif," notes 20, 33-44.

78. "Aesthetica in nuce," in Haynes 78 (N II, 206, 20f.) The Poet as "powerful speaker," "Aesthetica in nuce," in Haynes 67 (200, 7) (with Ps. 33:9). Cf. N I, 5.1 "God an author."

79. "Aesthetica in nuce," in Haynes, 74 (204.1).

80. "Fünf Hirtenbriefe," in N II, 368, 9f. Cf. note 78 (identity of the creator and judge).

mann's understanding of language and reason characteristically reaches its peak. Whoever wants to label it may describe it as an ontological hermeneutic or hermeneutical ontology. In any event Hamann seeks to answer the question of Being with a theology and philosophy of *language* effective as action in translation. He writes to Jacobi, "What is *Being* in your language I would rather call the *Word*."[81]

"Word" more clearly denotes the true universal community of communication, the community of justified sinners amidst their fellow creatures, as well as the authority creating this community. The word is the power "to unite Moses [Gen. 1:1] and John [John 1:1], Christianity and Judaism, the living and the dead, to make those who run wild and are socially scattered of one mind through the Spirit's dove-like simplicity, without tyrannical fetters, and to make commun[al] sinners brothers of the same mind. If you assume or believe a blind-eyed and hard of hearing public, then one must not seek to propagate the faith with arguments or rational discourse. . . ."[82]

If one wants to speak of Being at all, then only in such a way that God is meant to be a word of communication, as the truth communicating itself unmeritedly. In his controversy with Jacobi, Hamann writes that "original Being is truth; communicated Being is grace."[83] The original Being, the truth, is nothing but the name for God. Another Archimedean point "I neither recognize or know [other than] his word, his oath, and his *I am — and will be*, wherein consists the entire majesty of his old and new name."[84]

By virtue of his name God the author communicates with humans together with all creatures and in such communication performs the arduous labor of translating. In doing so he does not avoid making his way totally into the world, becoming man, and dying on the cross. In his pride the author is humble. In his omnipotence he descends in love to our weakness to address the creature through the creature. God is the Poet who speaks in the *genus humile*.[85]

---

81. H VII, 175, 17f. (to Jacobi; 1787). The text designated in note 13 preceded.
82. H VII, lines 18-26. On the unity of language, cf. H VII, 158, 5-10 (to Jacobi; 1787).
83. H V, 271, 28f. (to Jacobi; 1784).
84. H V, 333, 18-20 (to Jacobi; 1785). Cf. H VII, 427, 17f. (to Jacobi; 1787).
85. Besides the texts noted in notes 35 and 78: "Über die Auslegung der Heiligen Schrift," in N I, 5; 91, 7-17 (as well as in "Gedanken über meinen Lebenslauf," N II, 43, 28-40, especially 36-40; N I, 99, 24–100, 19). "The heathen, the philosopher recognizes the om-

In terms of the condescension of the triune God everything divine is human and everything human divine.[86] So reads Hamann's "final judgment on the divine and human origin of language"[87]: "This *communicatio* of the divine and human *idiomatum* (communication of properties) is a basic law and the main key to all our knowledge and all visible economy."[88]

This does not mean that for us the world and history would have been transparent and the problem of the relation between reason and language solved. But it means that the promised and awaited solution to the problem as the consummation of the world through judgment is the final, eternally new action in language of the human God. The unity of language and reason is therefore in the strict sense a matter of faith.

---

nipotence, the majesty, the holiness, the goodness of God; but knows nothing of the humility of his love for humankind" (ZH I, 394, 16-18; to Lindner; 1759).

86. Cf. especially "Last Will and Testament of the Knight of the Rose-Cross," in Haynes, 99 (N III, 27, 3-17). "As therefore a human assumes the throne of heaven and its majesty, so human language is the language of the court . . . in the Fatherland of the Christian!" (ZH I, 394, 3-6; to Lindner; 1759).

87. Addressed by the title of the writing ("Last Will and Testament . . . ," N III, 25-33) cited especially in "Criticism and Politics" (cf. also note 8).

88. "The Last Will and Testament of the Knight of the Rose-Cross," in Haynes, 99 (N III, 27, 11-14) (translation altered).

Chapter 10

Natural Right and Social Life

(Mendelssohn and Hamann)

In the first part of *Golgatha and Scheblimini* Hamann engages in dispute with Mendelssohn over the philosophy of right, to which he refers in the first section of *Jerusalem oder über religiöse Macht und Judentum (Jerusalem or On Religious Power)* (1783). In his extensive review of Hamann's writings Hegel recognized the significance of this dispute, and together with Hamann's *Metakritik* of Kant specifically singled out both pieces as the twin peaks of Hamann's authorship.[1] This is understandable. Hamann's criticism, in which he attacks Mendelssohn's dualism of "convictions" and "actions" and insists on their constitutive interrelation, anticipates Hegel's criticism of Kant, which in essence involves the nullifying of the dualism between morality and legality.

Just as in Kant, Hamann sees in Mendelssohn an "artist of divorce" ("chemist"), whose abstract separations he seeks to overcome by means of the Christological figure of the communication of properties *(Idiomenkommunikation)* as the "master-key of all our knowledge."[2] His controversy with Mendelssohn over the philosophy of right reaches its height in the question of the understanding of "natural right" and "social contract." Hamann metacritically enters Mendelssohn's distinctions and in this way accents a concept of "nature" from the perspective of a theology of creation.

Because Hamann appeals to the Old Testament for this purpose, and

1. Cf. above chapter 8, "History and Reason," note 105.
2. "The Last Will and Testament of the Knight of the Rose-Cross," in Haynes, 99 (N III, 27, 13); cf. above chapter 6, "Criticism and Politics," note 11.

especially to the biblical primeval history and its parallels such as in Psalm 33, the dispute is not only over problems relating to the constitution of modern subjectivity and sociality but also to the treatment of the Bible, the sensuousness and historicality of which the metacritical Christian sees as disappearing from the enlightened Jew. The attraction and volatility of the dispute lie not least in the question as to how the Bible can be claimed for fundamental anthropological insights that go towards shaping a political ethics. The thematic of this chapter is thus joined to the presentation of freedom as a basic anthropological concept.

For Hamann the sphere of right is in essence defined from the context of hearing and speaking, more particularly of assuring, of a promise given and the trust placed in it. Originally and beyond circumvention, not only social life but the entire context of nature as creation rests on "fidelity and faith." Thus, not least there must be spoken of a right of fellow creatures and of the human as the "trustee of nature," as is the case with Hamann. The idea of a contract with nature[3] passing itself off as totally new today was obvious to Hamann on the basis of his Bible exposition. It coheres with his diagnosis of the ecological crisis, which in its severity, as shown by the word about the creature as "a sacrifice and idol,"[4] has not yet been surpassed.

First, in what follows Hamann's dispute with Mendelssohn over the philosophy of right in *Golgatha and Scheblimini* will be presented. This will bring to view the most important text in Hamann's corpus on the problematic of institutions, which assumes and takes up the fundamental anthropological insights of the *Philologische Einfälle und Zweifel (Philological Ideas and Doubts).*[5] In the next chapter we can then learn Hamann's view of the problematic of institutions by way of the marriage example. Sexuality and marriage are not an arbitrary example of the problematic. Together with work and the institution of language and cult that embrace, penetrate, and establish them, they are the three basic conditions that Luther calls "estates" and to which the antitheses of the Sermon on the Mount refer.[6]

3. K. M. Meyer-Abich, ed., *Frieden mit der Natur* (Freiburg im Breisgau: Herder, 1979), especially 123-26.

4. Cf. above chapter 4, "The Modern Concept of Nature in Crisis," note 58ff.

5. Cf. above chapter 5, "Freedom as a Fundamental Concept of Anthropology," note 45ff.

6. Cf. O. Bayer, "Zukunft und Schöpfung," in *Schöpfung als Anrede* (Tübingen: J. C. B. Mohr [Paul Siebeck], 1986), 143; cf. above chapter 2, "Style and Form," note 64.

Claimant of Right or Trustee of Nature

Once more in cento style, Hamann responds to Mendelssohn's *Jerusalem*. According to Hamann's own testimony, *Golgatha and Scheblimini* is a "muse-like writing," a mosaic, "pieced together only from passages of Mendelssohn's Jerusalem."[7] For Hamann this style makes possible proceeding metacritically, in a "metaschematism." He is concerned "that the author be compared only with himself and to no standard other than the one which he himself professes."[8] He will not argue with viewpoints added to Mendelssohn's text from elsewhere but will defeat his opponent with his own weapons, or more appropriately, win him with his own arguments.

At the outset let us note the result of the dispute. It is indicated in titling the human as a "trustee of nature." Just as at the end of the same year (1784) Hamann dealt metacritically with Kant's discourse concerning self-inflicted *immaturity,* and uncovered his self-inflicted *guardianship,*[9] so in *Golgatha and Scheblimini* he opposes the one responsible for nature to the one who lays claim to it.[10] In a surprising turn of thought he takes seriously Mendelssohn's reference to the "laws of wisdom and goodness"[11] in which, as Hamann appropriately remarks,[12] he follows Leibniz.[13] From it Hamann draws a consequence from which he radically questions the individualism of possession dominating Mendelssohn's theory of right. If Mendelssohn had emphasized, "To me, and to me alone, appertains the right to decide whether, to what extent, when, for whose benefit, and under what conditions I am obliged to exercise

7. "Golgatha and Scheblimini," in N III, 319, 1f.; cf. above chapter 1, "Life and Work," note 47.

8. "Golgatha and Scheblimini," in N III, 165 (N III, 293, 19-21).

9. Cf. above chapter 7, "What Is Enlightenment?," especially notes 25-29.

10. "Golgatha and Scheblimini," in Haynes, 173 (N III, 299, 15). Here Hamann has Mendelssohn's theoretical foundation in view: "Since to explain his rudiments the theorist needs two races, the one holding right and the trustee." Cf. "Golgatha and Scheblimini," in Haynes, 168 (N III, 294, 40–295, 1) (translation altered).

11. Mendelssohn, *Jerusalem,* 46 and 50.

12. "Golgatha and Scheblimini," in Haynes, 170 (N III, 296, 30f.) and Haynes, 171 (N III, 297, 11).

13. Leibniz had defined: "*bonitas . . . cum Sapietia conjuncta Justitiam constituit*" ("goodness . . . joined to wisdom constitutes justice") (G. W. Leibniz, *Causa Dei Asserta per Justitiam Ejus, Cum caeteris ejus Perfectionibus, Cunctisque Actionibus Conciliatam* [Amstaeladami: apud Isacum Trojel, 1710], 50).

beneficence,"[14] then Hamann opposes such claimant to right with the human as "trustee." He contradicts Mendelssohn by Mendelssohn: "Not to him, not to him alone, is the moral capacity to make use of things as a means subordinated, but rather to those laws of wisdom and goodness which light our way in the immense kingdom of nature."[15]

This has made us initially aware of the explosive point of the dispute. In Hamann's judgment Mendelssohn shares that orientation, which, in view of the period between Hobbes and Locke, Macpherson has described as the "individualism of possession."[16]

Before we draw nearer to the explosive point of the dispute denoted by the title "claimant of right or trustee of nature" and just briefly explained, we shall take a step back to ask whether by making this point Hamann actually arrived at the intention of Mendelssohn's *Jerusalem or On Religious Power and Judaism*. Did Hamann see that Mendelssohn wanted to justify and explain his decided opposition to the "religious power," that is, to the church's or synagogue's bann,[17] that with borrowing from theories of contemporary enlightenment ecclesiastical law, and thus with taking up territorialistic but chiefly collegialistic ideas, he in no way betrayed his Judaism?[18] Did Hamann ever see what Mendelssohn was advocating in the context of painful modern history within the tension between "state and religion,"[19] that is, "liberty of conscience"?[20] It is enough for the moment to have thrown out these questions. Finally, we will be able to return to them and assert that though scarcely seen at first glance, Hamann enters into them with a will.

14. *Jerusalem*, 48; compare additionally Haynes, 174 (N III, 300, 2-4) and further Haynes, 196 (313, 26ff.).

15. "Golgatha and Scheblimini," in Haynes, 174 (N III, 299, 21-24).

16. C. B. Macpherson, *The Political Theory of Possessive Individualism: From Hobbes to Locke* (Oxford: Oxford University Press, 1962).

17. *Jerusalem*, 73-75.

18. Cf. M. Heckel, "Territorialsystem," in *Evangelisches Staatslexikon* (Stuttgart: Kreuz Verlag, ³1987), Sp. 2626-28; K. Schlaich, "Kollegialismus," in *Evangelisches Staatslexikon*, Sp. 1327-30. In addition the introduction by Altmann in JubA8, xxxvf.

19. Cf. Mendelssohn's insertion in *Jerusalem*, 33.

20. *Jerusalem*, 33.

Nature and Society

Hamann sets the lever of his immanent criticism at that excursus in *Jerusalem* where Mendelssohn, to arrive at the moot point of the relation between state and religion, discusses "the first fundamental propositions" of "natural right,"[21] thus its principles.[22]

Mendelssohn's discussion would collapse with the removal of the expedient of the distinction between a state of nature and a state of society.[23] According to his custom of detecting the organizing principle in his analysis of a book, of detecting that explosive point with which he can either agree or must disagree, Hamann sees this point in the distinction noted above. His metacriticism is set in relation to it: "Herr Mendelssohn believes in a state of nature, which he partly presupposes and partly opposes to society (as dogmatists do with a state of grace).[24] I grant him and every dogmatist his belief, even if I am myself incapable of making either a proper concept or use of this hypothesis so familiar to most of the men of letters of our century. I do no better with the social contract."[25]

One may devise several explanations for the invention of this "hypothesis so familiar to most of the men of letters of our century." It can more easily be said what it does. It offers the possibility of gaining a distance from the concrete historical and social situation, of criticizing, testing, judging, and altering it by comparing it with a primeval or natural state in its contingency, in its positive and thus in fact always particular modifications. In any event, whatever the authoritative orientation, it is expressed in the way in which the distinction between nature and society is conceived.

For Mendelssohn it is a *"law of nature"*:[26] that man, in the state of nature, is independent, that is, "under no positive obligation to any-

21. *Jerusalem*, 34.

22. Pages 45-57 comprise the actual excursus, Mendelssohn's "Theory of Rights, Duties, and Contracts," in *Jerusalem*, 56-57; cf. Haynes 165 (N III, 193, 11f.).

23. *Jerusalem*, 52. Further places: 47, 56, 70-71.

24. At issue here is not a casual comparison of Hamann. In fact the distinction between nature and society is formed according to the distinctions of salvation history — creation, the fall, redemption, consummation (above all the caesura between creation and fall).

25. "Golgatha and Scheblimini," in Haynes, 165-66 (N III, 293, 21-27).

26. *Jerusalem*, 52.

one,"[27] that in any case to him "alone belongs the right to settle cases of collision between [his] *own use* and *benevolence*."[28] "In this right lies man's *natural liberty*, which makes up a great portion of his felicity. . . . Man, in the state of nature, is the master of all that is *his*,[29] of the free use of his powers and capacities, of the free use of what he has produced by exercising them (that is, the fruits of his industry) or of whatever he has inseparably connected with the fruits of his industry,"[30] thus over his property. That a promise can be given and accepted and thus a contract concluded[31] assumes "the human's natural liberty," a "natural right" of independence in which the human is "under no positive obligation to anyone." The human is by no means always obligated.[32] In any event as regards the legal basis of an obligation, one always decides to be obligated on one's own. In principle, self-determination precedes the obligation of self to another; it first makes it possible. In the end this construction attempts to conceive the constitution of a rational society.

Hamann criticizes the idea Mendelssohn knows is a fiction,[33] the idea of a natural state conceived independently of the societal-historical world, not as to the time, however, but as to logic, and the claim to its validity, that is, linked to an individual right to self-determination.[34]

This criticism occurs in an extraordinary reversal totally identical to the move of that metacriticism of Kant described in the chapter titled:

27. *Jerusalem*, 49. Cf. for the parallel formulation *Jerusalem*, 52.

28. *Jerusalem*, 52.

29. Cf. Kant, *Metaphysics of Morals*, ed. Mary Gregor (Cambridge: Cambridge University Press, 1996), 166, in the Metaphysical First Principles of the Doctrine of Virtue. Introduction: "But two things are required for inner freedom: being one's own *master* in a given case *(animus sui compos)* and *ruling oneself (imperium im semetipsum)*, that is, subduing one's affects and governing one's passions."

30. *Jerusalem*, 52-53. Cf. "Golgatha and Scheblimini," in Haynes, 174 (N III, 299, 15-20).

31. *Jerusalem*, 54-55.

32. According to Mendelssohn this characterizes the human's relationship to God in a certain respect. Cf. *Jerusalem*, 58. In any event toward God there is no obligation to believe (cf. *Jerusalem*, 100f.).

33. Cf. A. Altmann, "Moses Mendelssohn über Naturrecht und Naturzustand," in *Die trostvolle Aufklärung. Studien zur Metaphysik und politischen Theorie Moses Mendelssohns* (FMDA II, 3) (Stuttgart–Bad Cannstatt: Frommann-Holzboog, 1982), 183f.

34. In judging Hamann's criticism we should note that he in no wise affirms what Mendelssohn rejects. He is not concerned with justifying poor political relationships. He too lays claim to liberty of conscience. But he does so within a particular context. He must not make the *usus politicus legis* the gospel, or theologically overload his liberty of conscience. His practical and political reason is finite, not unconditioned.

"Reason Is Language." There, as if in a salvo, Hamann gives first place to what Kant relegates to the margin, the question as to how the capacity for thought is possible, and turns the transcendental question regarding the condition for that possibility back to what is grammatically actual. So also here. And again, Hamann gives a transcendental reversal to the question regarding the condition for the possibility of social contracts, and thus moves away from the possible and conceivable to the actual and real. For him "nature" is not only the sphere of the possible and necessary, but above all of the real. Nature and society, nature and history[35] cannot be separated, indeed, not even distinguished, in any event, not in the way that Mendelssohn separates them.

Natural Contract

Hamann solicits Mendelssohn's agreement in his metacriticism with two arguments he may assume Mendelssohn shares. The first is the argument already cited and contained in the chiefly philosophical (though not excluded from the theological) reference to the "laws of wisdom and goodness."[36] The second is the decisive theological argument, not cited till now, by which the Christian sees himself attached to the Jew. At its very beginning, *Golgatha and Scheblimini* states that "the divine and eternal covenant with Abraham and his seed must be all the more important than theories of contracts by nature and by society because the blessing is based on this attested solemn contract, pledged and promised to all the peoples of earth."[37]

In the parallel passage in which Hamann takes up and unfolds the application and approach of his metacriticism, Yahweh's promise to Abraham (Gen. 12:1-3) is totally open to the primeval biblical history. Hamann moves within the universal, theological horizon of creation and sin. It contains the provocative term, "natural . . . contract,"[38] the contract with nature, an inconsistency for every advocate of the Enlightenment. The as-

---

35. Hamann understands nature as history and history as nature. His understanding is shown paradigmatically in his treatment of the biblical primal history: Haynes, 198 (N III, 308, 36–309, 26).

36. Cf. above note 12.

37. "Golgatha and Scheblimini," in Haynes, 166 (N III, 293, 28-31) (translation altered); cf. Genesis 12:1-3; Genesis 15 and 17, especially 17:7, 13.

38. "Golgatha and Scheblimini," in Haynes, 173 (N III, 299, 7f.).

sumption of a distinction and opposition[39] between nature and society as affirmed by Mendelssohn is relativized. The context reads:

> However, suppose that there is a social contract: then there is also a natural one, older and more genuine, and the conditions of the natural contract must be the basis of the social one. Through it all natural property becomes conventional again, and man in the state of nature becomes dependent on its laws, i.e., positively obliged to act in accordance with the very same laws which all of nature and especially the nature of man has to thank for the preservation of existence and the use of all means and goods contributing to it. Since man bears duties to nature, he accordingly has least of all an exclusive right to and hateful monopoly over his abilities, neither to the products thereof, nor to the sterile mule of his industry and the sadder bastards of his usurping acts of violence over the creature made subject, against its will, to his vanity [Rom. 8:20].[40]

This text is an artistic, metacritical weave. As usual, here too Hamann meets his requirement "that the author be compared only with himself and to no standard other than the one which he himself professes."[41] He has resorts to the above-named philosophical and theological argument in order to avoid the "great gulf between our religious and philosophical principle(s)"[42] and to bring forth the commonality of which he is certain. His metacriticism does not intend to lead to dissociation from Mendelssohn but to effect amity.

If "in the state of nature," of which Mendelssohn speaks, the human is "dependent" on its "laws," then "all natural possession" for its part is "conventional." It rests on a pledge, on a promise that will be heard and accepted. In brief, "nature" and its "laws" are not understood by themselves, they do not spring, say, from self-generation or parthenogenesis, but rest on an "establishment," an institution.[43]

---

39. "Golgatha and Scheblimini," in Haynes, 164 (N III, 293, 22f.); the context for the text is cited above (cf. note 27).

40. "Golgatha and Scheblimini," in Haynes, 173-74 (N III, 299, 7-20). The reference is to *Jerusalem*, 54-56. On "vanity" cf. also Haynes, 196 (N III, 314, 1-3).

41. Cf. above note 8.

42. "Golgatha and Scheblimini," in Haynes, 165 (N III, 293, 18f). Cf. Luke 16:26.

43. "Golgatha and Scheblimini," in Haynes, 175 (N III, 300, 34). Cf. "Einfälle und Zweifel," in N III, 37, 28-38, 3.

Now, Mendelssohn, who represented not only deism, but theism,[44] did not at all deny a creation[45] and establishment[46] of nature as such. But for him, unlike for Hamann, the knowledge of it was a matter of pure reason,[47] not a matter of reason dependent on language and thus on tradition and experience.[48] Hamann, however, makes precisely this claim and, noting his kinship with Luther,[49] conceives the *animal rationale* as a creature of language. In appeal to Cicero he shows RATIO as ORATIO, reason as language.[50]

This concept of reason as language, criterion of Hamann's metacriticism, is also the means by which he radically questions the right to distinguish natural right from social contract as transmitted from Hobbes to Mendelssohn in multiple variations. He absorbs this distinction into a unity in which nature and society, reason and the empirical, inner and outer, word and deed, intent and action are indissolubly united.

Accordingly, the result of Hamann's dispute with Mendelssohn reads:

> All social contracts derive, according to the law of nature, from the moral capacity to say Yes! or No!, and from the moral necessity to make good the word that has been given. The moral capacity to say Yes! or No! is based on the natural use of human reason and speech; the moral necessity to fulfill the word that has been given is

44. This makes use of Kant's distinction between Deism and Theism: *Critique of Pure Reason*, A 631f., p. 525 (524). "Thus the deist represents this being merely as a *cause of the world* (whether by the necessity of its nature or through freedom, remains undecided), the theist as the *Author of the world*."

45. Cf. especially *Jerusalem*, 58.

46. Cf. above notes 43 and "Golgatha and Scheblimini," in Haynes, 174 (N III, 299, 30) ("than the one intended for him and to which he is called").

47. "Golgatha and Scheblimini," in Haynes, 180-81 (N III, 304, 1-6). Hamann rejects Mendelssohn's idea of the immediacy of reason (cf. *Jerusalem*, pp. 90-91, 126, and the introduction by Altmann, pp. 20-21), with which the latter follows Spinoza (Introduction, xlvi).

48. Hamann's criteria for his metacritique of Kant (language, tradition, and experience) are also those of his metacriticism of Mendelssohn.

49. "Golgatha and Scheblimini," in Haynes, 177 (N III, 301, 40). (The reference is to Luther's Preface to the Psalter, 1528: LW 35, 254; WA DB 10/I, 100, 12-14). Cf. "Königsbergsche Zeitungen," in N IV, 425, 39f., and "Aesthetica in Nuce," in Haynes, 89, N II, 213, note 55.

50. "Golgatha and Scheblimini," in Haynes, 175 (N III, 300, 37–301, 2). Cf. L. Schreiner, HH VII, 86f.

based on the fact that our inward declaration of will can be expressed, revealed, or known only in speech or writing or action, and that our words like our deeds must be regarded as the natural signs of our convictions. Reason and language are therefore the inner and outer band of all social life. If that which nature, through having been established, has joined together is divorced or divided, then faith and fidelity are annulled, and lies and deceit, shame and vice, are confirmed and stamped as means to felicity.[51]

An exegesis of this key passage from *Golgatha and Scheblimini* would have to set forth its implicit Christology, the Christological figure of the communication of the properties *(idiomata)*, as well as the theology of creation concurrent with it. In fact, within the immediate context Hamann himself interprets that theology. The most important sentences read:

"For he spake, and it was done." [Ps. 33:9] — "and whatever the man called every creature, that was the name thereof" (Gen. 2:19). According to this model and image of definiteness, every word of a man ought to be and to remain the thing itself. It is on this likeness of stamp and motto to the perfect type of our race and to the guide of our youth . . . it is on this law of nature to make use of the word as the primary, noblest, and most powerful means of revealing and communicating our inward declaration of will . . . that the validity of all contracts is based, and this mighty fortress of truth in the inward parts is superior to all frenchified practices, machinations, pedantries, and mongering. The misuse of language and of its natural testimony is therefore the grossest perjury; it turns the transgressor of this first law of reason and its righteousness into the worst misanthrope. . . .[52]

What can be said in conclusion now is that the "first law of reason and its righteousness" is the *Word*, the context of hearing and speaking,

---

51. "Golgatha and Scheblimini," in Haynes, 175 (N III, 300, 22-36). Cf. Hamann's reference to the *"caput mortuum* of the divine and human form," in Haynes, 197 (N III, 314, 11f.).

52. "Golgatha and Scheblimini," in Haynes, 176-77 (N III, 300, 34) (translation altered), cited is Psalm 33:9 and Genesis 1 and 2. In his piece Mendelssohn discussed the question of perjury in detail; cf. *Jerusalem*, 63-72 (cf. also "Über die 39 Artikeln der englischen Kirche und deren Beschwörung," in JubA8, 158).

or better, of pledging, of promise given and the trust placed in it. On "fidelity and faith" rest originally and unavoidably not only social life and human right, but the *entire* context of the social and natural world — as creation. "Creation" is a world that is promised, a world that will be and as such is perceived by everyone or, however, is misjudged in the lie. For this reason there must not least be reference to a "right" of nature, a natural right even of inanimate fellow creatures, and correspondingly of the human as the "trustee of nature." Thus Hamann brings into view what is not considered in even such a circumspect theory of justice as that of John Rawls.[53]

In his metacriticism of Mendelssohn Hamann leads us into an expanse of responsibility that, probably, none of his contemporaries perceived or could perceive due to the prevailing individualism of possession — an individualism that not even Kant eliminated. But without the challenge of Mendelssohn's *Jerusalem* Hamann would scarcely have developed his doctrine of society and philosophy of right. In any event, measured by his other writings, not in the extended and easily reconstructable relation to contemporary thought, to particular traditions of the Enlightenment, as Mendelssohn represents them.

We scarcely need expressly add that Hamann, chiefly as concerns liberty of conscience, did not regress to the conditions out from which Mendelssohn wanted further to lead. However, in his own way he construed Mendelssohn's intentions more realistically, more aware of sin,[54] and more universally, conscious of the ecological crisis, not least brought about by the spirit of the individualism of possession. His word taken from Paul of the human's "usurping acts of violence over the creature made subject, against its will, to his vanity"[55] strikes the right note.

The Hebrew content of the Greek term *mataiotes* used by Paul and translated "vanity" by Luther, denotes the Nothing engaged with lying and deception,[56] thus with the "misuse of language,"[57] of the incapacity and willful refusal to hear and answer. Whoever along with the Old Tes-

---

53. J. Rawls, *A Theory of Justice* (Cambridge, MA: Belknap, 1971), 574. Rawls, admittedly, knows what is desired.

54. Cf. also the Introduction by Altmann: JubA8, xxxv, who speaks of Mendelssohn's thoroughly optimistic picture of humanity.

55. Cf. above note 40. "Aesthetica in nuce," in Haynes, 78 (N II, 206, 25-31).

56. Cf. above note 52.

57. Cf. above note 52.

tament and Paul's theology[58] is aware of the weight of sin will more than ever appreciate Hamann's reference to the human as trustee of nature and of the human's natural right as the moral ability to say Yes! or No! This awareness and reference is not, say, Hamann's private little esoteric discovery, but an interpretation of the Bible, and, if appropriate, does not aim past his contemporaries, but fundamentally engages them, and not least, in dissent.

"All social contracts derive, according to the law of nature, from the moral capacity to say Yes! or No!, and from the moral necessity to make good the word that has been given." This sentence about clear and distinct speech from Hamann's dispute with Mendelssohn over the philosophy of right interprets Jesus' word regarding proper speech and the appropriate word ("Let your word be 'Yes, Yes' or 'No, No'; anything more than this comes from evil," Matt. 5:37). It does so in a creations-theological and socio-ethical depth reached only by Hamann in his exposition of the Sermon on the Mount. It did not enter theological or churchly consciousness, and even less our general intellectual consciousness. The parallel passage in the Herder-Cycle was already noted in the chapter titled "Criticism and Politics." "This great architect and cornerstone of a system that will outlive heaven and earth, and a patriotism that overcomes the world, said: Let your word be yes, yes, no, no; everything else is of the devil — and herein consists the entire spirit of the Law and the social contract, have they names as they will."[59]

If in this sense Hamann's dispute with Mendelssohn on the theme of "natural right and social contract" is nothing but a sharp and discerning interpretation of the Sermon on the Mount, it is scarcely otherwise with Hamann's understanding of sexuality and marriage. According to his *Versuch einer Sibylle über die Ehe (Essay of a Sibyl on Marriage)*, "There would perhaps! Be nothing more beneficial for the human race and bourgeois society than to strive for that ideal of holiness for the state of marriage that the great Fulfiller of the Mosaic Law and the Prophets restored, and preached on that mount of beatitude as an imperial law of heaven and his new earth: 'Whoever looks at a woman and lusts after her, — and whoever separates from his wife — and whoever

---

58. In Romans 7:7ff. Paul takes up Genesis 3–11 in brief.

59. "Two Reviews," in Dickson, 458 (N III, 24, 7-13). Cf. above chapter 6, "Criticism and Politics," note 25.

woos a divorced woman, are adulterers' — Moses had specifically 'commanded us to stone such' and his law could not be dissolved, as are the schemes of our present morals and their vain preachers, but must be fulfilled, as a sure prophetic word. — "[60]

60. "Essay of a Sibyl on Marriage," in Dickson, 508 (N III, 200, 14-25); in addition cf. 2 Peter 1:19f.

Chapter 11

"Essay of a Sibyl on Marriage"

A s Hamann's other flying leaves, the modest *Essay of a Sibyl on Marriage*[1] is an occasional piece, composed in 1774 on the occasion of the marriage of Hamann's Riga publisher Hartknoch to a native of Königsberg. It can in no way be directly related to the biography of these two persons or to Hamann's marriage of conscience with Anna Regina Schumacher, though by way of Bible interpretation his own experiences emerge. Still, the personal confession is also a critical statement of the time with reference to the marriage law of the *Codex iuris Fridericiani*,[2] enacted in East Prussia in 1774, with reference to the gallant world of rococo as well as to the Herrnhutters' procurator of marriage,[3] to mention only a few aspects of a text rich in facets which, as all Hamann's writings, is a cento woven from quotations and allusions. The newspapers, the contemporary modes, opinions, and interests provoke Hamann's resistance, which to his mind follows from the sure prophetic word of the Bible. He sets the scene for what he has to say of marriage in a positive way by dealing chiefly with the primeval biblical history, with Jesus' Sermon on the Mount as the ultimate interpretation of the original creative will of God, and with the paraenesis on marriage in Ephesians. This does not reject the understanding of marriage as contract, but corrects it, conceived afresh from an anthropological depth misplaced by the Enlightenment.

1. Dickson, 505-15 (N III, 197-203).
2. Dickson, 508 (N III, 1-13).
3. Cf. below note 26.

In his essay on marriage, Hamann, delighting in inventing fables, combines intentions usually most often separated or which fall apart, that is, Bible criticism and criticism of the age. This occurs with a venturesomeness he reflects in an anonymous self-advertisement of his essay that likewise appeared anonymously in the *Königsbergsche Gelehrte und Politische Zeitungen* of December 18, 1775: The author seems "to border so closely on the modish, obscenely profane taste and superannuated mystical Gnosis as to contravene them both."[4] The intention Hamann pursues with his publication is stated clearly in a letter to his publisher, whose marriage was the occasion for the modest attempt on the great theme "of the mystical orgies of nature" (Clement of Alexandria):[5] "Whether you will be able to print it without offence to conscience, about this [I] await your frank confession, but I am notifying you beforehand that the whole nub of the thing lies in the fact that it intends to scandalize our moral century. And if it can have that effect I have reached my goal."[6] The sanctimonious moralism of his century along with the libertinism of the married man who keeps his mistress is repugnant to Hamann.

After the title and mottos Hamann begins his modest piece in this way: "Do not, blissful bridal pair! stop up your ears, open for the magical arts of harmony, but hear the voice of a sibyl, who can prophesy splendidly. May my teaching be wondrous, like love, and mysterious, like marriage!"[7]

Begun in this way the type of communication becomes immediately clear. Here there are no propositions to be defined such as we find, say, in Kant's or Hegel's philosophy of right, or in a theological ethics on marriage; no dogmatic or ethical tractate *de matrimonio*. What we hear is an address, not to the public in general, but to a single bridal pair, naturally, primordial in breadth.[8] The speech is as universal as it is concrete, the primordial breadth is not at the cost of intimacy and individual depth.

"Do not . . . stop up your ears . . . but hear the voice of a sibyl, who

---

4. "Königsbergsche Zeitungen," in N IV, 418, 8-10.

5. "Königsbergsche Zeitungen," in N IV, 418, 7. Cf. Clement of Alexandria, *Paedagogus* II, Chapter X, 96, 2.

6. ZH III, 128, 14-18 (to Hartknoch; December 4, 1774).

7. Dickson, 507 (N III, 199, 1-4).

8. The primeval biblical history (Genesis 1-11) is to be understood as primordially human, valid for every present period.

can prophesy splendidly." Particularly in matters such as love and marriage the chief thing is to find the magic word:

> There sleeps a song in all the things
> that keep on dreaming there.
> And the world begins to sing,
> if only you find the magic word.[9]

To this end Hamann slips into the shape of the sibyl which according to the judgment of the church fathers is to be set near the Old Testament prophets as witness to the true God. In the Sistine Chapel Michelangelo painted the prophets alongside the sibyls. But no decisive importance attaches to the figure of a sibyl as such, except to hear the voice "who can prophesy splendidly." The chief thing is to find the appropriate word so as not to be silent about marriage and love but to speak of them, but in such a way that its mystery is not talked to death and thus destroyed.

To prophesy unerringly of marriage seldom succeeds. Kierkegaard described the difficulty as follows:

> All questions about the significance of the sexual, and of its meaning where individuals are concerned, has undeniably been only sparsely answered till now . . . and above all very seldom answered in the right frame of mind. Making jokes about it is a miserable art; it is easy to warn against it, and it is just as easy to preach about it in such a way that the difficulties are glossed over. But to speak of it in a properly human way, is an art. To leave the answer to the stage and the pulpit so that the one part is embarrassed to say what the other says, with the result that the explanation of one side is as different as imaginable from that of the other, really means to renounce everything, and to lay on people a heavy burden not eased with so much as a finger: to find sense in both explanations while whoever the teachers may be present only one of the two.[10]

---

9. J. von Eichendorff, "Wünschelrute," cited according to *Neue Gesamtausgabe der Werke und Schriften in vier Bänden*, vol. 1: *Gedichte, Epen, Dramen*, ed. G. Baumann (Stuttgart: Cotta, 1978), 112.

10. Kierkegaard, *The Concept of Anxiety*, trans. Reidar Thomte (Princeton: Princeton University Press, 1980), 67 (translation altered).

However appropriately Kierkegaard described this nuisance crying out to this very day, he was no more able to remedy it in a theologically convincing way. Whoever would follow his tormented reflection and the tormented state on which he reflected would be poorly advised. For Kierkegaard the sexual is "the expression of that monstrous 'contradiction,' that the immortal spirit" is destined to be "man or wife," different in gender, sexually specific.[11] In support, Kierkegaard, as many others, appeals to Galatians 3:28 ("There is no longer male and female; for all of you are one in Christ Jesus"): "In Christianity the religious has suspended the erotic, not merely by ethically misunderstanding it as sinful, but as indifferent, since in the Spirit there is no distinction between man and woman."[12]

While Kierkegaard practices Christianity by repelling everything worldly, and marriage particularly, Hamann practices Christianity by taking in everything worldly, the sexual above all. In it he allows his sibyl to prophesy.

God and Sex

Hamann reflected on the difference between the sexes with an uncommon intensity. In doing so he arrived at such depths that it would be an exacting affair to follow him. He saw the difference between the sexes to be elementary and universal. It may "be more a physical need than an aesthetic imitation or philosophical invention when the concept of the sexual" is transferred "to the images of our concepts,"[13] when languages are not without genera, sexually not indifferent. In fact, Hamann assigns maximum theological significance to the difference between man and wife, maintaining that "the natural difference between the sexes is a *verum signaculum Creatoris*,"[14] a true sign of the Creator that one may only ignore with "Stoic and abstract coldness."[15] The Creator would deny himself in his love if Galatians 3:28 meant that ultimately he would allow the difference between the sexes to become meaningless and did not rather fulfill and consummate it toward its true destiny.

11. Kierkegaard, *The Concept of Anxiety*, 69.
12. Kierkegaard, *The Concept of Anxiety*, 70 (translation altered).
13. "Schürze von Feigenblättern," in N III, 212, 12-14.
14. "Schürze von Feigenblättern," in N III, 212, 12-14, lines 6f.
15. "Schürze von Feigenblättern," in N III, 213, 18.

Hamann cannot agree with the Enlightenment's Stoic and "Platonic"[16] reference to *the* human, the human as such. Whoever artificially abstracts from the sexual difference shares the yearning for androgynous perfection and repeats the old myth in a modern variation by assuming a neuter-neutral unity of the human, or by postulating anticipates it; such a one makes the human an "ambiguous hermaphrodite."[17] Longing for highest perfection, one arrives at abstraction.

By contrast Hamann clearly emphasizes how fundamental and essential it is that God did not create the human as human, but as man and wife. He diagnoses the reference to *the* human as an abstraction characteristic of the Enlightenment spirit. As early as in the *Fragments* he attempts a critical encounter with a corresponding understanding of the human self: "In order to fathom my own self it is not enough to know what man is, but also what his state is. Are you free, or a slave? Are you immature, an orphan, or a widow, and in what way are you related to higher beings who take it upon themselves to manage you, who oppress you, take advantage of you, and seek to profit by your ignorance and weakness and folly?"[18]

This text, altogether impersonalistic, strikingly expresses the concrete social character of every individual, not only the Christian, and belongs to the primary motif of Hamann's authorship. At issue in the wider context is the relation between love for God, for the neighbor, for self and free self-determination,[19] as in the corresponding summary in the *Biblical Meditations:* "The Christian alone is a man, a father, lord of the animals. He alone loves himself, his own and his goods, because he loves God who loved him before he was, and, when he was, was God's enemy."[20]

Just as God's love of humankind, reaching into the impure dust of the earth at its creating (Gen. 2:7), and redeeming (cf., e.g., John 9:6), is full of matter, earthly and sensuous,[21] so with human love. "The mysteries of our nature on which all taste and enjoyment of the beautiful, true and good are based, are related to knowledge and love, just as that tree of God in midst of the garden. Both are causes as well as effects of love.

---

16. Cf. "Schürze von Feigenblättern," in N III, 213, 18.
17. "Schürze von Feigenblättern," line 29.
18. "Fragments," in Smith, 164 (N I, 301, 32-38) (translation altered).
19. "Fragments," in Smith, 162 63 (N I, 299, 35–302, 35).
20. "Biblical Reflections," in Smith, 130 (N I, 71, 6-9).
21. Cf. ZH II, 415, 22ff. (to Herder; 1768).

Their glow is fiery and a flame from the Lord; for God is love and life is the light of men."[22]

Sensuousness and Morality

A brief comparison of Luther, Schleiermacher, Kant, and Hegel can help us understand how Hamann perceives the divine mystery of human love. Luther speaks in a drastic way of marital love: Sexual drive, God's word, and work (Gen. 1:28) are directed unrestrictedly toward the furtherance of life. However, as polymorphous, it needs to be defined by Jesus' express word regarding marriage and its indivisibility. Schleiermacher, especially the younger Schleiermacher of the *Vertrauten Briefe über die Lucinde,* places the accent elsewhere. The union of man and wife has its purpose in itself, not, first of all in the begetting of children. In the union of man and wife what is most sensuous and spiritual interpenetrate. An infinite harmony is awaited, that is, the fusion of one half of humanity with the other into a mystical whole. Kant's emphasis on the legal aspect is cold by comparison. With his understanding of marriage as "legally moral love"[23] *("rechtlich sittliche Liebe")* Hegel sought to unite and coordinate the constitutive elements, which did not deny the sensuous element though it clearly retreated, not least in the wake of the polemic against romanticism.

Hamann unites all these elements, but he clearly differs from Hegel, to whom he stands closest. And he differs from him chiefly in the fact that he regards the sensuous element in morality as much more permeating and determinative. What distinguishes Hamann's emphasis on the sensuous from early romanticism and the current libertinistic attitude is precisely what Hegel gives so much emphasis, the constitutive union of the sensuous with the moral-legal self-consciousness, emphasis on the evident reciprocity of knowing-oneself-in-the-other which alone constitutes true self-knowledge.

---

22. "Schürze von Feigenblättern," in N III, 213, 7-12.

23. Hegel, *Philosophy of Right,* trans. T. M. Knox (New York: Oxford University Press, 1981), 262 (cf. chapter 7, "What Is Enlightenment?" above note 7).

Mythical Tale of Self-Knowledge

Hamann allows his sibyl to tell of such self-knowledge given me by the other, become my own through the other, as a "short, mythical fairy-tale of my own case," thus from the female perspective. Introduced by renewed address to the "blissful bridal pair," it is formed in a clearly dramatic context, stands significantly at the end of the attempt, and is without doubt its high point. Hamann uses it chiefly to interpret the Yahwist creation narrative (Genesis 2), and mainly from it draws out the dramatic element. The fact that it cannot be everywhere exegetically supported does not detract from the path of the exposition as a whole, an exposition determined by the Hebrew word "to know" (cf. Gen. 4:1).

"Perhaps you would care to listen, blissful bridal pair! to a short, mythical fairy-tale of my own case, and how I am indebted to *one among thousands, of dovelike simplicity and serpentine cunning, the mysterious wisdom* of a sibyl." She tells of the "flash of fire of self-knowledge," how "the mirror of his sincerity threw back an answering gleam to my own heart, and I began to recognize in this the hemisphere of my sex *in naturalibus.* . . ."[24] The sibyl tells how she arrived at self-knowledge, that is, by being known. Naturally, the same applies to the male. Hamann is aware that his tale runs a great risk and, as is clear from his self-witness, that he is edging toward the profane-obscene taste à la mode. At the same time, however, he resists it.

Before the fairy-tale, in a way that seems cryptic to us and difficult to access but which for his contemporaries, especially in Königsberg, was an obviously polemical reference, Hamann had attacked the obscene, frivolous poems of Scheffner, composed à la Grécourt. It likewise attacked its extreme, the "vestal like" idea of the Herrnhut brotherhood,[25] according to which the wife, in intercourse with her husband, was permitted to see him only as the procurator of Christ, thus to direct her feelings not toward her husband, but only toward Christ, Lord of the community.[26]

Hamann also attacks mixing the Enlightenment notion of contract with the emotionalism that characterized von Hippel's *Über die Ehe,*

---

24. Dickson, 509-10 (N III, 201, 19–203, 2) (translation altered).

25. Dickson, 509 (N III, 201, 11f.) ("à l'enseigne de Barby": "according to the doctrine of Barby": training institute of the Moravians).

26. Cf. F. Tanner, *Die Ehe im Pietismus* (Zürich: Zwingli-Verlag, 1952), especially 143f.

which had just appeared (1774).[27] He agrees with von Hippel at various points. Naturally, on the basis of his own theological-anthropological presuppositions he can speak of marriage as a "covenant constructed by the power of will and decision, grounded in reason and fidelity."[28] In citing the divine word of blessing (Gen. 1:28) he states that "this *divine* is assimilated into the entire visible economy, and a development of the blessing pronounced at the beginning; yet none of our fellow-creatures is made for this purpose, for a deliberate and voluntary decision or a *covenant* and *social contract:* just as none is more capable of and more in need of a greater *education* than the human."[29] Since the human is a creature of deficiency, it must compensate; since it is unformed, it must take on form. Since its sexuality is polymorphous, it must be defined by language and able to be told in stories.

As this point precisely shows, Hamann's biblical interpretation is not only linked to a criticism of his time, but all throughout to agreement with significant elements of its anthropological, ethical, and legal thought. Yet, he takes hold more deeply and arrives at insights into the relation between love and death in anticipation of romanticism.

Love and Death

If the second title-motto with its reference to Proserpine in the quotation from Virgil conjured up the link between Eros and Thanatos,[30] this is reinforced in the essay itself. It does not occur uncritically, but in a way that expresses not only fertility and sadness, life force and death in their relation to each other, but specifically (in an existentialistically suggestive tone) recognizes "despair," whose booty are those who are damned to pleasure. If it knows nothing but mother earth the entire "search," the hunger for life, ends in death.[31] "What is all the fruitfulness of the breast and the womb of your All-mother, with the enjoyment of her fruits and her souls born of and damned to dust! . . . — Disguised sad-

---

27. Dickson, 509 (N III, 201, 7–203, 2).

28. Dickson, 507 (N III, 199, 33f.) (translation altered). Cf. Th. G. von Hippel, *Über die Ehe* (Berlin: G. Reimer, 1774).

29. Dickson, 507 (N III, 199, 17-23) (translation altered).

30. Dickson, 506 (*Aeneid* VI, 143-46).

31. Cf. H IV, 301, 33–302, 2 (to Herder; 1781).

ness and despair, and all your *search* a booty of the black, rich god of Hell, as the clever fable of *Ceres* and her daughter tells."[32]

Hamann no more deifies than demonizes the sexual. He attempts to speak of it in an authentically human way and tell of it in its mysteriously sensuous, bodily, and spiritual depth as in its other ethical, societal, and legal dimensions. Self-knowledge, founded on mutual awareness — "knowing" — and mutual recognition, is given its own free room. But it is not separated from handing on the life received. So begins the essay following the address: "I see in your tender, intimate glances the little pensive god of love, that took counsel with himself over the masterpiece of his work, whom he leads out and involves in all projects, conquests, and blind adventures and which culminates in this: '*Let us make human beings, an image, which is like us —.*'"[33]

32. Dickson, 509 (N III, 201, 13-18) (translation altered).
33. Dickson, 507 (N III, 199, 5-10).

Chapter 12

Created Time

Time is established, has become institution by a pledge. Conversely, institutions can be described as time given shape, as separate periods that in turn first of all "make" time, form the experience of "time." Individual and collective memory depend indissolubly on institutions, on shaped experiences mediated not least in liturgical worship forms.[1] Thus what is temporally inward is never without what is spatially outward. In his article for the Christmas festival of 1760, *Die Magi aus Morgenlande, zu Bethlehem,* Hamann writes, "Human life appears to consist of a series of symbolic actions by means of which our soul is able to reveal its invisible nature, and produces outside of itself, and communicates, a sensible knowledge of its effective existence."[2]

Time and Space

Time and space are linked to each other like hearing and seeing. The sense of hearing as that of time and the sense of sight as that of space collaborating with the sense of taste can no more be isolated from each other than painting, the oldest human writing, can be isolated from mu-

---

1. For what follows cf. my essay "Tempus creatura verbi," in *Schöpfung als Anrede* (cf. chapter 2, "Style and Form," above, note 64), 128-39.
2. "The Wise Men from the East in Bethlehem," in Smith, 191 (N II, 139, 26-29) (translation altered). Cf. "Ein fliegender Brief," in N III, 367, 5ff. and ZH I, 393, 28 (to Lindner; 1759).

sic, the oldest human language. Sounds and letters, sense of time and space unite in that synthesis ("speak, so that I see you") of the perception of self and the world, the reflection of which makes up the heart and core of Hamann's metacriticism of Kant's transcendental aesthetic:

> Sounds and letters are therefore pure forms *a priori,* in which nothing belonging to the sensation or concept of an object is found; they are the true, aesthetic elements of all human knowledge and reason. The oldest language was music, and along with the palpable rhythm of the pulse and of the breath in the nostrils, it was the original bodily image of all temporal measures and intervals. The oldest writing was painting and drawing, and therefore was occupied as early as then with the economy of space, its limitation and determination by figures. Thence, under the exuberant persistent influence of the two noblest senses sight and hearing, the concepts of space and time have made themselves so universal and necessary in the whole sphere of the understanding (just as light and air are for the eye, ear, and voice) that as a result space and time, if not *idea innatae,* seem to be at least *matrices* of all intuitive knowledge.[3]

With this argument Hamann sharply contradicts Kant and formulates his counterposition according to which language with its store of figures from which the affects are nourished determines time lived and experienced. Whoever abstracts from time conceived as language, thus also from the sensuous figures determining thought, must assume an empty capacity of soul for perceiving time or, as Kant, allow time to pale into a "pure form of sensible intuition."[4]

Over against such an understanding of time as well as Kant's transcendental aesthetic it is necessary to recognize as strictly as possible the institutional and physical-linguistic conditions of the experience of time as such. Without the twofold grace of breathing in and out, without the rhythm of heartbeat, without the rhythm of night and day, winter and summer, youth and old age, only artificially but never on principle

---

3. H V, 213, 29–214, 4 (= "Metacritique of the Purism of Reason," in Haynes, 211 [N III, 286, 14-28]). See the commentary: Oswald Bayer, *Vernunft ist Sprache: Hamanns Metakritik Kants* (Stuttgart: Frommann-Holzboog, 2002), 329-36. Cf. "Aesthetica in nuce," in Haynes, 63 (N II, 197, 15-27). Cf. also the interweaving of time and space: "Ein fliegender Brief," in N III, 385, 16-22.

4. Kant, *Critique of Pure Reason,* B 47, p. 75.

isolatable from the inner clock, and without the music and language linked to these rhythms in rising and falling, beginning and ending (say, of a story), no one knows what "time" is, "to know" being construed in the Hebrew sense of the term as a sensuous experience.

And, understanding Hamann's metacriticism of Kant's transcendental aesthetic requires a look back at Hamann's original motif. The root of his understanding of time is found in the *Biblical Meditations* and accompanying texts. If we search for this root and are aware of it without reservation, then there is total breakdown of the usual concepts of time and their demarcations: the accent is on a transcendental or actual historical, an existentialistic or *heilsgeschichtlich,* an individualistic or universal-historical, a kairological or chronological, an existential or natural scientific concept of time. In this way the complex perception of self and world is reduced to arbitrarily coined ideas, which in their isolation destroy and kill the life setting of my own history as well as that of the world, a life setting that can neither be constructed nor reconstructed.

It should be noted that Hamann's life-change in London, in 1758, was a specific experience of time. In his later years he never left it behind; it remained forever decisive. Hamann, to speak with Luther,[5] learned the "time of the gospel," which in its sharp and painful distinction from the "time of the law" creates the totally new that never grows old. The gospel as "the revelation of God in the flesh and the preaching of his kingdom is the sole new thing that would be significantly, universally and really new for all the earth and would never cease to be new." The "preaching of the gospel is therefore called the joyous tidings of the kingdom of God."[6] The law had accused Hamann, convicted him of his absent-mindedness, sadness, and despair. It accused him of his lack of communication in which, separated from his fellow human beings and from the God become his neighbor, he had become Cain, the "fratricide, the murderer of his only begotten Son,"[7] "restless and a fugitive."[8] Together with God's merciful nearness the gospel and its time brought him conquest of the deadly dissociation, of the separations, brought him the fertile fellowship, into the "marriage" with God, the world, others, and himself, brought him the liberty "to love ourselves and our neighbor. In

5. LW 26:336 (WA 40/I, 526, 21-32) (on Galatians 3:23).

6. "Biblical Reflections," in Smith, 136 (N I, 223, 23-33).

7. "Thoughts about My Life," in Smith, 153 (N II, 41, 9).

8. "Thoughts about My Life," in Smith, 153 (N II, 41, 6) (translation altered). Cf. N II, 31, 14f.

short, a man must be a true Christian in order to be a proper father, a proper child, a good citizen, a true patriot, a good subject, a good master and a good servant."[9]

"Understanding of the times gives us understanding of our duties."[10]

Time and Ethos

The significance of time for the conduct of life, for the ethos, most often overlooked in ethics, Hamann grasped at its core. "The Christian alone is lord of his days, because he is heir to the future. Our time is so bound up with eternity that one cannot separate them without extinguishing the light of their life. However dissimilar in their nature, their union is the soul of human life."[11] Human life is not only time for eternity,[12] but truly alive in a firm intertwining of the two. If, according to Schleiermacher's speeches *Über die Religion,* "to be one with the infinite in midst of the finite and to be eternal in a single moment is the immortality of religion,"[13] then Hamann brings such an understanding of religion down to earth and conceives time differently. He does so by virtue of the condescension of the triune God who has interlaced his eternity with time, not only with his incarnation and death on the cross but as the Creator who addresses the creature through the creature, and as the Spirit who kills and makes alive through modest, particular, temporal events, as narrated by the Bible.[14]

This eternal time of God, determinative for Hamann with his life's change, gives him a peculiar composure. But it immediately underwent contradiction by the modern idea of time, vocation, and work represented chiefly by Johann Christoph Berens, but also by Kant, according

9. "Thoughts about My Life," in Smith, 157 (N II, 44, 5-9). Cf. "Fragments," in Smith, 162 (N I, 299, 35–302, 35) and "Biblical Reflections," in Smith, 130 (N I, 71, 6-9); cf. above chapter II, "Essay of a Sibyl on Marriage," note 18.

10. "Biblische Betrachtungen," in N I, 125, 29.

11. "Biblical Reflections," in Smith, 130 (N I, 71, 13ff.).

12. Compare M. Trowitzsch, *Zeit zur Ewigkeit. Beiträge zum Zeitverständnis in der "Glaubenslehre" Schleiermachers* (Munich: Kaiser, 1976).

13. F. D. E. Schleiermacher, *On Religion: Speeches to Its Cultured Despisers,* trans. John Oman (New York: Harper, 1958), 101.

14. Cf. the Trinitarian inferences regarding time in many of Hamann's writings (cf. for example note 69 below) with the Trinitarian texts on condescension.

to which only the diligent, industrious citizen could find recognition as a useful member of society. Hamann, become a "lover of leisure"[15] for reading and writing, and tending to his sick father, was taken by his earlier friends to be a good-for-nothing and an idler. What seemed Bohemian to them was according to Hamann's self-understanding an expression of faith in justification worked by God's word alone and in eternal Providence, whose time, "distributed,"[16] granted, and remitted to him he wanted only to receive and enjoy. *Carpe diem!*

The peculiar perception of time given Hamann with his life's change is most evident in his capacity to distinguish between rest and work, *otium* and *negotium*. On March 31, 1759, he writes to Lindner with Berens in view: "My friend perhaps knows too little of what it is to work and be idle, how easy the former and how difficult the latter, how little one can boast of working and how proud one can be of *otium* like Scipio."[17] This makes for keen sight. "The hundred-eyed Argus was a man without occupations, as his name indicates."[18]

Living his life as a "lover of idleness," Hamann came practically and theoretically into conflict with the modern, secularized Protestant ethos of time and work that denies the strength of Sunday to promote life. Hamann, allowing Holy Scripture to be his "dictionary" and "linguistics," an art "on which all concepts and utterances are based and of which they consist and should be formed,"[19] takes special note of Psalm 90, the great psalm of time to which Luther had already devoted considerable exposition. From this psalm he learns the relations and distinctions between time and eternity, wrath and grace, time filled and idle, empty time, work and toil, and the blessing given by God to the "work of our hands" (Ps. 90:17).[20]

The "Moment"

"So teach us to number our days that we may gain a wise heart" (Ps. 90:12). Hamann senses the weight of this petition as early as in the *Bibli-*

---

15. Cf. "Socratic Memorabilia," in Dickson, 375 (N II, 57).

16. ZH I, 402, 3 (in the context of the entire letter to his brother; 1759).

17. ZH I, 311, 21-23 (to Lindner; 1759).

18. ZH I, 347, 21f. (to his brother; 1759).

19. "Biblische Betrachtungen," in N I, 243, 18-20.

20. Cf. for example ZH I, 294, 28-35 (to Lindner; 1759).

cal *Meditations,* which deliberately range over wide stretches in the language of prayer: "Lord, thy Word makes us wise, even if it teaches us nothing more than to number our days. What a nothingness, mere smoke, a spiritual nothingness they are in our eyes when reason numbers them! What a fullness, what a treasure, what an eternity when faith numbers them. Lord, teach me to number my days that I may apply my heart to wisdom. All is wisdom in thy ordering of nature, when the spirit of thy Word illumines our spirit. All is a labyrinth and disorder when we try to look for ourselves."[21]

In the *Socratic Memorabilia* Hamann takes up the wording in Luther's translation ("teach us to consider that we must die so that we become wise"), to question the current ranking of knowledge over faith: "What is more certain than the human end, and of what truth is there a more universal and confirmed knowledge? No one however is clever enough to believe it but the one who, as Moses gives us to understand, God himself teaches to remember that he must die. What one believes has therefore no need of proof; and a proposition can be irrefutably proven without being believed."[22]

Texts such as the one above or the other in the *Biblical Meditations* on Revelation 1:3 ("that the time of fulfillment is nigh and should make us aware of the end of the world which at death ceases for us and passes away and is no more, and makes us ready to travel"[23]) have given our generation cause to interpret Hamann as an existentialist.[24] But Hamann differs fundamentally from the existentialist summons to authentic existence in face of death as well as from the *meditatio mortis,* practiced since antiquity, and which promises self-knowledge.[25] The difference is that he does not think of the "moment," about which he can speak pithily, as something in isolation, or as the leap of decision, like Kierkegaard or Bultmann.

"In every moment slumbers the possibility of the eschatological moment. You must awaken it." With this appeal Bultmann concludes his

21. "Biblical Reflections," in Smith, 129 (N I, 70, 32-40).

22. "Socratic Memorabilia," in Dickson, 391 (N II, 73, 22-28).

23. "Biblische Betrachtungen," in N I, 248, 18-21. Cf. further: ZH I, 358, 36–361, 2 (to his brother; 1759); H VII, 161, 25-27 (to Jacobi; 1787); ZH I, 360, 21–361, 2 (to his brother; 1759).

24. Walter Lowrie, *Johann Georg Hamann: An Existentialist* (Princeton: Princeton Theological Seminary, 1950).

25. Cf. B. Mojsisch, "Meditation I," in *Historisches Wörterbuch der Philosophie,* ed. J. Ritter and K. Gründer (Basel: Schwabe, 1971-2007), vol. 5, 962.

Geschichte und Eschatologie.[26] In contrast to that, Hamann perceives the "moment" as an occasion that is granted, "that providence has intended for us."[27] From the infinitely wide and polyvalent context of God's providence the "moment" dawns and emerges on me, in midst of the community of the old and new covenant. But without that context, isolated from it, it is dead. When the "Lord of time," who alone knows "understanding of the times," does not tell us through his word "how important the moment is which he gives us," the "present moment is only a dead torso, without head or feet; it simply lies where it is. The past must be revealed to us, and the future likewise. In regard to the past our fellow-creatures can help us somewhat; the future is completely closed to us: even the breath of the succeeding hour is its own master, at least it depends on its predecessor as little as it can command its neighbour and successor. Every moment of time is perfectly rounded; that out of each moment a line comes, is due to the thread that Providence has drawn through it and which gives it an exact connexion, which our weak eyes cannot see. This thread makes the connexion of moments and parts of time so firm and inseparable, so grown into one another, that everything consists, and seems to consist, of one piece."[28]

Call and Response

What the third chapter of Ecclesiastes says of a time for every matter under heaven, of the moment, the proper occasion, Hamann meditates on to the extent that the element of truth in every Platonism, even of Whitehead, is retained, while the Platonic view as a whole is decisively corrected by emphasis on God's *call.* In this way a category is found that outstrips the correlation of accident and necessity. "Every finite thing has an eternity ahead of and behind it," an eternity that the human does not see through and much less rules. Every finite thing has "limits of time and place, but with God what happened at the beginning is present and what is about to happen at the end of time and days is present. How is it possible that with everything present to the eyes of God the least dis-

---

26. R. Bultmann, *History and Eschatology* (New York: Harper and Brothers, 1951), 155.

27. "Biblische Betrachtungen," in N I, 168, 29f. Cf. 169, 32-34.

28. "Biblical Reflections," in Smith, 131 (N I, 125, 20–126, 6); on "Lord of time" cf. Psalm 31:16; cf. ZH I, 393, 28–394, 3 (cf. above, note 2).

tinction could occur of which he should know nothing, and how much more should we fear a God who has seen and known us, not since yesterday or the day before, but since the beginning when he created heaven and earth. What was is present to God, and for him what is to be is as the past. He is not only Lord of the future, but also of the past, since what is borne along on the stream of time returns at his call and appears anew. By how much more does this suit the greatness of God than the necessary connection of all things, since this connection exists more by God's freedom and the omnipotence of his will."[29]

If God's freedom and omnipotence are to be understood solely under the category of call, of his efficacious word of address, by which he allows himself time and through which he allows us time, then God's omnipotence and human freedom are not at all mutually exclusive. "You are the one," as Hamann prays in the *Biblische Betrachtungen*, "who creates when he speaks, and yet allows nature time from morning till evening to do your will."[30]

The fact that Hamann's meditation on time in essence occurs in the form of prayer is neither accidental nor external to it. Just as Augustine arrives at his well-known meditation on time in the *Confessiones*, a meditation that still occupies theologians, philosophers, and philologists today, so too Hamann speaks in the form of confession, in prayer. He responds to the word, to the call that enables him to answer and gains him time, his time. Further, what seems to link him to Augustine is his use of meditation on time for the present, for "To-day." "It is not strictly correct to say that there are three times, past, present, and future. It might be correct to say that there are three times, a present of past things, a present of present things, and a present of future things. . . . The present of past things is the memory; the present of present things is direct perception; and the present of future things is expectation."[31]

Despite its personal setting, this Augustinian starting point of the meditation on time for the present proves to be rhetorical and philosophical, since what is acoustical is not only translated into the visual but replaced by it.[32] In the tradition of ancient rhetoric Augustine speaks of the halls of memory where remembrances lie. If for Augustine the

29. "Biblische Betrachtungen," in N I, 170, 3-18; cf. N I, 180, 31f.

30. "Biblische Betrachtungen," in N I, 63, 17-19.

31. Augustine, *Confessions*, XI, 20, 26, trans. R. S. Pine Coffin (London: Penguin, 1988), 269, 274.

32. Cf. E. A. Schmidt, *Zeit und Geschichte bei Augustin* (Heidelberg: Winter, 1985).

acoustical is reduced to the visual, for Hamann it induces the visual. What belongs to "To-day" he does not construe philosophically as spatial; he learns it directly from the language of the Bible, in its acoustics. He meditates on it in conjunction with the sight of God's voice[33] as narrated in Deuteronomy 4:12, a voice summarized in the single, primal promise: "I am the Lord your God!" (Deut. 5:6). The speaking God is not without shape, not least of all without the shape of the burning bush[34] and the fire.[35] In the context of such a synthesis of sight with hearing, Hamann (on Deut. 4:39: "So acknowledge today and take to heart . . .") emphatically affirms that

> the whole duration of time is nothing but a to-day of eternity. The whole of time made up a single day in God's economy in which all hours cohere and are included in one morning and one evening. The coming of our Saviour was the noon-day of time. The creation which cost God six days shall not last longer than to-day. God! what is eternity, and what is the Lord of eternity! How many millions of days it has taken, how many millions of revolutions the earth has made before it has reached to-day's; and how many millions will follow which Thou hast numbered as all that have passed have been numbered. Just as this eternity of days which have been and will be in the world are nothing but to-day for Thee, so the present day is an eternity for me. The whole duration of time is nothing but a to-day of eternity. The whole of time for me, even the present moment is an eternity for me.[36]

When Hamann seeks to interpret time in metaphors of space he proceeds once more from and takes aim at "To-day." He emphasizes that God

> allows the past to happen again, and what happens is nothing but a matrix of the future. Or rather, the plan for all time has a midpoint toward which all lines, all figures relate and unite. The building

33. "Biblische Betrachtungen," in N I, 64, 27-34; cf. 49, 29-32.

34. "Biblische Betrachtungen," in N I, 65, 31–66, 4.

35. "Biblische Betrachtungen," in N I, 60, 25 ("in fire . . ."). Cf. "Schürze von Feigenblättern," in N III, 207, 11f. Ezra 1:27.

36. "Biblical Reflections," in Smith, 129 (N I, 70, 19-32) (translation altered). Cf. "Betrachtungen zu Kirchenlieder," in N I, 279, 25–280.

consists of one single piece; the laws of relations are simple. The present is the front; the surface ahead of it is open to us but the entire body with its hindsight is withdrawn. The past and future are just this side we see in profile, in contraction. Each movement of the eye gives us another dimension or picture of it in another dimension; all these are mutilations of the whole and give us, as it were, an idea of perfection and beauty.[37]

The Present as Foundation and Reason for Past and Future

This start with "To-day," of the present in its fullness granted by God, characterizes Hamann's understanding of time. We need not expressly emphasize that this present is not the eternal present of Being, not the Parmenidean *nunc stans* of a timeless present. It is the present time of God in his name, in the promise of his accompanying presence, free in love (Exod. 3:14): I am who I am in freedom with you, and I will be the one who goes with you in freedom. Thus the key sentence of Hamann's understanding of time reads, "With God the present is the foundation and reason for the past and the future."[38]

This key sentence appears in Hamann's meditation on Revelation 1:3 and 4. The understanding of time in the *Biblische Betrachtungen* is concentrated in it. But here it explicitly appears in its Trinitarian structure, repeated in the final cadence of many of Hamann's writings:[39]

He is . . . he was . . . he will be. [The] time is at hand, it is nigh — only lately — scripture teaches us Christians to tell time, the whole length of it, by God's reckoning. We, his children, should also seek to learn how he tells it. Our life is as the duration of the whole world, nothing more than a To-day before God and every creature. What is our death? We must at least see it as near as every future moment. Is it we who die? No, it is the world that dies to us, passes away for us, and the dust where our head lies. One's death is thus the time where this revelation is in part fulfilled in every human soul. In this sense it is literally true that the time of fulfillment is

---

37. "Biblische Betrachtungen," in N I, 123, 38–124, 10.
38. "Biblical Reflections," in Smith, 138 (N I, 248, 31f.) (translation altered).
39. Cf. for example "Zwei Scherflein," in N III, 242, 12-18 (cf. below note 69).

nigh and should make us alert to the end of the world which at death ceases for us, passes away and is no more, should make us ready to travel.

How imperfect and inadequate men's ideas are to represent heavenly and spiritual things! God's eternity can only be grasped through the divisions of time, through a combination of three moments that in our inadequacy we are forced to compare and distinguish. The unchangeableness of God, in which, as James says (1:17), there is no variation or shadow due to change, can only be made clear to us by means of the transitoriness of earthly things. In our conceptions the past precedes the present; with God the present is the foundation and reason for the past and the future. What can give us a more wonderful and mysterious idea of God's unchanging and inexhaustible greatness and unfathomable heights than this destruction, or this surpassing, of all human ideas! In this Name of God there is not only an image of the Holy Trinity, but also in particular of our divine Redeemer. *He is* — I am with you always, till the close of the age — *he was* — the Word became flesh and dwelt among us, full of grace and truth — *he will be* — Behold, I come, is written of me in the book. Come, Lord Jesus![40]

With such a Trinitarian understanding of time Hamann is thinking neither of an origin nor a goal, but from out of a given middle. He is proceeding from a key event that discloses the meaning of events that precede and follow, and at the same time allows their fulfillment to be given beforehand. "I found the unity of the divine will in the redemption of Jesus Christ, so that all history, all miracles, all commands and works of God flowed towards this centre, to stir the soul of man from the slavery, bondage, blindness, folly and death of sins to the greatest happiness, the highest blessedness and an acceptance of goods. . . ."[41]

In order that seizure by such fulfillment should not be perverted into an autonomous and illusionary anticipation of the end that lays hold of nothing but an impenetrable night, I at the moment must be set at the midpoint of all of history. In Homer's poetic method Hamann sees a parable of God's speaking and acting as history. The *Iliad,* which begins with Homer's immediately setting his readers at the midpoint of the

---

40. "Biblical Reflections," in Smith, 138 (N I, 248, 8–249, 3) (translation altered).
41. "Thoughts about My Life," in Smith, 152-53 (N II, 40, 17-23).

whole story, "is like our life, when a higher muse controls its threads from the spindle of the first goddess of fate to the scissors of the last, and inserts its sketches into the weave."[42]

It is thus not a matter of setting myself at the center of histories that renders them as one history, so as to produce or take into myself an origin and goal related to me, or to find such a center already in me with the unity of my self-consciousness, as, per Schleiermacher, "the immediate presence of entire, undivided . . . existence."[43] And it is not a matter of perceiving this center on Kierkegaard's and Bultmann's terms as an isolated "moment." The center at which I am placed is rather a quite specific event, the self-mediating Word become flesh. "All philosophical resistance and the entire riddle of our existence, the impenetrable night of its terminus a quo and terminus ad quem, are dissolved by the charter of the Word become flesh."[44]

The Understanding of Time and the Concept of Science

Remarkably, Hamann did not attempt to abstract from his dictionary, from the language of the Bible. Yet he is so intense a contemporary of the Enlightenment, so much a modern thinker, that he was able to allow his understanding of time heard and learned from the Bible to effect scientific-theoretical reflection. Two chief evidences of this are the *Zweiter Hellenistischer Brief*[45] and his "division of the intellectual universe" in the *Fliegender Brief*,[46] which allows for meditation under the aspect of the relation between rationality and utopia.[47]

Hamann impressively ties his understanding of time gleaned from the Bible with the triadic concept of science of Francis Bacon.[48] The

---

42. ZH I, 360, 36–361, 2 (in relation to 360, 21ff., to his brother; 1759).

43. H. Steffens, *Von der falschen Theologie und dem wahren Glauben. Eine Stimme aus der Gemeinde* (Breslau: J. Max und Kamp, 1823), 99f. Cf. Schleiermacher, *The Christian Faith*, trans. H. R. Mackintosh and J. S. Stewart (Philadelphia: Fortress, 1976), §3.2, 6-7.

44. "Zweifel und Einfälle," in N III, 192, 22-26.

45. "Cloverleaf of Hellenistic Letters, Second Letter," in Haynes, 35-36 (N II, 174-78).

46. "Ein fliegender Brief," in N III, 396, 21.

47. On the subject cf. Bayer, *Umstrittene Freiheit* (UTB 1092), 135-51.

48. Francis Bacon, *De dignitate et augmentis scientiarum* II, c. 1. *The Works of Francis Bacon*. Facsimile reprint of the edition of Spedding, Ellis, and Heath (1857-1874) (Boston: H. O. Houghton and Co., 1963). Cf. S. Dangelmayr, *Methode und System. Wissenschafts-klassifikation bei Bacon, Hobbes und Locke* (Meisenheim [am Glan]: Hain, 1974).

concept had met with wide approval and been reviewed, for example, by Diderot and d'Alembert, in the *Discours préliminaire* (1751) of the *Encyclopédie,*[49] and by Buffon (1753).[50] Bacon divides science according to the three faculties of soul, that is, memory, perception of the present, and the power of imagination in respect of the future. Historical science is assigned to *memoria,* philosophy to *ratio,* and poetry to *phantasia.*[51] Hamann takes up this division without explicitly citing it. He speaks of the "scholar," thus of the historian, the "philosopher," and the "poet."[52] Then in the *Zweiter Hellenistischer Brief* he reverses the order and adopts a firm stance toward the old debate between poetry and philosophy, in vogue since Plato. He begins "with Homer, Pindar, and the poets of Greece"[53] in order to give preeminence to the poetic and utopian. This does not denote disparagement of the past and its remembrance. However, he sees this from the perspective of the future construed as hope in "a divine renewal of the past." "What would the most exact, most meticulous knowledge of the present be without a divine renewal of the past, without an intimation of the future . . . ? What kind of Labyrinth would the present time be for the spirit of observation without the spirit of prophecy and its guides from the past and future . . . for orienting the weathervane of philosophical speculation?"[54]

49. "Thus memory, reason strictly speaking, and imagination, are the three different ways in which our mind operates on the objects of its thoughts. These three faculties first of all form three general divisions of our system, and the three general objects of human knowledge; History, which relates to memory; Philosophy, the fruit of reason; and the Fine Arts to which imagination gives birth." Denis Diderot, Jean le Rond d'Alembert, *Encyclopédie, ou Dictionnaire raisonné des Sciences, des Arts et des Métiers,* Tome premier (Paris: Briasson, 1751-1765), *Discours préliminaire des Editeurs, XVI* (new printing in facsimile of the first edition of 1751-1780, vol. 1, 1966).

50. Cf. "Königsbergsche Zeitungen," in N IV, 425, 1f. Buffon, *Discours sur le style* (Paris: C. Delagrave, 1894); cf. chapter 2, "Style and Form," above note 3), XVIII.

51. Cf. note 48 above, vol. 1, 494: *"Historia ad Memoriam refertur; Poesis ad Phantasiam; Philosophia ad rationem"* ("history refers to memory, poetry to imagination, philosophy to reason").

52. "Aesthetica in nuce," in Haynes, 65-66 (N II, 199, 1-3). Cf. Haynes, 76 (N II, 205, 2-11) and also ZH I, 374, 12 ("Naturgeschichte, Philosophie und Poesie" ["natural history, philosophy, and poetry"]; to Kant; 1759).

53. "Cloverleaf of Hellenistic Letters, Second Letter," in Haynes, 44 (N II, 174, 31f.) in the context to Haynes, 43-44 (N II, 174, 31-176, 7). This applies despite the fact that "all authors are liars" (N IV, 457, 25).

54. "Ein fliegender Brief," in N III, 398, 10-26.

In this text of the *Fliegender Brief* already introduced in the chapter on "History and Reason,"[55] the dimensions of the past and future are perceived together over against the present, so that from a division into three has resulted a division into two. This clearly shows Hamann's interest in preventing the isolation of the present and the attention philosophy has given it, so that the "present moment" does not become a "dead torso, without head or feet."[56] To this end we are referred to the spirit of revealed prophecy: "The past must be revealed to us, and the future likewise."[57]

If the past like the future is revealed to us, then the past can also be read as future. Such a reading of past history is not, as Ernst Bloch directs, on the search for unrealized possibilities so as to realize them. Rather, it occurs through the spectacles of the Bible, which tells of God's activity in raising the dead and creating anew in such fashion that I am entitled "to a like hope" and can read "my own course of life" in a history already occurred, "in the history of the Jewish people,"[58] because I am addressed through it today by the triune God.

It is thus the sure prophetic word that has brought and brings the true future, the unsurpassably new, not, for example, a possibility immanent in the material of the diffuse and universal process of history, such as according to Bloch's ontology of the Not-Yet.

Hamann's biblical understanding of Word and Spirit determines that peculiar inversion found in the *Zweiter Hellenistischer Brief* which has continually fascinated theoreticians of time and history.[59] "The writer of history" is taken to be "the flimsiest author." "But can the past be understood when not even the present is understood? — And who will form correct ideas of the present without knowing the future? The future determines the present, and the present determines the past, as the purpose determines the nature and use of the means — we are nevertheless already accustomed here to a υστερον προτερον [later-earlier] in our

---

55. Cf. above chapter 8, "History and Reason," note 64.

56. Cf. above note 29 and referring to this "Biblische Betrachtungen," in N I, 180, 23 27.

57. Cf. above note 29 and referring to this N I, 180, 31f. ("What is forgotten calls us back and allows us to see into the future").

58. Cf. above chapter 3, "Original Motif," especially note 39 and referring to this "Biblische Betrachtungen," in N I, 178, 1f.

59. Cf. for example R. Koselleck, "Die unbekannte Zukunft und die Kunst der Prognose," in *Attempto*, Fascicle 70/71 (Tübingen: 1984/85), (80-85) 80.

way of thinking: through our actions we reverse all moments, like images in the eye without even noticing anything of it. —"[60]

Since Hamann notes this reversal and reflects on it, he contradicts the concept, in vogue since Aristotle, according to which "time" mainly is "that by which movement can be numerically estimated,"[61] in essence, linear, chronometric. He also contradicts the reflection and repetition of this linear concept of time in logic. If Aristotle and his successors insist on a linear, irreversible series of thoughts that does not allow "inferring the earlier from the later,"[62] if they want "no other proof to prevail but the rectilinear,"[63] Hamann radically questions the preeminence of this chronometric orientation and with it the preeminence of the notion of causality.[64] Analogous to the optical reversal in the eye, he reverses this usual orientation, not to replace it by giving preeminence to the temporal mode of the future together with the modality of possibility over past and present,[65] but in order to recognize the one "who as Lord has all times in his power and uses all times for our best,"[66] in whose hands are my times (Ps. 30:15), with whom "the present is the foundation and reason of the past and the future."[67]

However significant this understanding of time for a scientific concept, it cannot be secularized. The rigor of the factual would have to be denied or the human *ingenium* given the power to forgive sins and raise the dead. Only by hearing the "prophetic word more fully confirmed" (2 Peter 1:19) gone forth, the dead do not fall prey to a "past" wholly sealed off, and to the judgment of any given present, in the cult or judgment of the dead. In the community established by the confirmed prophetic Word they allow themselves not only to be asked about what they once wanted to say to their contemporaries, but what they have to say to us and ask today.

---

60. "Cloverleaf of Hellenistic Letters, Second Letter," in Haynes, 45-46 (N II, 175, 33-40).

61. Aristotle, *The Physics*, The Loeb Classical Library, trans. Wicksteed and Cornford (Cambridge, MA: Harvard University Press, 1963), IV, 11 (219 b 1), p. 387.

62. Aristotle, *Prior Analytics*, The Loeb Classical Library, trans. Hugh Tredennick (Cambridge, MA: Harvard University Press, 1962), II, 16, p. 485.

63. "Wolken," in N II, 98, 2f.

64. Cf. "Metacritique," in Haynes, 216 (N III, 288, 17f.).

65. "Wolken," in N II, 175, 37 (goal-means), is not to be understood in this way.

66. "Biblische Betrachtungen," in N I, 180, 32-34.

67. Cf. above note 38.

In the sphere of the communication of justified sinners, of those raised from the dead, one moves by hearing, asking, answering, contradicting, accusing, and excusing, not in a monologue of the mind, in imaginary space where everything is simultaneous. Faith in the promise of life through death and the hope grounded in this promise do not shut off from the world but disclose it in an unheard-of breadth and depth. Still, this does not happen in the anticipatory assumption that the world and its history are now transparent and the contemplating mind can see that it contains a "rational process."[68] Fragments are not rounded, faults not imagined to be necessary, the contrary not taken as ultimately meaningful. Guilt and forgiveness are not linked as immanent. Continuity is awaited solely from the fidelity of the One who does not allow the work of his hands to be abandoned.

The Trinitarian concluding cento of the *Zwei Scherflein* is an especially impressive text on time in the interlacing of its modes toward the present: The kingdom of God is now in your midst (Luke 17:21)! The cento reads and looks like this: "*Let there be!* — The first and *last word of triune creation!* — *And there was light! There was flesh! Let there be fire!* — *Behold!* a *new heaven* and a *new earth* — (without sea) — and a *new creation!* — The old has passed, *behold!* all has become *new. Behold! I am making all things new!* — LORD! Where then? — Where there is a carcass, there HE is!"[69]

68. Hegel, *Lectures on the Philosophy of World History: Introduction*, trans. H. B. Nisbet (Cambridge: Cambridge University Press, 1998), 27.

69. "Zwei Scherflein," in N III, 242, 12-18 (at the end of the text designated above in note 40 there is reference to the corresponding trinity). Cf. "Zwei Scherflein," in N III, 233, 27-29.

Translators' Epilogue

Johann Georg Hamann (1730-1788) is gaining recognition in the English-speaking world, not only in German studies but also in literary criticism, the history of ideas, and philosophy and theology.[1] This volume can serve as a further impetus for this momentum. Oswald Bayer, retired Professor of Systematic Theology at the Eberhard-Karls University in Tübingen, Germany, internationally known for his expertise in Hamann,[2] is well equipped to serve this growing interest in and appropriation of Hamann's thinking. Bayer's study ranks as an important contribution to Hamann; this manuscript presents the fruit of an intensive research to a general readership. It offers a series of lectures given to all the faculties at the University of Tübingen and is designed to be accessible even to undergraduates. Interweaving theological, philosophical, and literary perspectives within a historical and systematic ex-

---

1. Consider two recent texts, John R. Betz, *After Enlightenment: Hamann as Post-Secular Visionary* (Chichester, UK: Blackwell, 2009), and Gwen Griffith-Dickson, *Johann Georg Hamann's Relational Metacriticism* (Berlin: De Gruyter, 1995). Interest in Hamann has also impacted recent Anglican theology. See for instance "The Theological Critique of Philosophy in Hamann and Jacobi," in *Radical Orthodoxy*, ed. John Milbank, Catherine Pickstock, and Graham Ward (London: Routledge, 1999), 21-37.

2. See for instance (with C. Knudsen) *Kreuz und Kritik. Johann Georg Hamanns Letztes Blatt, Text und Interpretation* (Tübingen: J. C. B. Mohr [Paul Siebeck], 1983) and (with assistance from B. Gleede and U. Moustakas) *Vernunft ist Sprache. Hamanns Metakritik Kants, Spekulation und Erfahrung*, Texte und Untersuchungen zum Deutschen Idealismus, vol. 50 (Stuttgart–Bad Cannstatt: Frommann-Holzboog, 2002).

position, Bayer intentionally offers a multidimensional approach to Hamann. Most importantly, this text interprets Hamann from the context of his faith. While accessible to the general reader, the specialist will find the notes engaging for specific inquiries into Hamann's intellectual milieu and its ramifications for our own intellectual context. In this regard, Bayer ably exegetes Hamann's responses to Herder's anthropology, Kant's view of the Enlightenment and the relationship between language and reason, Lessing's perspective on the historicity of reason, and Moses Mendelssohn's stance on the foundation of social order. Bayer also provides a sharp corrective to Isaiah Berlin's book on Hamann, which presents Hamann as an irrationalist, and ignores the findings of recent Hamann research that form the background of Bayer's argument here.[3]

Bayer refers to Hamann as a contemporary — and he understands this in a twofold sense. First, Hamann is contemporary to the eighteenth century, the period of the High Enlightenment, and was not only a keen observer of his time but also one who was fully conversant with its literature and ideals. While rejecting the Enlightenment's reductionist views of truth as clear and distinct ideas and reason as instrumental, Hamann understood his colleagues' quest for a secularized Europe from the inside out. Hamann critiques several notions that arose during this time, including subjectivity as the unity of self-consciousness, freedom as the basic concept of anthropology and ethics, nature as devoid of spirit, reality construed as a metaphysical unity, and faith in scientific and social progress. The importance of Hamann's thought can be seen in that it was the impetus for the questions raised by Herder, the *Sturm und Drang* movement, Romanticism, and Søren Kierkegaard.

Second, Bayer presents Hamann as our contemporary — one who as a "radical Enlightener" can address our current concerns. Hamann does this by integrating features that modern inquiry separates, such as reason and sensuousness, and the contingent and the necessary, into a comprehensive aesthetic, a perception of reality with heart, mouth, and hands. This integration refuses to abstract conceptual reasoning from sensuousness, the empirical, and the historical, and from tradition, experience, and language. Hamann sought a new hearing and learning that is neither mere construction nor mere remembrance, grounded neither

---

3. Isaiah Berlin, *The Magus of the North: J. G. Hamann and the Origins of Modern Irrationalism* (London: Fontana, 1994); this is a new edition of a much earlier text.

in intuition nor in some irrational approach, but instead in rhetorical means — in the medium of history, philosophy, poetry, and the logic of thinking and imagery. He opposed all abstract disassociations between thought and experience devised by Enlightenment philosophers and argued instead for the integration of thought and experience. Specifically, Hamann's critique of Kant's "purism" of reason is akin to a postmodern critique of modern notions of abstract universality. Likewise, Hamann's critique of "truth as system" was already appropriated by Kierkegaard as a powerful antidote to Hegel. And, Hamann's views of the relationship between language and reason parallel those of Ludwig Wittgenstein with his view of language as "language games" intertwined with various "forms of life." His thinking has not only affinity with postmodern approaches, but is likewise indebted to a premodern approach, the "oldest aesthetic," as he put it, "to fear God and give him the glory"[4] — in other words, indebted to truth, which puts all other knowledge within the perspective of the alpha and omega of all creatures and creation itself.

Hamann's Life: A Brief Sketch

Primarily a journalist and writer, Johann Georg Hamann was born in 1730 in Königsberg, East Prussia, the native city of Immanuel Kant, a lifelong friend. His writings remarkably combine detailed philological work with philosophical depth and breadth. Hamann did not serve on the faculty of a research university as a professional member of the academic guild but instead was a man of letters. He was always first and foremost a reader, and then an author. He was predominantly a philologist — a lover of the word: for him all books were Bibles. And, for Hamann, God himself is an author, a poet. With Luther, Hamann contended that the most noble and powerful capacity of the human is the ability to speak. With this, he affirmed an aesthetic of receptivity, one that unites the author and the reader in a way akin to the unity of husband and wife.

Sent to London in 1756 on a mission by the Berens, a merchant family in Riga, Hamann underwent a crisis as a result of the failure of this mission and the profligate life he led that attended this letdown. Ultimately, his response to this crisis — an intense and thorough reading of the Bible

---

4. See *Aesthetica in Nuce* in Haynes, 95 (N II, 217, 16-17).

— transformed him and in effect rendered him an opponent of the Enlightenment. He began this reading of scripture on March 13, 1758. Isaiah Berlin writes that the crisis spelled Hamann's return to the religion of his childhood following a love-affair with the Enlightenment — a return to Lutheran Protestantism, and that his application of this new light "burned for him until the end of his days."[5] In this volume, Oswald Bayer writes that the "knot" of Hamann's depression was untied on March 31, while reading the story of Cain and Abel in Genesis 4, and added that this does not mean that Hamann had the experience in an isolated moment or by way of pure intuition.[6] As still another wrote, perhaps Hamann's "conversion" can only be referred to in figures, none of which yields more than a single facet of the event, an inaccessibility due to the event as veiled, as God's and Hamann's secret, not even accessible to Hamann himself.[7] In any case, in London, while reading the Bible Hamann experienced that in reading he was read, that in understanding — through "the descent into the hell of self-understanding"[8] — he was understood, and understood better, more critically and mercifully, than he could ever understand himself. In a bundle of pages titled "Biblische Betrachtungen eines Christen,"[9] the twenty-eight-year-old alluded to this crisis and the task of his life.

When he returned to Königsberg, Hamann's friends Johann Christoph Berens and Immanuel Kant sought to return him to Enlightenment ideals. Hamann's response was to author the *Socratic Memorabilia*, where, taking the voice of Socrates, he indirectly challenged his friends' uncritical absorption with the secular intellectual and economic ideals of the "public," which in its own way was an idol. Hamann was to serve as a "minister of the word," not as a clergyman or university professor (he was a stutterer) but as a journalist, for years a writer for the *Königsbergschen Gelehrten und Politischen Zeitungen*. Through Kant's intervention, he secured a position as a translator at the francophone customs office of the Prussian king, Frederick the Great, and later an administrator at the port. This position gave Hamann time to think and

---

5. See Isaiah Berlin, *The Magus of the North*, pp. 10, 13-14.

6. See above chapter 3.

7. See Harry Sievers, *Johann Georg Hamanns Bekehrung, Ein Versuch, Sie zu Verstehen*, Studien zur Dogmengeschichte und Systematischen Theologie, vol. 24 (Zürich: Zwingli Verlag, 1969), 104, 152ff.

8. "Chimärische Einfälle," in N II, 164, 18.

9. "Biblische Betrachtungen eines Christen," in BW, 65-311.

write. Most of his published works, however, were, as he put it, "flying leaves," not conventional, direct, linear essays favored in his day (like our own), but highly unconventional, indirect, tapestry- or matrix-like letters, reviews, or writings that sought to critique and evaluate the works of his contemporaries. Protesting against the sexual double standard of his time, where it was common for gentlemen to have both a wife and a mistress, he lived in a common-law relationship with his father's caregiver, Anna Regina Schumacher, the mother of his four children. Having obtained a pension, Hamann died in Münster (where he is buried), while visiting an admirer, the Princess von Gallitzin, a Roman Catholic, who along with her circle of intellectual colleagues was devoted to Hamann's oeuvre.

Against Kant's View of Immaturity

Kant's epoch-making work, the *Critique of Pure Reason*,[10] appeared in 1781. According to one report,[11] through the offices of the Riga publisher Hartknoch, Hamann assisted in the *Critique* and asked permission to read the proofs. He may thus have been the first reader of the printed copy of Kant's work, and in July 1781 received a bound exemplar from the author. On the basis of the advance-proof, Hamann had already written on July 1 a review of the *Critique of Pure Reason*, but did not publish it.[12] In a letter to his pupil Johann Gottfried Herder (1744-1803), he gave the reason: "I filed it because I did not want to offend the author who was an old friend, and, I must almost say, benefactor, since I have him almost entirely to thank for my first post."[13]

Isaiah Berlin writes of Hamann as "the first out-and-out opponent of the French Enlightenment of his time . . . the forgotten source of a movement that in the end engulfed the whole of European culture . . . the first writer in modern days to denounce the Enlightenment and all

---

10. Immanuel Kant, *Kritik der Reinen Vernunft* (Riga: Johann Friedrich Hartknoch, 1781). English translation: *The Critique of Pure Reason*, trans. Norman Kemp Smith (New York: St. Martin's, 1929).

11. Cf. Johann Georg Hamann, *Entkleidung und Verklärung, Eine Auswahl aus Schriften und Briefen des "Magus im Norden,"* ed. Martin Seils (Berlin: Eckart-Verlag, 1963), 293, n. 1.

12. See Oswald Bayer, *Vernunft ist Sprache, Hamanns Metakritik Kants*, 63-149.

13. Quoted in Oswald Bayer, *Vernunft ist Sprache*, 64.

its works . . . the first great shot in the battle of the romantic individual-ists against rationalism and totalitarianism."[14] Hamann stated his op-position to the Enlightenment in a December 18, 1784, four-page letter to Christian Jacob Kraus, Professor of Practical Philosophy and State-craft at Königsberg. The letter is a virtual exegesis of Kant's famous es-say "Was ist Aufklärung?" Hamann saw the source of Kant's error in his use of "the cursed adjective *self-incurred*," a term in the original connoting guilt[15] and on his view falsely applied to the immature, those who refused to dare to think for themselves. For Hamann, the guilt was that of the "wearisome tutor who is the correlative of the immature," a guilt consisting in his blindness even while pretending to see. The "tu-tor" had taken the balcony view, distancing himself from actual life, moving in cold abstraction, a theoretician skulking "in nightcap and behind the stove." He was blind to his separation of thought from ac-tual existence. With his distinction between a public or philosophical and a private or ordinary citizen's use of reason, Kant, this self-appointed guardian of the immature, was blind to the political effect of his philosophizing. Hamann insisted that it was the discourse of ordi-nary people that was best able to portray what was significant for life. In an ironic twist on Paul's word in 1 Corinthians 14 enjoining women to keep silence in the church, Hamann wrote that at home the women may of course chatter to their hearts' content, the private use of reason being their daily bread, and then concluded by describing the entire matter of a self-incurred immaturity as something with which his three daughters would never put up.

The upshot is that the harshness with which Kant presumed to judge the immature was now directed toward Kant himself, the tutor. Hamann insisted that thought and practical-sensuous existence belong together. The issue is thus to unite "the two natures" of the immature and the guide or tutor. In the guardianship of the one who lives in the "fear of the Lord," they are in fact united. Irritated by the philosophers' divorcing language from experience, separating what God had joined together, he argued for their reunification. Earlier, in an extended review of Kant's *Critique* titled *Metakritik über den Purismum der Vernunft,* and included in a letter to Herder in September 1784, Hamann had accused Kant of di-viding thought and speech, a divorce reflecting a "purism" that in effect

14. Berlin, *Magus of the North*, xv, 4, 22, 71, 107.
15. *Selbstverschuldet.*

puts reason to death.[16] "Reason is language, *logos*," wrote Hamann, "on this marrowbone I gnaw, and shall gnaw myself to death on it."[17]

Against Kant's Purism of Reason

The division between thought and speech in Kant only reflected what had been the principal method of the Enlightenment, that is, a separating the eternal from the temporal, the universal truths of reason from the accidental events of history, thinking from hearing or seeing, subject from object, the metaphysical from the historical. The separation had been given classic formulation in the philosophy of Descartes, and was repeated in Moses Mendelssohn. Hamann called them all *Scheidekünstler,* "artists of separation," and dedicated his life's work to contradicting this prevailing tendency. In his insistence on the unity of public and private reason in the letter to Kraus, or on the unity of thought and language as the true element of reason made visible in his *Metakritik,* Hamann worked from the background of the Protestant, Lutheran view of the "communication" between the "properties" of the two natures of Christ *(communicatio idiomatum),* or its view of the relation between the visible elements and the invisible grace in the sacrament. Hamann repeatedly asserted that this communication of the divine and human *idiomata,* or properties, is "a basic law and the master-key to all our knowledge."[18] He argued that the philosophers, on the other hand, wanted to be independent of the sensuous and accidental, but their claim to the timelessness of truth was a chimera; it was mysticism. In the Cartesian separation of subject from object, the subject was without a world, and the world was reified as a pure object. As the medium through which God speaks to humankind, the world, nature was reduced to total silence. And all that interest of the Enlightenment in historical research was also for the purpose of gaining a distance from, and not communicating with, what was researched.

An attention-getting exchange between Isaiah Berlin and James C. O'Flaherty, Professor Emeritus of German at Wake Forest University,

16. For an extended analysis of the letter and the *Metakritik,* cf. the volume by Bayer referred to above (note 2).

17. H V, 177, 18 (August 6, 1784; to Herder).

18. "The Last Will and Testament of the Knight of the Rose-Cross," in Haynes, 99 (N III, 27, 12-14).

suggests the need for caution when describing Hamann as an out-and-out anti-rationalist. In response to an essay on Hamann by Berlin,[19] O'Flaherty writes that Hamann's relation to the Enlightenment has undergone radical revision in recent years. He argues that despite Hamann's vehement attacks on reason, he allowed for the legitimate use of reason, and could actually say that "faith has need of reason as much as reason has need of faith." Thus, O'Flaherty concludes, "contemporary scholarship demurs on the charge of irrationalism against 'the Magus of the North.'"[20] Whether or not O'Flaherty's response led him to give greater precision to his characterization of Hamann's stance, Berlin writes that "to call Hamann an anti-rationalist is to say that he attacked the methods by which the great rationalists . . . stated, analyzed, and sought to justify their views," concluding with the statement that "it is this that makes the fact that Hamann is the first and most vehement opponent of the French Enlightenment and its descendants a phenomenon of historical importance."[21]

Freeing Theology from Kant

At one time, it was common to assume that the intellectual trajectory of the Reformation theologian Luther ultimately led to Kant, i.e., a skepticism about metaphysics' ability to get at reality as such and that the kingdom of God would be fulfilled on earth through following the categorical imperative, honoring self and others as ends-in-themselves. For Kant, the categorical imperative — the criterion for all ethical behavior — and not the senses offered a window into the noumenal, reality as such. What Bayer's interpretation of Hamann indicates, however, is that the evidence does not warrant the assumption that Luther leads to Kant. The theological ancestors of Kant are not the classical Reformers, such as Luther, but instead those who rose out of the Radical Reformation. Luther consistently appealed to an embodied word, a stance heightened by his encounters with Zwingli, and the Radical Reformers, the Ana-

19. Isaiah Berlin, "The Magus of the North," *The New York Review of Books* 40, no. 17, October 21, 1993.

20. James C. O'Flaherty, "The Magus of the North," *The New York Review of Books*, 40, no. 19, November 18, 1993.

21. "The Magus of the North," by James C. O'Flaherty; reply by Isaiah Berlin, *The New York Review of Books* 40, no. 19, November 18, 1993.

baptists and Spiritualists, such as Casper Schwenckfeld. The Radical Reformation was inclined to seek the Spirit outside the text, affirm soulful existence apart from the body, an ideal church over against the one we actually encounter, the one embedded in human society. In other words, these theologians' approaches unlike Luther's have Gnostic, mystic, and Manichean tendencies.

These are exactly the same tendencies expressed in Kant. For Kant, reason can and should be lifted out of the manifold of experience. Its powers can be discerned apart from the manifold of experience or the range and ability of the senses. Reason sees only what it has already produced with its own schemes.[22] Kant is a descendant of the Radical Reformers because he acknowledges no *verbum externum* but only a *verbum internum*. In contrast to this assumption, Hamann affirms that there is no pure a priori of knowledge but instead only a historical a priori of knowledge, of all comprehensive perceptions of the world — given especially in the Old Testament. For Hamann, similar to the postliberal thinker George Lindbeck, it is the text that absorbs the world and not the world the text.[23]

Hume is well known for his skepticism with regard to matters of faith. What is fascinating is that Hamann appealed precisely to Hume's skepticism — applying it to all matters where we claim knowledge. Ultimately, faith is all we have to go on in our dealings with nature. While it was Hume who — mediated by Hamann — woke Kant from his "dogmatic slumbers," Kant never secured or made room for faith as he claimed. Kant falsely assumed that knowledge operated outside faith, that is, knowledge of how we know. But, Hamann sees even this knowledge as a construct and thus as colored by language, culture, and history. Ultimately, Hamann's message to the Enlightenment is that reason is *only* rational when it acknowledges that it does its work in a context or framework *wider* than itself, a framework that includes language, culture, and history. The Enlightenment sought a rational security for matters for which security cannot be had — the continuity and the consciousness of the knowing subject, the reality of the world of things and objects, the confidence that some things can be known clearly and distinctly, and the rational basis for governance. In Hamann's metacritique, all such matters

22. *The Critique of Pure Reason*, B xiii, p. 20.

23. George Lindbeck, *The Nature of Doctrine: Religion and Theology in a Postliberal Age* (Philadelphia: Westminster, 1984), 118.

are expressions of faith. Counter to Enlightenment theologians, he agreed that God's transcendence cannot be domesticated — God, world, and self cannot be subsumed under a rational "spider web" of a metaphysical system — of whatever kind of order, including that of the Kantian. Hence, for Hamann, the dualisms of Enlightenment modernity, such as selves as subjects and things as objects (and the reduction of all experience into such subject/object schemata), a metaphysical matrix in which God, self, and world conform to a specific rational inquiry (since all share a place within the flattened scope of infinity), the quest for human freedom as autonomy independent of the social responsibilities that are pre-given or government as artificially grounded in a hypothetical construct of the consent of the governed — are all open to intense scrutiny. Ultimately the problem of the metaphysical enterprise is less the inability of the senses to chart supersensuous reality than the quest to achieve a schema more comprehensive than the scriptural narrative itself. It is the cross alone finally that shatters the vanity of the seamless metaphysical garment. All knowledge is ultimately through faith alone. The key is to test claims of knowledge in light of the cross.

The Bible as the Key to Nature and History

What is often missed in an appraisal of Hamann's work is that his faith as a response to the crisis of his youth extended throughout his life, "until the end of his days." For, once the Bible with its merciful nearness of God had given him conquest of the deadly dissociation of the philosophers' separations, had given him "marriage" with God, the world, others, and himself, it became his a priori. So he could write, "another *Dos moi pou sto* I do not recognize or know than his word."[24] For this reason the joining together of what the philosopher had separated began with an insight derived from the Bible. He wrote: "All the perceptions of nature are dreams, visions, riddles, which have their clear meaning and their obscure sense. The book of nature and the book of history are no more than ciphers, hidden signs, which have need of the key which the Bible offers and which is the object of their inspiration."[25]

---

24. The Greek phrase is Archimedes' "give me a place where I can stand." See H V, 333, 16-27 (to Jacobi; 1785).

25. "Brocken," in N I, 308.

Hamann's belief that the "pictorial" language of ordinary people was most adequate to portray what is significant for life was not merely reinforced by but drawn from his understanding of the Bible with its "poetic indirection." Similarly, his conviction that meaning depended upon visualization was not merely supported by but also derived from the Bible. For this reason, he decided to render his writings in a form similar to the language of scripture, and eschewed the treatise-like shape adopted by his contemporaries, a form that still irritates and puzzles his readers. Berlin notes Hamann's "hermetic style," his mysterious formulae intended to puzzle, intrigue, and waken the reader. But, if the poetically indirect or pictorial, the image or the metaphor was the chief ingredient of communication, obscurity could attach to it and result in misunderstanding. Augustine wrote of the image as chief ingredient in communication, with the result that one could never know with absolute certainty what the communicator had in mind.[26] As for Hamann's "hermetic style," it was a deliberate attempt at imitation of the biblical word.[27]

Hamann's allegiance to the Old Testament as yielding the union of opposites was a particular offense to his contemporaries, not least of all to Kant. Hamann wrote that one could hear from the Old Testament "historical truths, not only those of past times but also of times to come," that it is the primer by which one learns to spell history, "a living mind- and heart-rousing *primer of all historical literature in heaven, on and under the earth*." The same applied to nature. The Bible does not exclude nature; it rather discloses it. But nature like history was a "sealed book, a concealed witness, a riddle that cannot be solved, without plowing with another heifer than our reason."[28]

In his "Biblische Betrachtungen eines Christen" Hamann repeats his argument against reason detached from existence, this time in the context of his observations of key biblical passages. On the Pharisees' questioning Jesus' authority in Luke 20:1-8, Hamann writes that they use their reason, draw clever conclusions, presume an ignorance they do not

---

26. Cf. The *Confessions*, Book XII.

27. The title of Albert Anderson's essay, "Philosophical Obscurantism," reflects his observation of the poetic and prophetic function of biblical language as furnishing the basis for Hamann's philosophical reflections. See Albert Anderson, "Philosophical Obscurantism: Prolegomena to Hamann's Views on Language," *Harvard Theological Review* 62, no. 3 (July 1969).

28. "Socratic Memorabilia," in Dickson, 383 (N II, 64, 11-13).

have, all of it the consequence of pacifying "our stupid *(blöde)* reason."[29] Of the voice from heaven in John 12:29, he writes that the crowd's notion of it as thunder or an angel speaking reflects reason's two excesses: explaining the voice of God in terms of natural effects or as a subordinate miracle.[30] On Paul's encounter with the altar to an "unknown god" in Acts 17:23, Hamann writes that reason is inclined to serve but is infinitely distanced from an unknown God, adding that it refuses to know him, and what is even more amazing, when it does know him, ceases to serve him.[31] On Romans 1:16 he writes that reason might be expected to know and accept this doctrine which of all others is best suited to the imperfection of our nature, and in the easiest and most probable way is raised to a level suited to our inclinations, yet nothing is more difficult and impossible for the natural man than this faith.[32]

Hamann was not an exegete in the classical sense of the term. As his *Biblische Betrachtungen eines Christen* indicates, his interest lay more in registering of observations respecting biblical texts. On the other hand, questions dealing with the biblical canon, with scriptural inspiration and the manner in which the Bible was to be read and understood, as well as its effect, occupied him throughout his life. Respecting the canon, Hamann wrote that it appears to have come about by way of an "enormous detour," despite whatever may have been gained by it. He wrote that the history of canon formation could not be decisive for the Bible's authority. He did not trust the power of church fathers and councils to canonize a book any more than he could trust the Septuagint's becoming canonical through the passages cited by the evangelists and apostles. Orthodoxy's danger was precisely in that it was convinced that it possessed eternal life in the scripture, omitting to test it as Christ required (John 5:3). To this principle of tradition Hamann opposed what he called "freedom in Christ." In its witness to Christ lay the importance of scripture.[33]

---

29. "Biblische Betrachtungen," in N I, 215.

30. "Biblische Betrachtungen," in N I, 217.

31. "Biblische Betrachtungen," in N I, 224.

32. "Biblische Betrachtungen," in N I, 227.

33. J. G. Hamann, "Hierophantische Briefe," explained by Evert Jansen Schoonhoven, *Mysterienschriften* (Gütersloh: Gütersloher Verlagshaus [Gerd Mohn], 1962), 83-85.

Hamann's Relevance for Theology Today

Against Kant's attempt at a "purism" of reason or any attempt to divorce thought from language, feeling, or the body, Hamann's work seeks to affirm the quest for knowledge within a total perception of life. He acknowledges a total context of life without a totalizing approach to reason. In this regard, he curiously comes close to the position of many postmoderns. However, since his confidence is in the truth of the Christian faith, he acknowledges the scriptures as the only basis for making sense of the world. He refuses the nihilism that today we see so readily in the postmoderns. Ultimately, life has meaning, purpose, and scope — and it is the scriptures that provide the key by which nature and history can be deciphered and thus how we can be in touch with the divine purpose written into the fabric of both. Hamann concedes no totalizing approach to reason, and yet creation itself as God's continual and constant address to us provides a meaningful context for life and vocation. Indeed, the only way that reason can be rational is when it is relative to a context wider than itself. Otherwise, it gnostically overextends itself. We may very well grieve the limits of reason but it is always better to live within reality rather than avoiding it. The "others" of reason, such as sensuousness, mythology, and embodiment, refuse to be diminished or marginalized.

Much of current theology is done in the *Scheidekunst* that Hamann decries. It is difficult if not impossible to think of contemporary theologians for whom understanding is not opposed to sensuousness or the contingent to the necessary. We are so very much children of these Enlightenment dichotomies. And, all too often, postmodernity simply tends to favor one side of these oppositions, that of the irrational, the sensuousness, or the playful, over the other side — and thereby ultimately becomes nihilistic. We need an approach that can wed what never ought to have been separated in the first place. This Hamann can do — and without favoring reason over the irrational, the necessary over the contingent, or the understanding over the sensuousness — or vice versa.

The core of this ability to wed experience and reason, sense and concept, history and idea is the Christological conviction that God was in Christ reconciling the world to himself (2 Corinthians 5:19). That is, the basis for Hamann's faith in the holding together such opposites is nothing other than the conviction that God was incarnate in Jesus Christ "for us and for our salvation." All this means that the standard ways in which theology is done today, grounding theological truth under the rubrics of knowing, doing, or feeling, needs to be challenged. Those metaphysical- and Hegelian-inspired theologies that ground truth in a comprehensive, encyclopedic knowing overestimate the power of human reason and sub- sume the wider context of experience into that of reason. These views fail to understand that in this life we walk by faith, not by sight (2 Corinthi- ans 5:7). Kantian- (or Marxist-)inspired theologies that accentuate the utopian quest for God's kingdom on earth by seeking to advance the ex- ercise of human autonomy as much as possible, ignore that we are recipi- ents at our core, receivers of God's categorical gift. Schleiermacherian- influenced theologies look to feeling as the basis for the doing of theol- ogy. At present, this has given rise to countless hyphen-theologies. This perspective looks to an internal word and not the *verbum externum* and thus ultimately if inadvertently construes theology as anthropology writ large, as Feuerbach put it. More than anything, a Hamannian-inspired approach to theology eschews the dichotomy between a private piety and a public theology. Instead, as Bayer has elsewhere claimed, "Theology be- gins and ends with the divine service."[34]

Given current concerns about the ecological crises, Hamann's work is especially pertinent. He criticized the Enlightenment approach to na- ture which on the one hand "sacrificed" nature for human exploitation and on the other "deified" it as a Mother. The quest to exploit nature for human interests was sanctioned by the Cartesian subject/object split in which the subject as such, as nonextended in space and thinking, was fundamentally separate from the world, while the world, as a collection of things or objects, was bereft of spirit. As *res extensa*, nature is subject to experimentation and utilization. Nature and spirit are separated, and nature is no longer read as the "book" of creation.

Others respond to this splintering between nature and spirit by posit- ing nature as an alter ego, "Mother Nature," as we see in some forms of Romanticism. Both perspectives fail to honor humans who as political animals possess a judicial and administrative dignity. Likewise, Hamann argues that nature is best seen as creation, a word through which God speaks to us. Nature is not finally for human exploitation but for enjoy- ment and learning.

---

34. See *Theology the Lutheran Way*, ed. and trans. Jeffrey Silcock and Mark Mattes (Grand Rapids: Eerdmans, 2006), 93.

For Hamann, we are ever addressed. We are recipients — God is ever gifting us with existence and life, in harmony with all other creatures. Likewise, God is ever and always addressing us, not only in the words of scripture, in which God speaks most clearly, but also in all creatures. To be human is to be open to this address — to let go of those defenses that close us off to God. For Hamann, dependence and autonomy must be reconfigured in light of receptivity and spontaneity. We are simultaneously lords and servants, since always we have power over others and others have power over us. Thus we need to be merciful to those under us but also courageously address those over us.

This translation is offered to the English-speaking public in the anticipation that it can make both Hamann's and Bayer's works better known, help offer a path beyond the impasse between irrationalism and fideism on the one hand and a kind of Gnostic, disembodied rationalism on the other, provide a model for the integration of scriptural hermeneutics and systematic theology, encourage a theology as thoroughly systematic yet fully grounded in and accountable to lived experience, and foster a concern for neighbor-focused politics free from an utopian political theology.

Roy A. Harrisville
Luther Seminary
St. Paul, Minnesota

Mark C. Mattes
Grand View University
Des Moines, Iowa

Chronological Table

1730   Johann Georg Hamann, born on the 27th of August in Königsberg, eldest son of the barber Johann Christoph Hamann (1697-1766) and Maria Magdalena nee Nuppenau.

1746   Matriculation at Albertus University, Königsberg. Studies include jurisprudence and political science, philosophy, languages, and literature.

1749/50   Publication of the weekly *Daphne,* with friends Johann Christoph Berens, Johann Gotthelf Lindner, and others.

1752-56   Studies without final examinations, travel to Livonia and Kurland as private tutor. Continuation of philosophical and political-economic studies, extended readings of English and French authors. Translation and *Beilage* (supplement) for a commercial-political writing at Berens's request.

1756-58   Position obtained at the commercial firm of Berens in Riga. Travel to London on a presumably commercial-political assignment. Failure of assignment effects a crisis leading to a life-change resulting in *Biblische Betrachtungen eines Christen* and *Gedanken über meinen Lebenslauf,* not intended for publication.

1758/59   In Riga again, the courtship of Catharina Berens goes awry, due to tense relationship with Johann Christoph Berens. Return to Königsberg.

1759-64   In summer of 1759, arrival of Johann Christoph Berens in Königsberg. Attempts made with Kant to effect Hamann's reconversion to the Enlightenment. The *Sokratische Denkwürdig-*

keiten appear as response and mark the onset of Hamann's authorship. Invitation to cooperate on the *Literaturbriefe* rejected but several small pieces published, of which the most important such as the *Aesthetica in nuce* appear in the omnibus volume *Kreuzzüge des Philologen* (1762). Cooperation on the *Königsbergsche Gelehrte und Politische Zeitungen.* Study of Greek, Hebrew, and Arabic, of Luther and Bengel, and lively participation in the literary and philosophical discourse as expressed in small polemical writings. Beginning of a friendship with Johann Gottfried Herder. Attempt to find a post in the Magistracy and the Departments of War and the Interior.

1764-67   Travel to Frankfurt am Main in hopes of a position tendered by Friedrich Carl von Moser. Moser defaults. By way of Berlin, Hamann meets Moses Mendelssohn and Friedrich Nicolai. Returns to Königsberg. In 1765 travel to Mitau as secretary to the attorney Tottien. Travel to Warsaw.

1767-72   Return to Königsberg. With Kant's help receives the post of translator at a French customs office. Marriage of conscience with Anna Regina Schumacher. The first of four children born. The economic situation severe. Smaller French writings, translations from the English, and magazine articles are produced.

1772-77   In response to Herder's prize essay *Über den Ursprung der Sprache* and as criticism of Friedrich II's political system, composition among others of the dual *Philologische Einfälle und Zweifel über eine akademische Preisschrift* and *Au Salomon de Prusse. Des Ritters von Rosenkreuz letzte Willensmeinung über den göttlichen und menschlichen Ursprung der Sprache* written on the problematic of the origin of language. In correspondence with Kant, opinion given of Herder's *Älteste Urkunde des Menschengeschlechts.* Connection with Matthias Claudius and Johann Kaspar Lavater.

1775-79   Attack on the moral hypocrisy of the age in *Versuch einer Sibylle über die Ehe.* The *Hierophantische Briefe* document the religious-historical and theological dispute with the enlightener, Freemason, and Crypto-Catholic Starck on the origin and nature of Christianity. The *Konxompax. Fragmente einer apokryphischen Sibylle über apokalyptische Mysterien* devoted also to the question of a natural religion. As the subtitle indicates, the "Fragments" dispute entered upon with response to Lessing. Promotion to overseer of a rental property.

1779-86   Strong attack on Kant's *Beantwortung der Frage: Was ist Aufklärung?* in a letter to the mutual friend and Königsberg professor of practical philosophy, Christian Jacob Kraus. The *Metakritik über den Purismum der Vernunft* of Kant's *Kritik der reinen Vernunft*, as well as *Golgatha und Scheblimini* directed against Mendelssohn's *Jerusalem oder über religiose Macht und Judentum*, form the height of Hamann's authorship. During these years friendship with Friedrich Heinrich Jacobi and Franz Caspar Bucholtz. The latter assists Hamann out of financial difficulty. Beginning of connection with the circle around Princess Gallitzin in Münster. *Entkleidung und Verklärung. Ein fliegender Brief an Niemand, den Kundbaren* concludes Hamann's authorship.

1787/88   Request for a leave met with dismissal and a small pension. A long-planned trip to Westfalia for a visit with Jacobi, Bucholtz, and Princess Gallitzin. Plagued by illness, the last year spent as their guest with thinking and activity concentrated in the *Letzte Blatt*, composed as an album entry. On June 21, 1788, death in Münster.

(This time tablet is offered in dependence on: Johann Georg Hamann, *Sokratische Denkwürdigkeiten/Aesthetica in nuce*, with a commentary, edited by Sven-Aage Jørgensen, Stuttgart, 1968 [Reclam Universal-Bibliothek] 926/26a], 155-57.)

Index of Persons

Index of Scripture References